Microsoft® Office
User Specialist:

Microsoft®
Access® 97
Exam Guide

Joe Habraken

A Division of Macmillan Computer Publishing
201 W. 103rd St., Indianapolis, IN 46290 USA

MW00966151

Microsoft Office User Specialist: Access 97 Exam Guide

By Joe Habraken

©1998 Que Corporation

All rights reserved. No part of this book shall be reproduced, stored in a retrieval system, or transmitted by any means, electronic, mechanical, photocopying, recording, or otherwise, without written permission from the publisher. No patent liability is assumed with respect to the use of the information contained herein. While every precaution has been taken in the preparation of this book, the publisher and author assume no responsibility for errors or omissions. Neither is any liability assumed for damages resulting from the use of the information contained herein. For information, address Que Corporation, 201 West 103rd Street, Indianapolis, IN 46290. You can reach Que's direct sales line by calling 1-800-428-5331.

Library of Congress Catalog Card Number: 97-81449

International Standard Book Number: 0-7897-1507-4

99 98   8 7 6 5 4 3 2 1

Interpretation of the printing code: the rightmost double-digit number is the year of the book's first printing; the rightmost single-digit number is the number of the book's printing. For example, a printing code of 98-1 shows that this copy of the book was printed during the first printing of the book in 1998.

Screen reproduction in this book were created using Collage Plus from Inner Media, Inc., Hollis, NH.

Printed in the United States of America

Executive Editor
Mary Foote
Acquisitions Editor
Al Valvano
Development Editor
Nancy D. Warner

Technical Editor
Ricardo Birmele
Managing Editor
Sarah Kearns
Project Editor
Lori A. Lyons
Copy Editor
June Waldman
Book Designer
Glenn Larsen
Cover Designer
Jay Corpus
Indexer
Chris Wilcox
Production Team
Mike Henry
Linda Knose
Tim Osborn
Staci Somers
Software Specialist
Jack Belbot

Contents at a Glance

1   **Planning Access Databases** 5

2   **Creating a New Database** 17

3   **Creating Tables** 31

4   **Entering Data in a Table** 47

5   **Modifying Data in a Table** 59

6   **Modifying a Table** 69

7   **Sorting Records** 81

8   **Finding and Filtering Records in a Table** 91

9   **Building a Relational Database** 103

10   **Maintaining Data Integrity in a Table** 115

11   **Working with Forms** 135

12   **Advanced Form Design** 153

13   **Designing Queries** 177

14   **Working with Advanced Queries** 195

15   **Creating Reports** 215

16   **Modifying Report Design** 231

17   **Integrating Data from Other Applications** 249

18 **Access and the Internet** 263

19 **Fine-Tuning Your Databases** 277

20 **Access Security** 289

21 **Getting Help** 299

 A **Student Preparation Guide** 307

 B **Glossary** 313

    Index 319

Table of Contents

Introduction 1

1   Planning Access Databases 5

   Understanding Access Relational Databases 6

   Working with Access Objects 7

      Using Tables 7

      Using Forms 7

      Using Queries 8

      Using Reports 8

      Using Other Access Objects 10

   Planning a New Database 10

   Normalizing a Database 11

   Review Questions 13

   Review Question Answers 13

   Practice Lab 14

      Answers to Practice Lab 14

2   Creating a New Database 17

   Creating a Blank Database 18

      Starting Microsoft Access 18

      Using the Access Dialog Box 18

   Using the Database Wizard 20

   Viewing the Database Objects 24

   Opening a Database 25

      Navigating the Open Dialog Box 26

      Finding a Database File 27

   Review Questions 29

   Review Question Answers 29

   Practice Lab 30

      Opening a Database 30

      Modifying the Presentation of a Database 30

3 Creating Tables **31**

Understanding Table Layout 32

Creating a Table in Design View 32

    Setting Up Fields 33

    Understanding Field Properties 36

    Selecting the Primary Key 37

    Saving the Table Structure 38

Creating a Table in Datasheet View 39

Using the Table Wizard to Create a Table 40

Review Questions 44

Review Question Answers 44

Practice Lab 45

4 Entering Data in a Table **47**

Entering Data in Datasheet View 48

Navigating the Table 50

Entering Data with an AutoForm 51

    Closing the AutoForm 52

    Updating the Table 53

Printing a Table 53

Closing the Table 54

Review Questions 55

Review Question Answers 55

Practice Lab 56

    Enter Data into a Table 56

    Enter Data in a Form and Add a Record Using a Form 56

    Navigate Through a Table 57

5 Modifying Data in the Table **59**

Changing Field Content 60

    Replacing Field Content 60

    Editing Field Content 61

Moving and Copying Data 62

Inserting New Records 63

Deleting Data from a Table 64

Deleting a Record 64

Deleting a Field 65

Review Questions 66

Review Question Answers 66

Practice Lab 67

Modify Data in a Table 67

Delete Data in a Table 67

6   Modifying a Table 69

Moving a Field 70

Switching Between Datasheet View and Design View 71

Changing Field Column Widths 72

Changing Column Widths with the Mouse 72

Changing Column Widths with Menus 73

Changing Table Row Height 74

Changing the Font for the Table 74

Hiding a Field 75

Adding New Fields to a Table 76

Changing Field Properties 76

Review Questions 78

Review Question Answers 78

Practice Lab 79

Modify Field Layout 79

Modify Field Properties 79

7   Sorting Records 81

Sorting Records in a Table 82

Sorting by a Single Field 82

Sorting by Multiple Fields 83

Creating Advanced Sorts 84

Freezing Columns 86

Review Questions 88

Review Question Answers 88

Practice Lab 89
    Sort Data on Single Fields 89
    Sort Data on Multiple Fields 89

8   Finding and Filtering Records in a Table 91

Using the Find Command 92
    Setting Search Parameters 92
    Using Wildcards with Find 94
    Using Replace 95
Filtering Records 96
    Filtering by Selection 97
    Filtering by Form 98
Review Questions 100
Review Question Answers 100
Practice Lab 101
    Find a Specific Record 101
    Add and Remove Filters 101
    Find a Specific Record 101
    Add and Remove Filters 102

9   Building a Relational Database 103

Understanding Table Relationships 104
Creating Table Relationships 105
    Working in the Relationships Window 106
    Referential Integrity 107
    Relationship Type 107
    Join Type 108
    Completing the Relationship Creation Process 108
Differentiating Relationship Types 109
Deleting Table Relationships 111
Editing Table Relationships 111
Review Questions 112
Review Question Answers 112
Practice Lab 113

10 Maintaining Data Integrity in a Table 115

Strategies That Ensure Data Integrity... 116

Specifying a Default Value in a Field 116

Using Validation Rules 118

Entering Validation Rules 118

Understanding Validation Rule Operators 120

Setting Required Fields 121

Setting Field Size.. 122

Specifying a Format and Input Masks 123

Specifying a Format 123

Input Masks 124

Enforcing Referential Integrity in Table Relationships 126

Using Lookup Fields 128

Review Questions 131

Review Question Answers 131

Practice Lab 132

Validate Text 132

Set Required Properties 132

Set Validation Rules 132

Set Lookup Fields 133

11 Working with Forms 135

Creating Forms 136

Using the Form Wizard 136

Switching Between Views... 139

Customizing Forms 141

Creating a Form Title 141

Using the Forms Toolbox 141

Formatting Text and Borders.. 143

Creating a Form from Scratch 144

Adding Fields to the Form 145

Moving a Field 146

Adjusting Field Label and Control Sizes 147

Saving the Form 147

Entering Data in a New Form 147

Viewing Multiple Records in a Form 148

Review Questions 149

Review Question Answers 149

Practice Lab 150

    Create a Simple Form 150

    Modify a Form and Switch Between Views............................... 150

    Add a Record Using a Form 151

    View Information in a Form.. 151

    View Multiple Forms 151

12   Advanced Form Design 153

Creating Controls on a Form 154

    Understanding Form Controls 154

    Entering a New Control in the Form Footer 155

    Using the Expression Builder to Create Calculated Controls ... 156

Calculations in a Form 158

Improving Data Accuracy Using Combo and List Boxes on Forms ... 159

    Creating a Combo Box 160

    Using a Combo Box 163

Creating Subforms 164

    Viewing Related Records 167

    Adding New Records to a Compound Form 167

Modifying Controls 168

    Changing Tab Order 168

    Formatting Control Text and Colors... 169

    Adding Graphics 170

Printing a Form 172

Review Questions 173

Review Question Answers 173

Practice Lab 174

    Create and Modify Controls 174

    Improve Accuracy in Forms.. 174

    Merge Two Tables into a Form 175

Add Records with a Main Form and Subform 175

Modify and Enhance Form Design 175

Print a Form 175

13   Designing Queries **177**

Understanding Queries 178

Creating a Simple Query for One Table 178

Adding Fields to a Query 180

Removing Fields 181

Hiding or Showing a Field 181

Adding Criteria to the Query 181

Designing Queries with Multiple Criteria 183

Sorting Records in a Query 184

Saving a Query 185

Running the Query 185

Using the Simple Query Wizard 185

Creating Queries Involving Multiple Tables 189

Joining Tables in a Query 190

Removing Joins in a Query 191

Review Questions 192

Review Question Answers 192

Practice Lab 193

Create a Simple Query 193

Create a Query with Multiple Criteria 193

Sort a Query 194

Add Fields to a Query 194

Join Tables in a Query 194

Remove Joins in a Query 194

14   Working with Advanced Queries **195**

Calculating Fields in Summary Queries 196

Using the Totals Section in the Query Grid 196

Calculating Fields in the Total Row 198

Calculating Fields Using Expressions 200

Using the Expression Builder 201

Creating Crosstab Queries 203
  Using the Crosstab Query Wizard 205
  Building Crosstab Queries in Design View 207
Printing Query Results 207
Using Append Queries 208
Using Delete Queries 209
Other Query Types 210
Indexing Fields 210
Review Questions 212
Review Question Answers 212
Practice Lab 213
  Build a Summary Query and Calculate Fields 213
  Set Crosstab Queries 214
  Print the Results of a Query 214

15 Creating Reports 215
Understanding Access Reports 216
Creating a Report 216
Using AutoReport 216
Using the Report Wizard 218
  Grouping Data in a Report 219
  Sorting Data in a Report 220
  Working with Multiple-Table Reports 221
  Completing the Report 222
Printing and Viewing Reports in Print Preview 223
Modifying a Report 224
  Modifying Report Controls 225
Creating a Report in Design View 225
  Selecting Fields for Grouping and Sorting Data 225
  Moving Labels and Controls 226
Review Questions 228
Review Question Answers 228
Practice Lab 229
  Create a Report 229

Grouping and Sorting Data 229

Modify a Report 229

16 Modifying Report Design 231

Modifying Reports in Design View 232

Adding a New Label to a Report 232

Creating Report Controls 233

Inserting Date and Page Number Controls 233

Making Calculations on a Report 235

Creating a Chart 238

Adding Custom Pages to Reports 241

Adding Subreports to a Report 242

Inserting Page Breaks in a Report 243

Inserting an Image into a Report 244

Getting the Most from Your Reports 245

Review Questions 246

Review Question Answers 247

Practice Lab 247

Modify and Label a Report 247

Customize Headers and Footers 247

Make a Calculation on a Report 247

Add Custom Pages 248

Present Information in a Chart 248

17 Integrating Data from Other Applications 249

Understanding Object Linking and Embedding 250

Linking Objects 250

Embedding Objects 253

Adding Pictures to Records 253

Viewing Images in Forms 256

Importing Data from Other Applications 256

Exporting Data from Access to Other Applications 259

Copying and Pasting 259

Using OfficeLinks 260

Review Questions 261

Review Question Answers 261

Practice Lab 261

   Import Data 262

   Linking Data 262

   Add Pictures to Records 262

18   Access and the Internet **263**

Using Access Internet Integration Tools 264

Creating Hyperlinks in Database Objects 264

   Creating a Hyperlink in a Table Field 264

   Placing a Hyperlink in a Table Field 265

   Placing a Hyperlink in a Form or Report 268

Saving Access Objects in HTML Formats 269

Building Internet Order Forms 270

   Creating the ODBC Data Source 270

   Saving an Access Form as an ASP File 272

Exporting Reports as Static HTML 273

Review Questions 275

Review Question Answers 275

Practice Lab 275

   Create Hyperlinks 276

   Build Order Forms for Internet Use 276

19   Fine-Tuning Your Databases **277**

Using the Performance Analyzer... 278

   Understanding the Optimization Tip Types 280

   Optimizing the Object 280

Using the Table Analyzer 281

   Placing the Fields in New Tables 282

   Completing the Process 284

Documenting Database Objects 285

Compressing a Database 286

Repairing a Database 287

Review Questions 288

Review Question Answers 288

Practice Lab 288

20   Access Security **289**

Securing Your Databases 290

Assigning a Password to a Database 290

Working with User Levels 292

Assigning Users to Security Groups 292

    Users 293

    Groups 293

    Change Logon Password 293

Using the Security Wizard 294

Data Protection on Forms 296

Review Questions 298

Review Question Answers 298

Practice Lab 298

21   Getting Help **299**

Using the Office Assistant 300

    Working with the Office Assistant 301

    Asking the Office Assistant a Question 301

Using the Access Help Topics 302

    Using the Contents Tab 302

    Using the Index 303

    Using Find 303

Managing Help Topics You've Located 304

Getting Help with Screen Elements 305

Review Questions 306

Review Question Answers 306

Practice Lab 306

A   Student Preparation Guide **307**

Studying for the Tests 308

Levels of Certification 308

Required Tasks 308

Registering for the Exams 312

Taking the Tests 312

B   Glossary **313**

Index **319**

Dedication

To my wonderful spouse, Kim; thanks for loving me, Kim, even when I'm writing.

About the Author

Joe Habraken is a computer technology professional, instructor, and author with more than 15 years of experience in the computer application training field. He has taught computer software seminars across the country. Joe has a Masters degree from the American University in Washington, D.C. and currently serves as the lead instructor for the Networking Technologies program at Globe College in St. Paul, MN. Joe's recent book titles include *The Complete Idiot's Guide to Microsoft Access 97, The Big Basic Book of the Internet,* and *The Ten Minute Guide to Microsoft Outlook 98.*

Acknowledgments

Creating a user-friendly and technically sound book like the *Access 97 Exam Guide,* requires a team effort by a number of publishing and computer technology professionals. I would like to thank Al Valvano, who served as the acquisitions editor for this project and put together the team that made this book a reality. His insights into the organization and coverage of the book are also greatly appreciated. A big thanks goes out to Nancy Warner, our developmental editor, who worked closely with the technical editor and the author to create this book and who came up with many great ideas for improving its content. Also a tip of the hat and a thanks to Ricardo Birmele, who as the technical editor for the project did a fantastic job making sure that everything was correct and suggested a number of additions that made the book even more technically sound. Finally, a great big thanks to our project and copy editors, Lori Lyons and June Waldman, who ran the last leg of the race and made sure the book made it to press on time—what a great team of professionals!

Trademarks

All terms mentioned in this book that are known to be trademarks have been appropriately capitalized. Que cannot attest to the accuracy of this information. Use of a term in this book should not be regarded as affecting the validity of any trademark or service mark.

Que Publishing

Que Corporation has a long-standing reputation for high-quality books and products. To ensure your continued satisfaction, we would like to know if you enjoyed this book, if you have trouble with the information or examples presented, or if you have a suggestion for the next edition.

Please note, however: Que staff cannot serve as a technical resource during your preparation for the MOUS certification exams or for questions about software- or hardware-related problems. Please refer to the documentation that accompanies Microsoft Access for Windows 97 or to the application's Help systems.

If you have a question or comment about any Que book, there are several ways to contact Que Publishing:

Publisher
Que Corporation
201 West 103rd Street
Indianapolis, Indiana 46290
USA

If you prefer, you can fax us at 317-581-4663, or you can send email to the following Internet address:

```
certification@mcp.com
```

Please be sure to include the book's title and author as well as your name and phone or fax number. We will carefully review your comments and share them with the author. Please note that due to the high volume of mail we receive, we may not be able to reply to every message.

Orders, Catalogs, and Customer Service

To order other Que or Macmillan Computer Publishing books, catalogs, or products, please contact our Customer Service Department at **800/858-7674** or fax us at **800/835-3202** (International Fax: 317/228-4400). Or visit our online bookstore at **http:// www.mcp.com/**.

INTRODUCTION

Congratulations on your decision to become a Certified Microsoft Office User! This is your opportunity to present to the world your qualifications as a proficient or expert user of Microsoft Office products.

Microsoft has developed one level of certification in Access: the Access Expert User. The Expert certification requires that you perform a wide range of basic, intermediate, and advanced skills. This guide, approved by Microsoft, will assist you in preparing for the Expert certification exam.

The *Microsoft Office User Specialist: Access 97 Exam Guide* is your pathfinder to certification success! Using this guide, you can review tasks that are included in your certification test and prepare yourself for the Microsoft Access 97 Expert exam. Here you will find tutorials that step you through tasks, review questions, and practice labs. All that you need to learn, study, and prepare for your Microsoft Access certification can be found in the *Microsoft Office User Specialist: Access 97 Exam Guide*.

Who Should Use this Book

The *Microsoft Office User Specialist: Access 97 Exam Guide* is for anyone who:

▶ Wants to expand their Access 97 skills

▶ Is seeking certification in Microsoft Access 97

▶ Wants to learn or reference tasks in short, concise lessons

▶ Is an instructor or trainer preparing groups of people for the Microsoft Access 97 Exam

Why *This* Book?

We present to you, in a reasonable and concise method, the tools and information you need to prepare for your certification test. The author is an experienced trainer and consultant, having taught computer applications, operating systems, hardware, networking, and programming classes for many years.

The *Microsoft Office User Specialist: Access 97 Exam Guide* includes tutorials, review questions, and practice labs. Required Tasks for passing the Certification exams are covered not once, but three times. Tasks are presented first in tutorial format, using a proven step-by-step format. Tasks are then reviewed in a set of review questions. Last, skills are reinforced through practice labs provided in each lesson.

How This Book Is Organized

Microsoft Office User Specialist: Access 97 Exam Guide contains:

▶ **Lessons**   You can work through the book lesson by lesson, building upon your skills, or you can use the book as a quick reference when you want to perform a new task or practice for the exam. Organized by Skill Area (according to the Certified Microsoft Office User exam), each lesson first identifies the Skill Area and the Required Tasks for that Skill Area that are covered in the lesson. Each lesson then contains:

  ▶ **Tutorials**   Step-by-step instructions to completing required tasks for Skill Areas identified in the Certified Microsoft Office User exam.

  ▶ **Review Questions**   Thought-provoking questions and answers built to reinforce how a task is performed and alternate methods to completing tasks.

▶ **Practice Labs**   Exercises that apply tasks in a "real life" situation without the aid of step-by-step instruction. This is your chance to test yourself in the Required Tasks and Skills Areas.

▶ **Instructor Tips**   Productivity or study tips, "inside" information on using Access 97, and real life experiences from the author/instructors to help you in your quest to master Access.

▶ **Cautions**   Tips on techniques that might give you trouble and suggestions for how to use the technique safely.

▶ **Tear Card**   The Microsoft Office User Proficiency Guidelines for the Access Certification exam mapped to the contents of the book, to assist you in quickly locating Required Tasks and Skill Areas.

▶ **Student Preparation Guide**   Information on how to use this book to prepare for the Access exam, what to expect during the exam process, and how to sign up for an exam.

▶ **Glossary**   List of terms and definitions found throughout the book and in the software and exams.

Conventions Used in This book

Commands, directions, and explanations in this book are presented in the clearest format possible:

▶ Titles of windows and dialog boxes will be capitalized to distinguish them from regular text. For example, the Custom Conventions box refers to an onscreen box whose title bar reads "Custom Conventions."

▶ A series of menu selections that you must click will be separated by commas. For instance, "Select **Start**, **Programs**, **Access**" means that you click the Start button, the Programs menu choice, and then the Access option.

▶ As a further help, commands you are directed to type will also be in **bold** type so that you can see them clearly.

▶ You might also be directed to hold down several keys simultaneously, as in the command "Press **Ctrl+F2**." The two keys that you press will be connected with the plus sign (+).

Some information is offset in sidebars to draw your attention:

 Skill Area   Lists the Microsoft Skill Area in which a task is found. When applicable, Skill Areas are identified as *Proficient* or *Expert* skills, according to the exam guidelines.

 Required Tasks   Identifies the Required Tasks for each Skill Area.

 Instructor Tips   Provide timesaving shortcuts and workarounds and insider information to learning and applying new skills.

 Cautions   These warn you of situations that can land you in trouble.

Planning Access Databases

This lesson covers one Required Task for the Skill Area Create a Database for the Expert User level.

In this lesson you learn the following Required Task for the Expert User "Create a Database" Skill Area:

▶ Plan a database

Understanding Access Relational Databases

A *database* is a collection of organized data relating to a particular topic: a list of very important clients, a catalog of your personal compact disc collection, or all the data related to the running of a small business—information regarding customers, employees, suppliers, sales, and inventory. People use databases everyday. Your local phone book, the collection of business cards piled on your desk, and the product and price information that grocery store checkout clerks use every time they scan a purchased item are examples of information collections—databases.

For a database to be of any value, you must be able to access, retrieve, and use the information kept in that database. Computerized database management systems provide the greatest flexibility for working with data in a database.

Microsoft Access 97 is a special kind of database management system. It enables you to create relational databases. A *relational database* divides information into discrete groups—*tables*—which can then be related to each other. For instance, one table may contain customers, another table may show products, a third table may consist of suppliers, and a fourth table may contain orders. A relational database enables you to set up relationships among these tables and then create queries, reports, and forms that tie together and display the information in various ways. The relationships among tables in a typical Access database are shown in Figure 1.1.

Figure 1.1

Access databases hold their data in a collection of related tables.

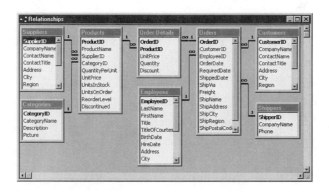

Relational databases, like those built in Access, help you in two important ways: First, they enable you to avoid entering repeated or redundant data; and second, their basic design (a group of related tables) enables you to easily manipulate and then view the data in many different ways. You learn how to build a relational database in Lesson 9, "Building a Relational Database."

Working with Access Objects

Access provides various ways of entering, viewing, and manipulating data, and Access objects are the tools that enable you to accomplish these data manipulations. You can think of your Access database as a container that will hold a collection of various database objects, such as tables, forms, queries, and reports.

Using Tables

The most important Access object and the basic building block of its databases is the table. Each table holds a category of information. Access tables look like spreadsheets, displaying the data that they hold in rows and columns. Each row holds all the information for a particular person, place, or thing; table rows are called *records*. Each column contains a different piece of information pertaining to that person, place, or thing; the columns are referred to as *fields*. A typical Access table is shown in Figure 1.2.

Figure 1.2

Tables divide information into records and fields.

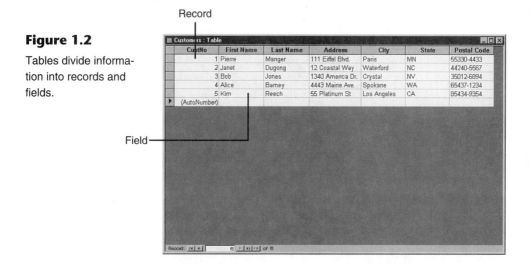

Most Access databases consist of two or more tables, and you do most of your data entry in the table. Lesson 3, "Creating Tables," covers the creation of Access tables.

Using Forms

Even though your tables will hold the data that you enter into your database, another Access object provides an alternative way for entering and viewing the information—*forms*. Forms enable you to view and enter data one record at a time, as shown in Figure 1.3. You can also design custom forms that enable you to enter information into more than one table. Forms can also be used to view special data types such as linked objects (an employee photo for example). You learn how to create forms in Lesson 11, "Working with Forms," and how to work with advanced form design in Lesson 12, "Advanced Form Design."

Figure 1.3

Forms provide an alternative way to view and enter data into your tables.

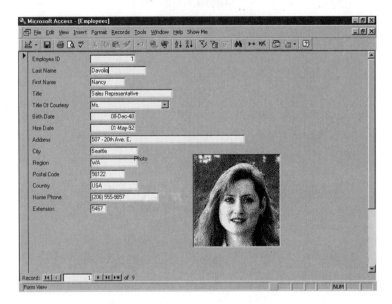

Using Queries

A *query* is the Access object that enables you to manipulate data in your table. You can use queries to sort and select data from your Access tables. You can also design queries that summarize and perform calculations on the information found in a table or tables. You can use queries to delete records that match a certain criteria or to update information in a particular field of a table. Figure 1.4 shows the view you use to design a new query in Access.

When you run a query, the results appear in a table format (Figure 1.4 shows the Query Design view), providing you with the familiar geography of an Access table. You learn to design simple queries in Lesson 13, "Designing Queries." More advanced queries are covered in Lesson 14, "Working with Advanced Queries."

Using Reports

A *report* is the database object that enables you to format the data in your table so that it is suitable for printing. Reports provide various format and layout options for presenting data. An Access report appears in Figure 1.5.

Figure 1.4

The Query Design window enables you to set parameters that select, sort, or summarize data found in an Access table.

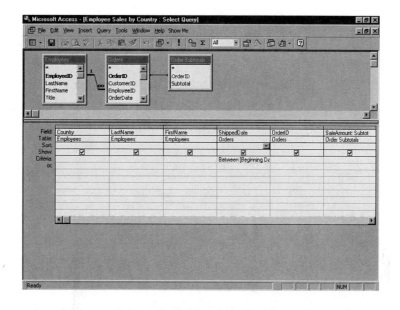

Figure 1.5

Reports provide various formats for printing the data in your database tables.

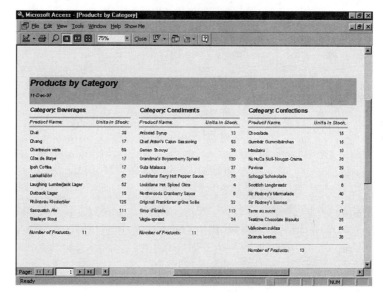

Access reports can pull information from more than one table or provide a printable review of information in a query. Reports can also perform calculations and summarize data. You learn to create reports in Lesson 15, "Creating Reports," and to work with advanced report design in Lesson 16, "Modifying Report Design."

Using Other Access Objects

Two additional Access objects enable you to create custom databases:

▶ Macros

▶ Modules

Programmers familiar with the Microsoft Visual Basic for Applications programming language use both of these objects.

 Macros and Modules Knowledge of these highly advanced Access objects is not required for the Access End-User Certification. You can learn about macros and modules from the book *Special Edition, Using Microsoft Access 97* by Que.

Planning a New Database

The truly hands-on nature of Microsoft Access and its capability to get a new database up and running quickly may entice you into creating a new database without any pre-planning. A little up-front planning can help you avoid the painful trial-and-error process that many users experience when they first work with Access.

The data that your database holds is very important, and a poorly designed database will only make it more difficult for you to extract the information that you need, when you need it. One way to start the planning process for your new database is to ask yourself several questions:

▶ What information do you want to get out of the database when it is operational? This answer will drive how the your data is stored and organized and will dictate the number of tables you will need.

▶ How do you want to input the data, and how would you like to view this data? This question should prompt you to consider how you can use forms to make your data entry easier and more reliable.

▶ How will you want to manipulate the data after it has been entered in your tables? This question should help you begin to consider the type of queries you may want to run.

▶ What type of printouts will you need from the database, and how should the data be arranged on the printed page? This question should start you thinking about what kind of reports you will want to design for your database.

The brainstorming that should result from these questions is the first step in your database planning. It will give you a fairly broad view of what your database will eventually look like and the types of objects you will use to manage it. A good second step in planning your database is to more precisely determine the tables you will have in the database and the information you will include in each.

Normalizing a Database

Normalizing a database simply means that you need to structure your tables so that you are not constantly reentering the same information. A properly designed database should avoid unnecessarily redundant data. Table 1.1 holds the customer data for a small business, but is a poorly designed table.

Table 1.1   **A poorly designed table.**

Customer Name	Customer Address	Customer Phone	Order Date	Order Total
ABC Plumbing	201 W. 44th St.	(317) 555-2394	2/5/98	$155.90
ABC Plumbing	201 W. 44th St.	(317) 555-2394	2/12/98	$90.25
ABC Plumbing	201 W. 44th St.	(317) 555-2394	3/17/98	$225.00
Jack's Place	15 Conway	(317) 555-1234	4/1/98	$1500.00
Kim's Pizza	11 Fair Rd.	(317) 555-2222	4/4/98	$990.00
Jack's Place	15 Conway	(317) 555-1234	4/12/98	$40.00

Notice that the table contains a lot of redundant information. Each time a transaction is recorded, all the customer's information (such as the company name, address, and phone number) must be entered into the table. Consequently, the same information is entered over and over for repeat customers.

The best way to avoid the repetition of data as seen in Table 1.1 is to assign a unique customer number to each customer. You then can break the data into two tables: a customer table and an orders table, as shown in Table 1.2 and Table 1.3.

Table 1.2   **Customer table.**

Customer ID	Customer Name	Customer Address	Customer Phone
1	ABC Plumbing	201 W. 44th St.	(317) 555-2394
2	Jack's Place	15 Conway	(317) 555-1234
3	Kim's Pizza	11 Fair Rd.	(317) 555-2222

Table 1.3 Orders table.

Order ID	Customer ID	Order Date	Order Total
1	1	2/5/98	$155.90
2	1	2/12/98	$90.25
3	1	3/17/98	$225.00
4	2	4/1/98	$1500.00
5	3	4/4/98	$990.00
6	2	4/12/98	$40.00

The customer number ties together the two tables. Breaking down large tables with redundant data into smaller tables that are linked by a common field (in this case, customer number) is the essence of normalizing a database. The concepts and practices of relating tables in a database by common fields are discussed in Lesson 9.

In addition, in Lesson 3 you learn that each table needs to have a field that uniquely identifies the records. Keep this rule in mind when planning new database tables. (Notice that Tables 1.2 and 1.3 have an ID number that uniquely identifies each record.)

 Even Good Plans Can Go Awry No matter how well you plan your new database and the objects that you want to include in it, you will probably find that your database needs fine-tuning—maybe even drastic alterations—after you've entered your data. Access is extremely flexible, and you can adjust the structure of most database objects without damaging the data or the object itself. Access actually provides a number of tools to help you fine-tune an existing database; they are described in Lesson 19, "Fine-Tuning Your Database."

Review Questions

The Certified Microsoft Office User Exams are task oriented. The following types of questions are not representative of the test. These questions are designed to help you understand the required tasks and methods of performing those tasks prior to taking the test.

1. Describe the design strategy embraced by relational databases.

2. Which Access object houses the data in your database?

3. How do you normalize a table containing redundant data?

4. If you want to print information from a database, which Access object would you most likely use?

5. When you normalize an unnecessarily redundant table, what do you use to link the tables created during this process?

Review Question Answers

1. A relational database holds its data in a group of related tables. Each table holds a specific category of information such as customers, products, or suppliers. For more information, see the section "Understanding Access Relational Databases."

2. The table is the Access object that contains the data you input into your database. For more information, see the section "Using Tables."

3. You break the table holding the redundant data into two or more tables. Each table then holds a specific category of information, such as customers or orders. For more information, see the section "Normalizing a Database."

4. Reports provide the best printouts of the data in your database. For more information, see the section "Using Reports."

5. When you normalize a table, the resulting new tables are linked by a common field. For instance, a customer table and an orders table could be linked by a CustomerID field, which would appear as a column in both table. For more information, see the section "Normalizing a Database."

Practice Lab

The Microsoft Access Expert User Exam lists planning a database as one of the Required Tasks in the "Create a Database" Skill Area. The following practice lab covers all the skills required to plan a database.

 Required Tasks   One of the Required Tasks for this Skill Area is plan a database.

1. List on paper the types of database objects you want to create for a mail-order shoe business. Keep in mind that tables hold data, forms are used for viewing and entering data, queries enable you to select and sort data, and reports enable you to print the information.

2. Use the information in Table 1.4 as the data for a new database. Determine the number of tables you want to create to hold the data. Remember to avoid designing tables that will lead to redundant data; also remember to link the new tables.

Table 1.4   **Data for new database.**

Employee Name	Address	Ext.	Training Date	Class Taken	Credits
Phil Sharp	211 W. 16th	234	02/17/98	Access Database	6
Becky Rowan	40 West St.	543	03/19/98	Customer Service	3
Phil Sharp	211 W. 16th	234	03/19/98	Customer Service	3
Nick Gianti	59 Point St.	122	03/20/98	Leadership 101	9
Martha Donat	72 Warren Blvd.	333	3/23/98	Customer Service	3
Becky Rowan	40 West St.	543	03/24/98	Access Database	6

Answers to Practice Lab

1. A mail-order shoe business would require several tables to properly manage the information in a database. These tables would include the following:

    ▶ Customer table (used for customer information such as name and address)

    ▶ Product table (provides stock numbers and other information related to the shoes your business sells)

▶ Supplier table (contains information on your shoe suppliers)

▶ Invoice table (contains information on items purchased by your customers)

These tables are the minimum you would want to begin with.

The database would probably include at least two forms: a Customer form for the entering customer information and an Invoice form.

Queries for the database would include a query that sorts your products by number sold and a query that would give you the total value of all the merchandise you have in stock.

Reports for this database would include printed invoices, shoe types ordered by supplier, and total sales detailing the sales on each shoe type.

 Use This Practice Lab as a Pre- and Posttest Until you've had the opportunity to work with the different Access objects, your initial database planning will probably be somewhat vague as far as the number of objects you want in the database. To test your understanding of database planning and the role of the various Access database objects, redo this practice lab when you finish the book.

2. Tables 1.5, 1.6, and 1.7 were created after normalizing Table 1.4. Note that each table contains an identifier field to uniquely identify the records and that common fields link the tables.

Table 1.5 **Employee table.**

Employee ID	Employee Name	Address	Ext.
1	Becky Rowan	40 West St.	543
2	Phil Sharp	211 W. 16th	234
3	Nick Gianti	59 Point St.	122
4	Martha Donat	72 Warren Blvd.	333

Table 1.6 Class table.

Class ID	Class	Credits
C1	Customer Service	3
C2	Leadership 101	9
C3	Access Database	6

Table 1.7 Training table.

Class ID	Employee ID	Training Date
C3	2	02/17/98
C1	1	03/19/98
C1	2	03/19/98
C2	3	03/20/98
C1	4	03/23/98
C3	1	03/24/98

LESSON

2

Creating a New Database

This lesson covers two Required Tasks for the Skill Area Modify a Database for the Expert User level.

In this lesson you learn the following Required Tasks for the "Modify a Database" Skill Area:

▶ Open a database

▶ Modify the presentation of a database

Creating a Blank Database

Before you can create any Access objects, such as a table, or enter data into a database, you must create a database file. The database file is basically a container that holds all the Access objects (tables, forms, queries, and reports) that help you manage your database information.

You have two options for creating a new database file: You can create a blank database and then build all the objects that will be used in the database; or you can create a ready-made database by using the Access Database Wizard. The Wizard-created database is ready-made in the sense that a collection of tables, forms, queries, and reports will be built for you automatically.

The approach you take to creating your own database depends on how well the objects that the Database Wizard creates match your particular database needs. A highly specialized database may require that all the objects be built from scratch. This lesson explores both methods of database creation.

Starting Microsoft Access

Before you can use either method to create your new database file, you must start the Access software. Complete the following steps:

1. Click the **Start** button. The Start menu appears.

2. Point at **Programs**.

3. Click the **Access** icon on the **Programs** menu. The Access window opens.

Alternative Way of Starting Access   You can also use the Microsoft Office toolbar to start Access. With the toolbar displayed on the Windows desktop, click **Office, Customize.** In the Customize dialog box, select the **Buttons** tab. Scroll down through the list in the Show These Files as Buttons scroll box. Click the **Microsoft Access** check box to add the Access button to the toolbar. Click **OK** to close the dialog box.

Using the Access Dialog Box

When you start Microsoft Access, the Microsoft Access dialog box appears (see Figure 2.1). This dialog box prompts you to create a new database from a blank database or by using the Database Wizard. This dialog box also gives you the option of opening an existing database.

Figure 2.1

The Access Database dialog box opens when you start Access; it gives you the options of creating a new database or opening an existing one.

To create a blank database, click the **Blank Database** radio button in the Access dialog box. Click **OK** to complete the process.

The File New Database dialog box opens (see Figure 2.2). You must give your new database a name and determine where you want to store this new file.

1. Type a name for the file in the **File Name** text box.

2. To select the drive and folder in which you want to save the new database, click the **Save In** drop-down button and select a drive.

3. After you select the drive, a list of the folders on that drive appears in the folder box. Double-click the folder you want to use.

Figure 2.2

The File New Database dialog box is where you name your new database and select the drive and folder in which you want to store the file.

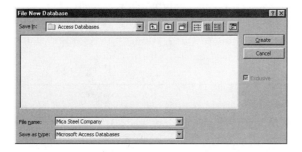

4. Click the **Create** button.

A new Database window appears, as shown in Figure 2.3. The Database window contains a tab for each Access database object type: Tables, Queries, Forms, Reports, Macros, and Modules.

Because this is a blank database, the tabs for each object type are empty. You must create each object that you want in the database.

Creating a Blank Database When Access Is Already Running You can also create a blank database when Access is up and running and you have already passed the selections available in the Access dialog box. Click the **New** button on the Database toolbar to open the New Database dialog box. Make sure the **General** tab is selected in the dialog box, and then click **OK**. The File New Database dialog box appears. Name the new database and select the location in which you want to save the file. Click the **Create** button to complete the process.

Figure 2.3

The Database window contains a tab for each Access object type.

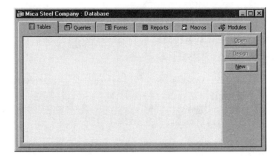

The Access window also has a toolbar that provides the commands you will use when you work with objects at the database level. When you create a blank database, most of the buttons on the toolbar are dimmed. These commands are not available until the Database window contains objects on the various tabs. To view a ToolTip for any button on the toolbar, place the mouse on the particular button. When you click the tab for a particular database object, such as the table or form, the toolbar changes. Each object in Access has a specific toolbar that relates to the features of the object.

 Access differs from Windows applications like Microsoft Word and Excel in that you can have only one database open at a time (in Word and Excel you can have multiple documents or worksheets open). To close the current database window, click the **Close** button in the upper-right corner of the window or click **File, Close**.

Using the Database Wizard

You can also use the Database Wizard to create a new database. The Wizard can create objects for the new database and can create a number of tables, queries, forms, and reports automatically.

When you use the Wizard to create a new database, you are asked to select a database template. These templates are blueprints for a particular type of database, such as an address book, a contact management database, or video collection; the templates contain ready-made database objects that you would use when building this type of database from scratch. How closely your database needs fit one of the Access templates determines how many new objects you will need to create for the database or how much restructuring you will need to do to the built-in tables, queries, forms, and reports.

To create a new database using the Database Wizard, follow these steps:

1. If you just started Access and the Access dialog box is onscreen, click the **Database Wizard** radio button and then click **OK**. If you've already closed the dialog box or have been working with another database, select **File, New Database**. In either case, the New dialog box appears (see Figure 2.4).

2. Click the **Databases** tab to display a list of available database templates.

Figure 2.4

The Databases tab of the New Database dialog box contains the various templates that the Wizard uses to build a new database.

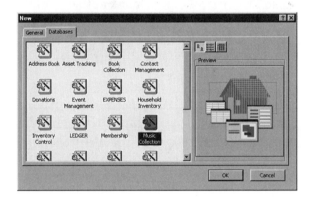

3. Choose one of the database templates and double-click it (for example, choose the Music Collection template). The File New Database dialog box appears.

4. Type a name for the new database and select an appropriate drive and folder for the new file. Click **Create** to continue. The Database Wizard opens with a screen that explains what type of information the new database will store. (For example, the Music Collection database stores information about recording artists, recording information, and individual track information.)

5. Click the **Next** button to continue. The next screen lists the tables that the Database Wizard will create for the new database and the fields that will make up each table, as shown in Figure 2.5.

Optional field

Figure 2.5

The Database Wizard window contains a tab for each type of Access object.

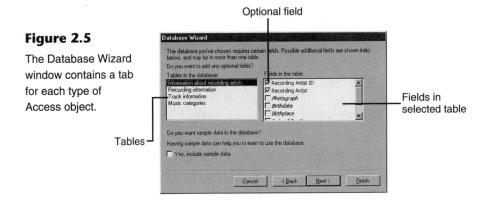

Tables

Fields in selected table

6. Click the table in the **Tables in the Database** box to view the fields for the table. The fields in the table appear in the scroll box to the right. Required fields for the new table already have a check mark in their selection box.

7. Click any optional fields (in italic) that you want to include. Click the **Yes, Include Sample Data** check box if you want the new database to contain sample data. Adding sample data will provide you with a ready-made database that can serve as an excellent learning tool.

 The Wizard's Tables and Fields   The Wizard's tables and the fields they contain are included by default in the new database, even if you do not need them. If you try to deselect a preselected field, Access displays a `Sorry, This Field Is Required` and `Must Be Selected` message.

8. Click the **Next** button to continue.

9. The next screen asks you to select a screen display style for the new database. This style determines the "look" of the forms that the Wizard builds automatically. Click a style in the list box, and Access displays a sample in the sample window. After making your style selection, click the **Next** button to continue.

10. The next screen asks you to select a report style for the new database. Click a style to preview it. After making your report style selection, click the **Next** button to continue.

11. The next screen asks you to provide a title for the new database, as shown in Figure 2.6. You also have the option of selecting a picture to include on the forms and reports in the database (for example, a company logo). If you want to include a picture, click **Yes, I'd Like to Include a Picture**. Select the picture by clicking the **Picture** button. Use the dialog box that opens to move to the appropriate drive or folder and select the picture. Click **Open** to return to the Database Wizard. Click **Next** to continue.

Figure 2.6

The Database Wizard asks you to name your database and gives you the option of including a picture (graphic file) on forms and reports in the database.

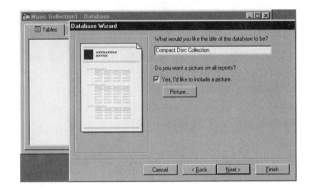

12. The Finish screen asks you if you want to start the new database. Make sure the **Yes, Start the Database** check box is selected and then click **Finish**.

The Wizard will create the new database. When the database is completed, a Main Switchboard window appears (see Figure 2.7). A *switchboard* is a form that provides easy access to the various tasks that you perform on the database, such as entering new data or running predesigned reports. Switchboards provide a good interface for the novice user but prevent you from directly viewing the objects in the new database. You learn to create your own switchboards in Lesson 12, "Advanced Form Design."

Figure 2.7

The Main Switchboard window provides easy access to many tasks associated with maintaining a database and its objects.

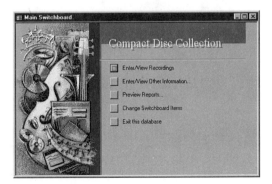

To remove the Switchboard window, click its **Close** button. The minimized Database window appears in the Access window. Click the **Maximize** button on the Database window to display the new database (its name appears on the Access title bar) and its tabs for each database object. You can click the various tabs to view the new objects that the Database Wizard created.

To open an object, such as a table or a form, double-click the object; it will open in its own window. When you finish viewing the object, click its Close button to return to the Database window.

 Wizard-Built Databases Provide Food for Thought The Wizard-built database includes excellent examples of the types of tables, forms, and reports you can use in a typical database. Building a database with sample data is a powerful learning tool.

Viewing the Database Objects

Access provides several ways to view the objects listed on a particular tab in the Database window. The default view is a list of the objects. For instance, if the **Tables** tab is selected, Access displays the names of the tables in the database in a list format.

The Database toolbar contains buttons that provide different views of the objects on a Database window tab. They are described in Table 2.1.

Table 2.1 Database toolbar icons.

Button	Button Name	Description
	Large Icons	Lists the objects on a tab as Large Icons.
	Small Icons	Provides a horizontal view of the objects as small icons.
	List	Provides the default view with the objects arranged in a vertical list.
	Details	Provides a vertical list of the objects along with a description of the object (if available), the date the object was created, and the date the object was last modified (see Figure 2.8).

Figure 2.8

Details view includes information on when the object was created and the last time it was modified.

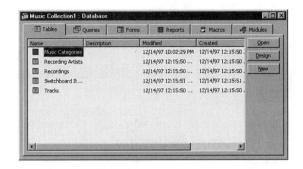

You can also sort the objects on a Database window tab. Click **View**, **Arrange Icons** and then select one of the sort choices on the submenu: **By Name**, **By Type**, **By Created**, or **By Modified**.

When you finish working with the new database, you can close the Database window or exit Access. You can close the database window in any of the following ways:

▶ Double-click the Control menu button (in the top-left corner) for the database.

▶ Click the Database window **Close** (x) button.

▶ Select **File, Close**.

▶ Press **Ctrl+F4**.

▶ Press **Ctrl+W**.

Although the Database window closes, the Access program window remains open. You will notice that only a few options (such as **New** and **Open**) are available on the toolbar.

Opening a Database

You can open a database in several ways. The method you use to open a database file depends on whether Access is currently running on your computer.

▶ When you start Access, the Access dialog box opens. Recently used databases are listed in the **Open an Existing Database** list box. Make sure the **Open an Existing Database** radio button is selected; then double-click the filename.

▶ If the database file you want to open is not on the recently used list, double-click **More files** in the recently used list. The Open dialog box opens. (See the next section "Navigating the Open Dialog Box.")

▶ If Access is already running, you can open a recently used database from the **File** menu. Click **File;** the four most recently used databases are listed at the bottom of the **File** menu.

▶ If the file you want to open is not listed at the end of the **File** menu, click **Open;** the Open dialog box appears, as shown in Figure 2.9.

After the Open dialog box is on the desktop, you can select the database file that you want to open (see "Navigating the Open Dialog Box").

Figure 2.9

The Open dialog box enables you to open database files that are located on various drives and in various folders.

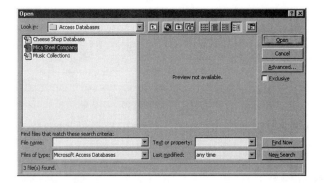

 Toolbar Buttons Provide Fast Results You can also open a database file by clicking the **Open** icon on the Database toolbar.

Navigating the Open Dialog Box

The Open dialog box enables you to select a Database file, change to a different folder or drive, or search for a Database file. The Open dialog box also provides several ways to view the files that appear in the file box (refer to Figure 2.9):

▶ The **List** button shows the files in a vertical list.

▶ The **Details** button provides a list of the files, the file size, and date created.

▶ The **Properties** button provides a list of the filenames and a separate Property box that details the properties of the selected file.

▶ The **Preview** button lists the files and provides a separate pane that gives a preview of the file. The preview feature cannot provide previews of Access database files. It previews only Word and Excel files.

Locating a particular database file may require you to look on a different drive or in a specific folder. To change the drive or folder in the Open dialog box, follow these steps:

1. Click the **Look In** drop-down box arrow.

2. Select the drive you want to use. The folders on the selected drive appear in the **Open** box.

3. Double-click the folder you want to open. The files in that folder appear.

4. Double-click the file you want to open, or select the file and click the **Open** button.

The Database window opens for the selected file.

Finding a Database File

If you are having trouble finding a particular database file, the Open dialog box can also help you search for the file. To find a file using the Open dialog box, complete the following steps:

1. Click the **Open** button on the Database toolbar or select **File**, **Open Database**.

2. Type the name of the file you're searching for in the **File Name** box at the bottom of the Open dialog box.

3. You can also enter additional search criteria—for example:

   ▶ If you're looking for a file type other than an Access database (.mdb), choose it using the **Files of Type** drop-down list.

 Not all Access databases will have the MDB extension. Encrypted Access databases have the MDE extension. Use the **Files of Type** drop-down list when the file you want to open does not have the standard MDB extension.

   ▶ To find a file containing certain text, type the text in the **Text** or **Property** box.

   ▶ If you know when the file was last modified, choose a time interval from the **Last Modified** drop-down list.

4. When you are ready to conduct the search, click the **Find Now** button.

5. You can also fine-tune the search; click the **Advanced** button in the Open dialog box. The Advanced Find dialog box appears, as shown in Figure 2.10.

Figure 2.10

The Advanced Find dialog box enables you to set additional parameters and conditions for your file searches.

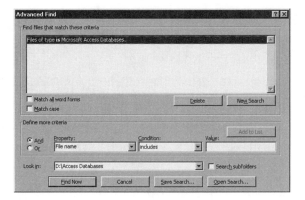

6. You can define more criteria related to such things as the filename, contents, or the date the file was created. You can apply conditions such as *includes*, *begins with*, and *ends with* to the items you select in the **Property** box. Values can also be set in the criteria by typing information or text strings into the **Value** box.

7. You can use the **Look In** box to restrict the search to a certain drive or folder. If you select a particular drive, make sure the **Search Subfolders** check box is selected.

8. After setting and selecting the Advanced Find options, click the **Find Now** button.

Whether you run your search from the Open dialog box or the Advanced Find dialog box, the results of your search will appear in the Open dialog box. Figure 2.11 shows the results of a search for Access files on the D: drive of a computer.

Figure 2.11

The Find feature displays the files that met the criteria of the search in the Open dialog box.

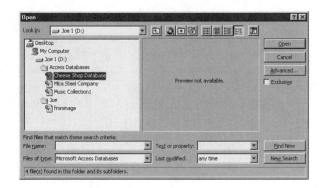

Review Questions

The Certified Microsoft Office User Exams are task-oriented. The following types of questions are not representative of the test. These questions are designed to help you understand the required tasks and methods of performing those tasks prior to taking the test.

1. If Access is already running, how would you create a new database?

2. What are the advantages of creating a new database with the Database Wizard?

3. When Access is already running, what is the fastest way to open an already existing database file that has been recently used?

4. When you are using the Open dialog box to locate an existing Access database, how do you change to a different drive or folder?

5. Is it possible to change the presentation view of the objects on a particular tab in the Database window?

Review Question Answers

1. Click the **New** button on the Database toolbar; alternatively, select **File**, **New**. Choose the Blank template on the **General** tab of the New dialog box and then click **OK**. Type a name for the new database and select a drive and folder for the file in the File New Database dialog box. Click **Save** to save the file and to open the new database in Access. For more information, see the section "Creating a Blank Database."

2. The Database Wizard provides a number of database templates (sample databases) that have been designed for certain tasks such as home inventories, contact lists, or asset tracking. Each template includes premade tables appropriate for the kind of data you will store in the database. (The record collection template, for example, contains tables that you can use to catalog your collection of albums or compact discs.) An obvious advantage of the Database Wizard is that you walk through all the necessary steps to create a database containing ready-made objects, such as tables, forms, and reports. For more information, see the section "Using the Database Wizard."

3. To open a recently used database from the Access window, click **File** and then select the name of the database file from the list at the bottom of the File menu. For more information, see the section "Opening a Database."

4. Click the **Look In** drop-down arrow and select a drive from the drop-down list. The folders for the drive appear in the Open dialog box. Double-click a particular folder to open it. For more information, see the section "Navigating the Open Dialog Box."

5. Yes, a group of buttons on the Database toolbar (Large Icons, Small Icons, List, and Details) provides various views of the objects on a particular tab. For instance, to show file details, select the Object tab (such as **Tables** or **Forms**) and then click the **Details** button on the Database toolbar. For more information, see the section "Modifying the Presentation of a Database."

Practice Lab

The Microsoft Access Expert User exam lists open a database and modify the presentation of a database as Required Tasks for the "Modify a Database" Skill Area. Both tasks have been covered in this lesson. Following you will find a practice lab for each Required Task.

Required Tasks   The two Required Tasks for this Skill Area are open a database and modify the presentation of a database.

Opening a Database

1. Create a new database using the Access Database Wizard. Base the new database on the Contact Management template. Save the file as **Mica Steel Contacts.mdb**. Close the database when you have completed the steps provided by the Database Wizard. Open the file from the Access window.

2. Exit from Access. Start Access and open the **Mica Steel Contacts** database from the initial Access dialog box that appears.

Modifying the Presentation of a Database

1. Open the **Mica Steel Contacts** database. Select the **Forms** tab. View the tables in the **Table** tab as Large Icons, Small Icons, File List with Details, and File List with Properties.

Open the database **lesson2a.mdb** on the companion CD to see a completed version of the Mica Steel Contacts database used in this lab.

LESSON 3

Creating Tables

This lesson covers one Required Task for the Skill Area Create a Database for the Expert User level.

In this lesson you learn the following Required Task for the Expert User "Create a Database" Skill Area:

▶ Create a table

Understanding Table Layout

Databases are collections of data; the database object that actually holds that data is the *table*. Access tables, the basic building block of your databases, are arranged in a column and row format that looks very much like a spreadsheet. This *spreadsheet* view of a table is called a *datasheet*.

Each row in the table is called a *record*. A record holds information that relates to a particular person or thing. For instance, a Customer table holds records (rows) for each of your customers.

Records consist of more discrete pieces of information called *fields*. The columns in the table serve as the fields and hold information such as a customer name or address. Each column in the table has a field heading. The field (column) heading, known as the *field selector*, has a name that describes the field's content. A field for your customer's first name could be labeled First Name. Figure 3.1 shows an Access table in Datasheet view.

Figure 3.1

Tables are divided into rows and columns. Each row is a record and each column holds a particular field.

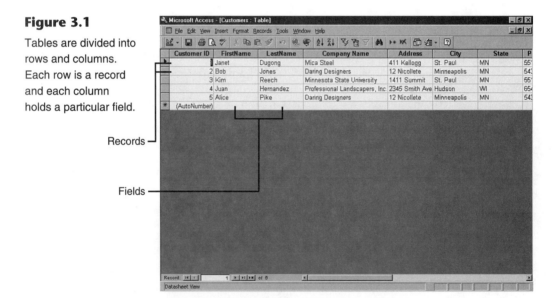

Creating a Table in Design View

The most flexible way to create a new table is in Table Design view. Design view enables you to select the names you want to use for the fields in the table as well as the parameters related to the fields, such as data type and field size.

To create a table in Design view, complete the following steps:

1. Create a new database or open an existing database. Make sure the **Tables** tab is selected in the database window.

2. Click the **New** button on the right side of the database window. The New Table dialog box appears.

3. In the New Table dialog box, select **Design View** (as shown in Figure 3.2) and then click **OK** to enter Table Design view.

Figure 3.2

To create a new table from scratch, select Design View in the New Table dialog box.

Setting Up Fields

Table Design view provides all the tools you need to design a new table. Design view is divided into two panes: the top pane is the Field Grid pane, and the bottom pane is the Field Properties pane.

The Field Grid pane is where you specify the fields that will be in the table. Each field must have a unique *field name* and a *data type*. The field name provides a label for the field. For instance, a field named State would specify where the state data would be entered in each record. Field names can be a maximum of 64 characters and include spaces.

The Field Properties pane is where you can set field-related items, such as field size and format. Figure 3.3 shows the parts of the Table Design window.

You may want to actually map out your table fields on a piece of paper before actually creating the table. This approach will help you make sure that you have all the fields you will need when you begin the data entry process.

 Map Out Your Tables   Mapping out your tables on paper also helps you design tables that can easily be related. See Lesson 9, "Building a Relational Database," for more information about building relational databases.

To set up a new field in Table Design view, follow these steps:

1. To create the first field in the table, make sure that the insertion point is in the first row of the Table Design area. Type the field name.

2. Press the **Tab** or **Enter** key to advance to the Data Type column.

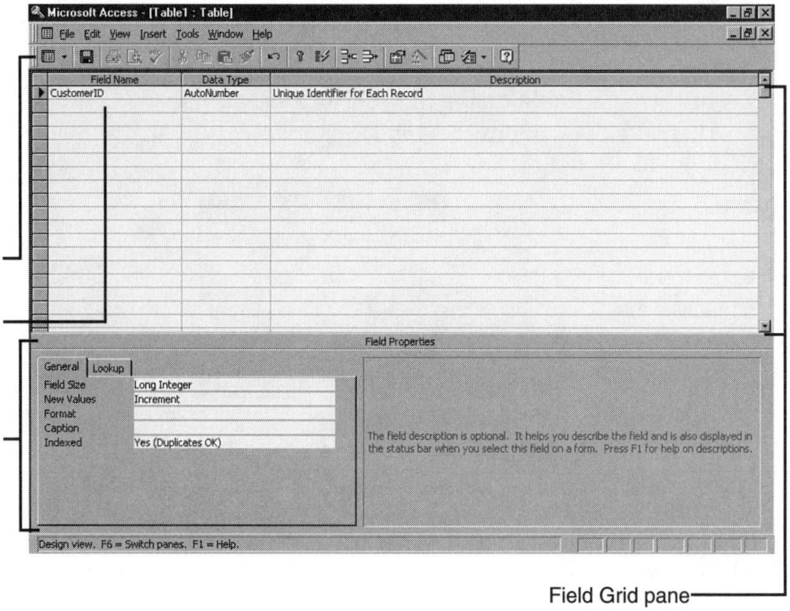

Figure 3.3

Table Design view provides all the tools you need to set up the fields for your new table.

Table Design toolbar —

New field —

Field Properties pane —

Field Grid pane —

Keep Field Names Descriptive but Short When you actually enter data into your table, you will be in Datasheet view, which is divided into rows and columns. Extremely long field names will limit the number of field columns that you can see in the table window at any one time. Single-word names are best. If you do use multiple words in a field name, you may want to connect them with underscores rather than spaces. (Access prefers the underscores to spaces, especially in complex queries.)

The data type is related to the kind of information that you want to enter in the field. Access provides 10 field data types. Table 3.1 describes each data type and includes sample fields.

Table 3.1 Data types.

Data Type	Description	Sample Fields
Text	Alphanumeric (text) or numeric entries; a text field can contain up to 255 characters.	Name
		Address
Memo	Lengthy text entries; the field can contain up to 64,000 characters.	Comments
		Notes

Data Type	Description	Sample Fields
Number	Numeric information; this data type will not accept non-numerical entries such as text.	Number in Stock Number Ordered
Date/Time	Date and time values; display date and time information in a particular format.	Date Hired Order Date
Currency	Monetary values; formats number as currency.	Available Credit Item Price
AutoNumber	Access provides numbers in sequence.	Customer Number Order Number
Yes/No	Answers a true/false question; field can be toggled between yes and no.	Order Filled Customer Contacted
OLE Object	Object Linking and Embedding (OLE) field; enables you to link or embed an object from another software program such as a picture, spreadsheet, or other file type.	Employee Photo (embedded picture) Current Sales Chart (linked Excel chart)
Hyperlink	Enables you to jump from the current field to another file or location on the Internet.	Suppliers Web Page Part Specifications (hyperlink to spreadsheet file)
LookUp Wizard	Provides a list of values for the field; this field type enables you to select the field values from a list based on another field column in a table or query, or a list that you create. The LookUp Wizard is not really a field type but a tool that helps provide a list of values for the field.	SuppliersID ProductSKU#

Selecting the appropriate field type for the fields in your table is important; for instance, fields holding text must have the Text data type. A field that will hold numerical values (values that have mathematical significance such as number of items) should be set up as a Number data type. This field type scheme is not a hard and fast rule; there can and will be exceptions.

Numbers That Are Not Numerical Fields for postal code, phone number, and Social Security number should not have the Number field type. These numbers hold no numerical value; they are only designators and should be set up as Text fields.

After naming the field, press the **Tab** key. When the insertion point is placed in the Data Type column, a drop-down box arrow appears. To select the field type for the field, follow these steps:

1. Click the **Data Type** drop-down box arrow to select from the list of data types. Select the appropriate data type from the list.

2. The data type will be placed in the Data Type column for your field. Press the **Enter** or **Tab** key to advance to the Description column.

The Description column is optional. It is useful, however—especially if someone other than you is going to enter the actual data into the table. The information that you place in the Description column appears on the status bar of the Table window when you are in Datasheet view and enter the field. This description tells the person entering the data about the particular field.

Understanding Field Properties

You set the field properties for a field in the Field Properties pane. Field properties can affect the way the data entered in the field looks or can limit the number of characters that can be placed in a field. For instance, Field Size determines the number of characters that can be placed in a text or number field during data entry.

The default field size is 50; the maximum field size for a text field is 255 characters. In certain instances, you will want to increase or decrease the field size. For example, a State field that requires the two-character abbreviation for a state (such as OH or MN) only needs a field size of 2. Limiting the field size assists you in getting the appropriate kind of data (two-character state abbreviations) into the field during data entry.

 Field Properties Maintain Data Integrity The field properties that you can set in the Field Properties pane go way beyond simple items like field size and format. You can set default values for a field and even set validation rules that allow only a certain range of values to be entered in the cell. Lesson 10, "Maintaining Data Integrity in a Table," shows you how to modify basic field properties such as Format and Input Masks and also covers the full range of field properties available for maintaining data integrity in your tables.

To change the field size for a particular field, make sure the field is currently active (the insertion point is in the field's row) and follow these steps:

1. Double-click the **Field Size** box in the Field Properties pane to select the current field size.

2. Type the new field size.

After you enter all your field names and data types (and adjust field sizes appropriately), you are ready to complete this initial structure for your table. An important aspect of the table structure is designating the primary key.

Selecting the Primary Key

As you set up the fields for your new table, you must make sure you create a field that will uniquely identify each record that will eventually appear in the table. This field is called the *primary key*. The primary key must contain a unique entry for each and every record in the table.

In a Customer table, you might think that a LastName field will suffice as a key field. However, remember that last names can be repeated in a table. Having more than one Smith or Jones in the table makes a LastName field inappropriate for the primary key. Fields such as customer number, product code, supplier identification number—fields that assign a unique number or identity code to each record—make excellent primary keys.

To designate a field as the primary key, complete the following steps:

1. Place the insertion point in the field row that you want to designate as the primary key.

2. Click the **Primary Key** button on the Table Design toolbar.

A Key icon will appear on the row button for the field that has been designated the key field. If you inadvertently assign the primary key status, click the **Primary Key** button a second time to remove the Key icon from the field row.

 Use the AutoNumber Data Type for Key Fields   To assure that primary key fields such as customer number or product code always have a unique value entered during the data entry process, use the Counter data type. Access will place a unique, sequential number in the key field for you as you enter the data into the other fields for each new record.

Figure 3.4 shows several completed fields—including a primary key—for a Customer table; note that the active field, State, has a field size of 2.

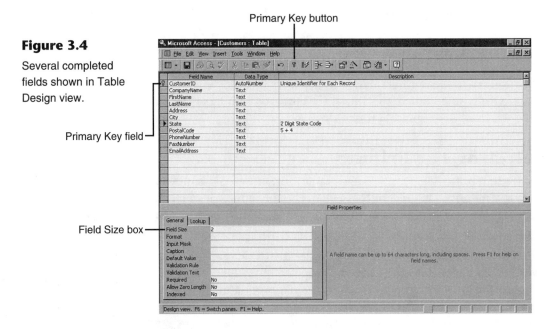

Figure 3.4

Several completed fields shown in Table Design view.

Primary Key button

Primary Key field

Field Size box

Saving the Table Structure

You should always save the table structure for the new table as soon as you begin to enter the field names and data types. You don't want to lose any of your work if the machine locks up or your electricity goes off. (Access also demands that you save the table before you exit the Design view.) To save the new table, complete these steps:

1. Click the **Save** button on the Table Design toolbar.

2. The **Save As** box appears, as shown in Figure 3.5.

Figure 3.5

Enter a name for your new table in the Save As dialog box and then click OK to save the table's structure.

3. Enter an appropriate name for the new table, and then click **OK** to save the table.

You also should always save the table structure before you close the Table Design window. After you've named the table, each subsequent click of the **Save** button saves any changes you make to the structure. If you forget to save the structural changes and attempt to close the Table Design window, Access prompts you to save your work.

Creating a Table in Datasheet View

You can also create a table in Datasheet view. This method immediately creates a table with 20 field columns and 30 record rows. However, you still have to enter Table Design view to specify the key field, the field data types, field descriptions, and any field property changes.

To create a table in Datasheet view, follow these steps:

1. Open the database in which you want to create the table; make sure that the **Table** tab is selected in the Database window.

2. Click the **New** button on the right side of the Database window.

3. The New Table dialog box appears (see Figure 3.6). Select **Datasheet View** in the dialog box and then click **OK**.

Figure 3.6

The New Table dialog box enables you to select the method you want to use to create your new table.

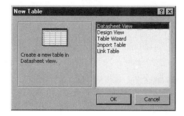

4. A new, blank table will appear in Datasheet view. To enter the field names, double-click any of the field column headings (Field1, Field2, and so on).

5. Type in your new field name. Figure 3.7 shows a new table that has been created in Datasheet view.

To switch from Datasheet view to Table Design view, click the **View** button on the Table Datasheet view toolbar. Switching to Design view enables you to set up each field in the table as you did when you created a table from scratch in Design view.

Figure 3.7

A table created in Datasheet view can be fine-tuned in Table Design view.

View button

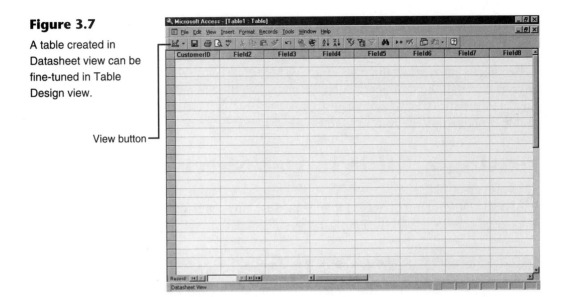

Using the Table Wizard to Create a Table

A third way to create a new table in Access is to use the Table Wizard. The Table Wizard creates the new table by using a list of sample tables and the fields that you would typically find in them. You select a particular sample table type and then determine which of the sample fields you want to include in your new table.

The upside of using the Table Wizard to create a table is that the sample fields are often assigned a data type and format to make your data entry easier. The downside is that if you don't fully understand how a particular data type or field property operates, you may find these ready-made fields more trouble than they are worth.

Open the database in which you want to create the new table. To use the Table Wizard to create the table, follow these steps:

1. With the **Table** tab selected, click the **New** button in the Database window.

2. Select **Table Wizard** in the New Table dialog box, and then click **OK**.

3. The Table Wizard window appears, as shown in Figure 3.8.

4. Click one of the tables in the **Sample Tables** box. The fields available in the sample table appear in the Sample Fields box.

Figure 3.8

The Table Wizard provides sample tables that contain sample fields you can use to build your new table.

Add button

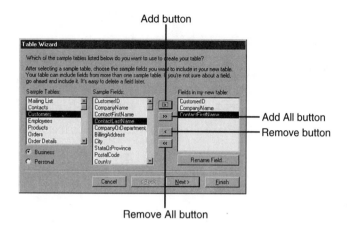

Add All button
Remove button

Remove All button

 Business or Personal   The Table Wizard provides two different groups of sample tables. Click the **Business** radio button to see a list of business-related tables. The **Personal** radio button shows a list of tables you can use for home inventories or personal mailing lists.

5.   Select a field in the **Sample Fields** box, and then click the **Add** button to add the field to the **Fields in My New Table** box. Click the **Add All** button to add all the fields to your table.

 Remove and Remove All Buttons Let You Change Your Mind   If you inadvertently add a field to the Fields in My New Table box, select the field and then click the **Remove** button. To remove all the fields, click the **Remove All** button.

6.   If you want to rename any fields you place in the Fields in My New Table box, select the field and then click the **Rename Field** button.

 If you do rename a field, be aware that the properties for the field remain the same. Renaming a field that is meant to hold numeric data does not change the data type. You must make Properties changes in Design view.

7.   A Rename Field box appears. Type the new name in the text box and click **OK** to continue.

8.   After you select all the fields for your new table, click the **Next** button.

On the next screen, you are asked to provide a name for your table. This screen also asks whether you want Access to select the primary key for you or whether you want to select it yourself. When you initially select the fields for the new table, remember that customer numbers, product codes, and other sequential numbering systems provide the best primary keys. In a customer table, for instance, a CustomerID field would be an appropriate key field.

9. Type a new name to replace the default that Access has placed in the **Name** text box.

10. Select either the **Yes, Set a Primary Key for Me** radio button, or the **No, I'll Set the Primary Key** radio button. Click **Next** after making your choice.

If you selected **Yes, Set a Primary Key for Me**, the next screen asks whether any relationships exist between the new table and tables already in the database; click **Next** to continue with the table creation process. Table relationships and how to create them are covered in Lesson 9.

If you selected **No, I'll Set the Primary Key**, the next screen asks you to select a field to serve as the primary key and to choose a data type for the key field, as shown in Figure 3.9. You choose the primary key in the drop-down list box.

Figure 3.9

If you select your own primary key for the new table, you must also designate a data type for the field.

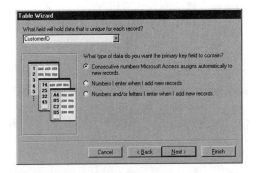

Three data types are provided for your primary key:

▶ **Consecutive Numbers Microsoft Access Assigns Automatically to New Records**   Choose this if your primary key field is a simple record number that Access can assign consecutively as you enter the data in the records.

▶ **Numbers I Enter When I Add New Records**   Choose this data type if you want to enter your own numbers for the records. This choice precludes you from entering any alphanumeric characters (letters of the alphabet) in this field. This data type works well for license numbers or product numbers such as numerical bar codes.

▶ **Numbers and/or Letters I Enter When I Add New Records**   Choose this data type if you want to enter your own identification numbers that are a combination of text and numbers.

After selecting the primary key and the data type, click the **Next** button to continue. Access asks about table relationships in the database, as discussed earlier in the lesson. Click **Next** to continue.

The Finish screen provides three options:

▶ **Modify the Table Design**   This option takes you into Table Design view so that you can modify the new table's structure.

▶ **Enter D Directly into the Table**   This option takes you to the Datasheet view, where you can begin to enter records into the table.

▶ **Enter Data into the Table Using a Form the Wizard Creates for Me**   This choice creates a form that enables you to enter data as you view only one record at a time. Forms and how to create them are covered in Lesson 11, "Working with Forms."

After making your choice, click the **Finish** button to end the table creation process and jump to the option that you selected. If you are finished with the table for the moment, you can close any open windows by clicking the window's **Close** (**x**) button.

If you close the table, you return to the Database window. Your new table will appear on the table list when you select the **Table** tab.

Review Questions

The Certified Microsoft Office User Exams are task oriented. The following types of questions are not representative of the test. These questions are designed to help you understand the required tasks and methods of performing those tasks prior to taking the test.

1. Create a new table using Design view.

2. Create a field in Design view.

3. Change the field size in Design view.

4. Select a primary key for a table in Design view.

5. Save a table's structure.

6. Create a new table using the Table Wizard.

Review Question Answers

1. Open a database or create a new database. Click the **Table** tab in the Database window, and then click the **New** button in the Database window. Select **Design View** in the New Table dialog box. Enter field names, data types, and descriptions in the Field Grid pane. For more information, see the section "Creating a Table in Design View."

2. In Table Design view, click in a new field row in the Field Grid pane. Type the name of the new field. Press the **Tab** key and select the data type from the drop-down list box. Press the **Tab** key and type in an optional description for the field. For more information, see the section "Setting Up Fields."

3. Place the insertion point in the field's row in the Field Grid pane; click the **Field Size** box in the **Field Properties** box. Select the current field size and then type in the new size. For more information, see the section "Understanding Field Properties."

4. Place the insertion point in the field row of the field you want to designate as the primary key. Click the **Primary Key** button on the Table Design toolbar. For more information, see the section "Selecting the Primary Key."

5. In Table Design view, click the **Save** button on the Table Design toolbar. For more information, see the section "Saving the Table Structure."

6. Open a database or create a new database. Click the **Table** tab, and then click the **New** button in the Database window. Select **Table Wizard** in the New

Table dialog box and then click **OK**. Select a sample table in the **Sample Table** box; select and add fields from the **Sample Fields** box. Click **Next** to advance through the various Table Wizard screens and make the appropriate choices, including the table name, the primary key, and the view the new table will open in when the Table Wizard process is complete. For more information, see the section "Using the Table Wizard to Create a Table."

Practice Lab

The Microsoft Access Expert User Exam lists create a table as one of the Required Tasks in the "Create a Database" Skill Area. The following practice lab covers all the skills required to create a table in Access.

 Required Tasks   One of the Required Tasks for this Skill Area is create a table.

Open the Database **lesson3.mdb**. Use the information in Table 3.2 to create a new table in Design view.

Table 3.2   Practice Lab table information.

Field Name	Data Type	Notes
EmployeeID	AutoNumber	Automatically assigns a number to each employee
First Name	Text	
Last Name	Text	
Department Code	Text	
Phone Extension	Text	Enter a three-character extension
Home Address	Text	
City	Text	
State	Text	Enter a two-digit abbreviation
Zip	Text	
Home Phone	Text	
Salary	Currency	

Set the EmployeeID field as the primary key. Set the Phone Extension field size to 3. Set the field size for the State field at 2. Save the table as Employees.

Create a second table by using the Table Wizard. Use the Suppliers table in the Wizard's **Sample Table** box for a list of sample fields. Include the following fields in your table: SupplierID, SupplierName, ContactName, Address, City, PostalCode, StateOrProvince, PhoneNumber, and FaxNumber.

Rename the StateOrProvince field to State. Name the table Current Suppliers. Have the Table Wizard open the new table in Design view when you click **Finish**. In Design view, change the field size of the State field to 2. Save the table structure and close the table.

Open the database **lesson3a.mdb** on the CD to see completed versions of the tables created in this Practice Lab.

4

Entering Data in a Table

This lesson covers Create a Database and Use Forms Skills for the Expert User level.

In this lesson you learn three Required Tasks for the Create a Database Skill Area and one Required Task for the Use Forms Skill Area:

- ▶ Enter data into a table
- ▶ Enter data in a form
- ▶ Navigate through a table
- ▶ Add a record using a form

Entering Data in Datasheet View

After you create a table in Design view or by using the Table Wizard, you are ready to begin the data entry process. Open the database into which you want to enter data and select the **Table** tab in the Database window. Double-click a table on the **Table** tab to open it in Datasheet view.

 Columns Are Fields and Rows Are Records Remember that the columns in the Table datasheet are fields and that the rows are individual records.

You may want to maximize the table by clicking its **Maximize** button. To enter data in the table, follow these steps:

1. Click the first empty field in the record in which you want to enter data.

2. Type the data for the field. If you make a data entry error in a field, press the **Backspace** key to delete the character to the left of the insertion point. Press the **Tab** or the **Enter** key to advance to the next field.

3. Enter the appropriate data in the field. Continue to advance through the fields using the **Tab** key. Complete the records for which you have data.

4. If you need to move back a field and reenter data, press **Shift+Tab**. A table with completed records appears as in Figure 4.1.

 Be Aware of AutoNumber Fields If you've set up an AutoNumber field (such as customer number or employee ID) to automatically enter sequential numbers for the records, you don't need to type a value in those cells.

 Using the Mouse You can also use the mouse to advance to the next field by clicking in the field; the insertion point will appear. However, when you are entering data, it's better to keep both hands on the keyboard. Reaching out to grab the mouse will slow you down. Use the mouse when you enter the editing phase of your data entry work.

Figure 4.1

Enter data in a field and then press the Tab key to advance to the next field.

Records

Current field

Fields

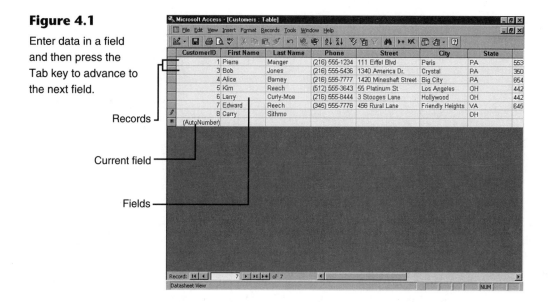

Entering data is really nothing more or less than taking the time to get all the information into your database tables. It is certainly the least glamorous and most time-intensive aspect of building databases. You can use the following data entry tricks to reduce the amount of typing:

▶ If you need to enter the current date into a field, press **Ctrl+;** (semicolon).

▶ If a certain value already exists in your table, you can copy and paste it into another field. Use the **Tab** key to move to the field information you want to copy (it will be automatically selected) and then press **Ctrl+C** to copy the data. Move to the field into which you want to paste the information and press **Ctrl+V** to paste the data. Moving and copying data are covered in Lesson 5, "Modifying Data in a Table."

▶ If you have entered data in a field in a record (such as the State field) and now you want to place the same data in the field in the next record, press **Ctrl+;**. Access automatically repeats the data.

▶ If you want to enter repeating values, use field masks. When you create your fields during the table design process, you can create a field mask for a field; the mask will enter repeating display characters. An example of a field mask is the parentheses around a phone number's area code: (216)555-1212. You learn how to create field masks in Lesson 10, "Maintaining Data Integrity in a Table."

▶ Specify a default value for a field. For example, if all your customers live in Minnesota, have Access enter the value MN automatically. You can assign a default value to a field in Table Design view. You learn how to create default values for fields in Lesson 10.

 Maintaining Data Integrity A number of other features and commands are available that can help you enter data into your tables and verify that the data has been entered accurately. These features are covered in Lesson 10.

When you enter data into a table, your natural inclination is to click the **Save** button or to click **File**, **Save** to save the information. This is not necessary, however. As soon as you enter information into a field and then advance to the next field, Access saves the data to the database table.

Obviously, if you use other applications, such as Word or Excel, you have gotten into the habit of saving your valuable work. The fact that Access is automatically saving your data entry takes some getting used to. You will, however, have to save any changes that you make to a table's structure—for example, widening a field column or moving a field. Always click the **Save** button after making changes like this.

Navigating the Table

After you enter data into the table, you will want to move about the datasheet to view its contents. You already know that the **Tab** key and **Shift+Tab** will move you one field at a time through the table either forward or backward, respectively. Table 4.1 summarizes the keyboard shortcuts you can use for moving around a table.

Table 4.1 Keyboard shortcuts.

Keystrokes	Results
Tab	One field forward
Shift+Tab	One field back
Up arrow	One field up
Down arrow	One field down
Ctrl+down arrow	Same field in the last record
Ctrl+up arrow	Same field in the first record

Keystrokes	Results
Home	First field in a record
End	Last field in a record
Page up	Up one screen of records
Page down	Down one screen of records
Ctrl+Home	First field in the first record
Ctrl+End	Last field in the last record

You can also use a mouse to navigate through a table. A set of navigation buttons is visible at the bottom-left corner of the table window. Figure 4.2 displays the buttons and their functions. The navigation buttons enable you to move to the first record in a table, to the last record in a table, or to the last row in a table and enter a new record. The navigation buttons are particularly useful when the table has many records.

Figure 4.2

You can use the table navigation buttons to move around a table with the mouse.

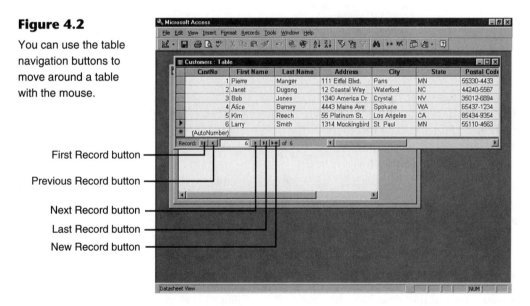

First Record button
Previous Record button
Next Record button
Last Record button
New Record button

Entering Data with an AutoForm

As you enter data in Datasheet view, you may find that the task of entering information into each field becomes more difficult as the number of records increases. The AutoForm feature helps you focus on one record during the data entry process. AutoForm creates a form (the ideal Access object for data entry) that includes all the fields in the current table.

The form displays only one record at a time, allowing you to focus on the data for that particular record.

To create an AutoForm for data entry, complete the following steps:

1. Click the **New Object** drop-down arrow button on the Table toolbar. A list of possible new objects appears.

2. Click **AutoForm**. A form appears in the Access window. The form incorporates all the fields from the table, as shown in Figure 4.3.

Figure 4.3

The AutoForm feature provides a ready-made form that uses all the fields in the current table.

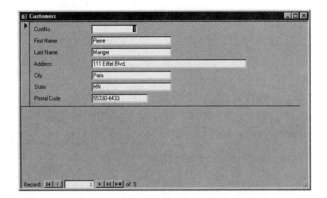

Each record in the table appears separately on the form. In the form window's lower-left corner, you can see the same set of navigation buttons that you found in the Table window (refer to Figure 4.2). You can use these buttons to navigate through the records contained in your database table. You can also use the keyboard shortcuts from Table 4.1 to navigate through the forms.

If you want to enter a new record using the form, click the **New Record** button (it's the navigation button with the asterisk on it). A blank form appears. Enter the data in the new record as you would enter data in a table. Use the **Tab** key to move to the next field or press **Shift+Tab** to move to the previous field.

Closing the AutoForm

When you have completed data entry using the AutoForm, you can close the form and return to the table. Click the form's **Close** button.

When you close the form, Access displays the message box shown in Figure 4.4. Access gives you the option of saving the AutoForm or closing it without saving.

Figure 4.4

You can either save the form created using AutoForm or discard the form without saving it.

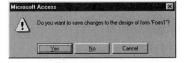

If you select **Yes**, a Save As dialog box prompts you to enter a name for the form. After entering the name, click **OK**. You can find the saved form on the **Forms** tab of the Database window. If you select **No**, the form closes without saving.

Updating the Table

When you close the data entry form, you will notice that records added by using the form do not appear in the table. You must update the table.

Click anywhere in the table. Press **Shift+F9** (function key). Records entered using the AutoForm now appear in the table.

 Moving the Form   If you need to move your table while you are working with the AutoForm, drag the form off the table by its title bar.

Printing a Table

A printout of an Access table is not the ideal way to display your data. It will appear as it does on the computer screen: a datasheet consisting of columns and rows. A very large table will also spread over several pages, making it difficult to get an overall picture of the significance of the data. You will find that reports are really the ideal object for Access printouts; their use and design are covered in Lessons 15, "Creating Reports," and 16, "Modifying Report Design."

However, you may want to print out a table just as a visual reference. If the table is open, click the **Print** button on the Table toolbar. If you are in the Database window, select the table you want to print on the **Table** tab and click the **Print** button on the Database toolbar. Both of these options send the print job directly to your printer.

You can also print the table by clicking the **File** menu and then clicking **Print**. The Print dialog box appears (see Figure 4.5), which gives you more control over the print job.

Figure 4.5

The Print dialog box gives you control over the parameters of the print job you want to initiate.

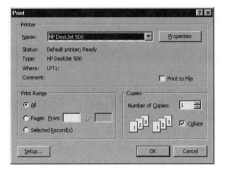

Closing the Table

When you have finished working with a table, click the table's **Close** (**x**) button to close its window. You return to the Database window. You can also close the table by clicking **File, Close** or by double-clicking the table's Control menu button.

 Click the Appropriate Close Button   If you are working with a table or any other database object in a maximized window and you want to close it, click the lower of the two **Close** buttons in the Access window. If you click the upper **Close** button, you will exit from Access.

Review Questions

The Certified Microsoft Office User Exams are task-oriented. The following types of questions are not representative of the test. These questions are designed to help you understand the required tasks and methods of performing those tasks prior to taking the test.

1. How do you create an AutoForm?

2. What are two methods for moving through a table?

3. How do you update the records in a table that have been entered using the AutoForm?

4. How do you print a table (what are the steps)?

5. True or False: You must save an AutoForm after using it to enter data.

Review Question Answers

1. Open the table for which you want to create the AutoForm. Click the **New Object** drop-down arrow and then click **AutoForm**. For more information, see the section "Entering Data with an AutoForm."

2. The **Tab** key and **Shift+Tab** provide forward and backward movement through the table. You can also use keyboard shortcuts to move through the table; for example, **Home** moves to the first field in a record, and **End** moves to the last. You can also use the navigation tools at the bottom left of the Table window to move through the table with the mouse. For more information, see the section "Navigating the Table."

3. After entering records using the AutoForm, you can close the form or click the Table window to select it. Press **Shift+F9** (function key) to update the records in the table. For more information, see the section "Updating the Table."

4. To print a table, open the table or select it in the Database window and click the **Print** button. You can also print the table by clicking **File, Print**. For more information, see the section "Printing a Table."

5. False, you do not have to save an AutoForm after using it for data entry. For more information, see the section "Closing the AutoForm."

Practice Lab

The Microsoft Access Expert User Exam lists enter data into a table, enter data into a form, and navigate through a table as Required Tasks for the "Create a Database" Skill Area. Add a record using a form is a Required Task for the "Use Forms" Skill Area. The following practice lab covers these Required Tasks.

 Required Tasks   Three of the Required Tasks for the "Create a Database" Skill Area are enter data into a table, enter data in a form, and navigate through a table. One of the Required Tasks for the "Use Forms" Skill Area is add a record using a form.

Enter Data into a Table

Copy the **lesson4.mdb** database from the CD that accompanies this book to a folder on your computer using Windows Explorer. Open the database. Open the **Customers** table and enter the data from Table 4.2.

Table 4.2   Customers table data.

CustNo	Fname	LName	Address	City	State	Postal Code
1	Pierre	Manger	111 Eiffel Blvd.	Paris	MN	55330-4433
2	Janet	Dugong	12 Coastal Way	Waterford	NC	44240-5567
3	Bob	Jones	1340 America Dr.	Crystal	NV	35012-6894
4	Alice	Barney	4443 Maine Ave.	Spokane	WA	65437-1234
5	Kim	Reech	55 Platinum St.	Los Angeles	CA	85434-9354

Enter Data in a Form and Add a Record Using a Form

Use the AutoForm feature to create a data entry form for the Customers table. Use AutoForm to enter the data in Table 4.3.

Table 4.3   AutoForm customers table data.

CustNo	Fname	LName	Address	City	State	Postal Code
6	Larry	Smith	1314 Mockingbird Lane	St. Paul	MN	55110-4563

Save the AutoForm as **Customer Entry Form**. Update the table. Print the table and then close the table.

Navigate Through a Table

In the **lesson4.mdb** database, open the **Suppliers** table. Use the keyboard shortcuts and the navigation buttons explained in this lesson to move through the records and fields in the table.

Open the database **lesson4a.mdb** on the CD to see a completed version of the Customers table you worked with in this lab.

Modifying Data in a Table

This lesson covers two Required Tasks for the Skill Area Create a Database for the Expert User level.

In this lesson you learn two of the Required Tasks for the "Create a Database" Skill Area:

▶ Modify data in a table

▶ Delete data from a table

Changing Field Content

The accuracy of the data in a table is crucial to the value of the database as an informational tool. However, entering data is one of those repetitive tasks that can sometimes lead to errors.

Access makes it very easy for you to edit or modify the data in your tables. You can replace the entire field entry or change the current entry by editing.

Replacing Field Content

If the contents of a field are wrong, it's probably best to reenter the information completely. To replace the old data, follow these steps:

1. Select the field content by moving to the field using the keyboard (**Tab**, **Shift+Tab**, and so on). You can also select the field's content using the mouse.

2. Position the mouse pointer on the left edge of the field. The mouse pointer becomes a plus sign (see Figure 5.1). Click once to select the field's data.

3. Enter the new data in the field. The new data will replace the old information. Move to the next incorrect entry and repeat the data-replacement process.

Figure 5.1

Place the mouse on the edge of the field and click to select the field contents.

Field Selection tool ———▶

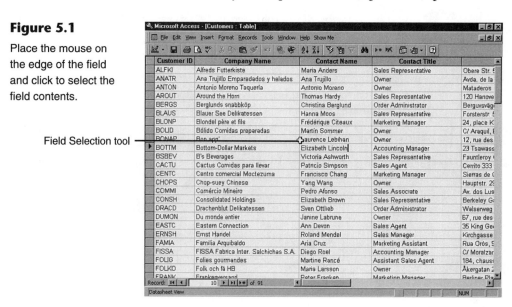

Editing Field Content

If you need to change a portion of the data in a particular cell, you can edit that portion rather than completely re-entering the information. The mouse is the best tool for positioning the insertion point in a specific place in a field that must be edited.

1. Position the mouse pointer in a field where you want to place the insertion point.

2. Click once to place the insertion point in the cell, as shown in Figure 5.2.

Figure 5.2

Use the I-beam mouse pointer to place the insertion point in a field.

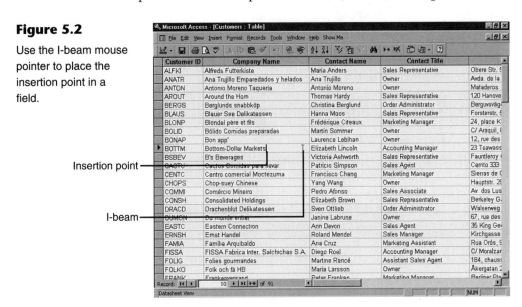

Insertion point

I-beam

3. To delete characters to the left of the insertion point, use the **Backspace** key. To delete characters to the right of the insertion point, use the **Delete** key. You can also use keyboard shortcuts to move around the field as you edit the data. These keyboard shortcuts are described in Table 5.1.

Table 5.1 Keyboard shortcuts.

Keystroke	Movement
Right arrow	One character to the right
Left arrow	One character to the left

continues

Table 5.2   Continued

Keystroke	Movement
Ctrl+right arrow	One word to the right
Ctrl+left arrow	One word to the left
End	End of the line
Ctrl+End	End of the field
Home	Beginning of the line
Ctrl+Home	Beginning of the field

 Use the Mouse to Select Incorrect Data   You can also use the mouse to select portions of a field's data by clicking and dragging the I-beam over the characters to be selected.

Moving and Copying Data

You can also use cut, copy, and paste to enter or edit data in the table.

1. Select the field or field information you want to move or copy. Click **Edit**; then click **Cut** or **Copy**.

2. Click in the field into which you want to paste the information (select the field's data if the paste is to replace the entire entry); then click **Edit**, **Paste**.

You can also cut, copy, and paste using the Table toolbar buttons. Keyboard shortcuts are also available for cut, copy, and paste (see Table 5.2).

Table 5.2   Cut, copy, and paste keyboard shortcuts.

Command	Keyboard	Toolbar Button
Copy	Ctrl+C	
Cut	Ctrl+X	
Paste	Ctrl+V	

Cut, Copy, Paste Objects   You can move and copy entire database objects. For instance, to copy a table to a different database, you could select and copy the table in the current database window. Open the destination database and select **Paste** to insert a copy of the table.

Inserting New Records

New records are inserted automatically at the bottom of the table. You can't insert new records between existing ones. However, you can sort records in any order you like; sorting records is covered in Lesson 7, "Sorting Records." To insert a new record, follow these steps:

1. Click the **New Record** button (it's the table navigation button with the asterisk on it) and enter the field data in the new record.

2. You can also click **Records**, **Data Entry**. This method hides the current records in the table, as shown in Figure 5.3, and places you in a blank record row. Enter the data into the fields of the record.

3. To return all the records to Datasheet view, click **Records**, **Remove Filter/ Sort**.

Figure 5.3

You can use the Records menu to temporarily hide the records in the table so that you can work on a clear datasheet containing a new blank record.

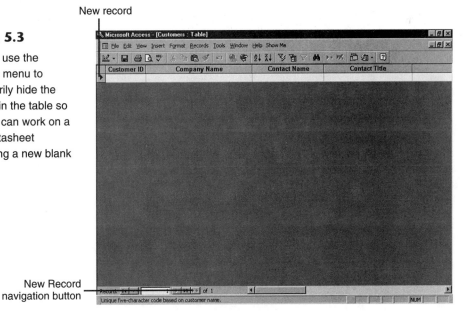

New record

New Record navigation button

Deleting Data from a Table

If you want to simply delete field information and leave a field blank, your best option is to select the field and press the **Delete** key. You can delete portions of the field information by selecting it with the mouse and then pressing **Delete**.

Deleting a Record

Access also enables you to delete entire records from a table. To delete a record, complete the following steps:

1. Click the record's selection button, shown in Figure 5.4, or click **Edit**, **Select Record**. All the fields in the record are selected.

Figure 5.4

Each record has a selection button to the left of the first field column.

Record Selection button

2. Click the **Delete Record** button on the toolbar or press the Delete key on the keyboard. A message box tells you that the selected record will be deleted if you continue. Click **OK**. Access removes the record from the table.

 Use Delete Record You can also delete a record without selecting it. Click in any field of the record and then select **Edit**, **Delete Record.** (This method does not work for tables that are in a relationship with another table in which referential integrity has been enforced. See Lesson 10, "Maintaining Data Integrity in a Table," for more information.)

When you delete a record from the table, you cannot use the Undo feature to get it back. Deleting a record from a table is permanent.

 Regular Backups You should back up your Access databases regularly. You can use backup software (Windows 95 has a backup program) or simply copy the database files to disk. Backups of your databases are your only recourse if your computer fails. A backup can even help you out if you inadvertently delete records or database objects.

If you want to delete more than one record, you can select several records in a series (the records must be contiguous) by clicking the first record you want to select and then Shift-clicking the last record you want to select.

In a worse-case scenario, you can also select all the records in the table and delete them. Click the selection box at the intersection of the row and column headings in the table. Or you can Click **Edit**, **Select All Records**. Pressing **Delete** or clicking the **Record Delete** button on the toolbar removes all records from the table.

 Be Aware of AutoNumbered Fields AutoNumbers will be lost if you delete a record in a table that is using the AutoNumber format to assign numbers to a particular field (such as customer number). AutoNumber does not reuse numbers that have been deleted from the table.

Deleting a Field

You can also delete a field column from a table in Datasheet view. This method deletes all data in this field in all the records in the table. Deleting an entire field obviously has a dramatic effect on the table. To delete a field column from the table, follow these steps:

1. Place the mouse pointer in one of the fields of the field column you want to remove.

2. Place the insertion point in the field.

3. Click **Edit**, **Delete Column**. As Figure 5.5 shows, Access warns you that the field and all the data it holds will be deleted (that is, all the data in this field in each record).

4. If you want to delete the field column, click **Yes** in the dialog box. Access removes the column from the table.

5. You can remove contiguous fields from a table by clicking on the first field heading and then Shift-clicking on the last field column heading. Use the Edit menu to remove a group of fields as you did in step 3 to remove a single field.

Figure 5.5

Access warns you that deleting a field also deletes all the data that was in the field.

Deleting a field column from a table removes a field from the table's structure. Make sure that you click the **Save** button on the toolbar to save the changes you have made.

Review Questions

The Certified Microsoft Office User Exams are task-oriented. The following types of questions are not representative of the test. These questions are designed to help you understand the required tasks and methods of performing those tasks prior to taking the test.

1. What is the easiest way to select a field's contents using the mouse?

2. How do you edit a portion of a field's data?

3. How do you copy data from one field to another?

4. What is the most straightforward method for deleting a record in a table?

5. How would you delete an entire field from a database table?

Review Question Answers

1. Place the mouse pointer on the left edge of the field; the mouse pointer becomes a plus sign. Click to select the contents of the cell. For more information, see the section "Replacing Field Content."

2. Use the mouse to click and drag to select a portion of the data in a field. Type the new information; it replaces the selected data. For more information, see section "Editing Field Content."

3. Select the data in the field and then click the **Copy** button on the table toolbar. Click the I-beam mouse pointer in the field where you want to copy the data; the insertion point appears in the field. Click the **Paste** button on the toolbar. For more information, see the section "Moving and Copying Data."

4. Click the record's selection button on the left side of the table; the entire record will be selected. Press the **Delete** key or click the **Delete Record** button on the toolbar. Access asks you to verify the deletion; select Yes. For more information, see the section "Deleting a Record."

5. Click in any of the fields in the field column you want to delete. Click **Edit**, **Delete Column**. Access asks you to verify the deletion. Click **Yes**. For more information, see the section "Deleting a Field."

Practice Lab

The Microsoft Access Expert User Exam lists modify data in a table and delete data from a table as Required Tasks for the "Create a Database" Skill Area. The following practice lab covers these tasks.

 Required Tasks Two of the Required Tasks for this Skill Area are modify data in a table and delete data from a table.

Modify Data in a Table

Copy the **lesson5.mdb** database from the CD that accompanies this book to a folder on your computer by using Windows Explorer. Open the database. Open the **Customers** table and modify the data as follows:

- ▶ Change the Company Name in record 1 to **Mica Steel Incorporated**.
- ▶ Change the State in record 5 to **WI**.
- ▶ Change the Last Name in record 2 to **Smith**.
- ▶ Change the Address in record 5 to **111 Fourth St**.
- ▶ Change the City in record 5 to **Evansville**.
- ▶ Change the Area code in record 5 to **215**.
- ▶ Change the Address in record 3 to **14 Summit Ave**.

Open the database **lesson5a.mdb** on the CD to see a completed version of the Customers table you worked with in this portion of the lab.

Delete Data in a Table

Delete the following data from the Customers table in the **lesson5.mdb** database:

- ▶ Delete the abbreviation Ave from the Address field in record 4.
- ▶ Delete the email address from the E-Mail Address field in record 3.
- ▶ Delete records 2 and 5.
- ▶ Delete the Fax Number field column.

Open the database **lesson5b.mdb** on the CD to see a completed version of the Customers table you worked with in this part of the lab.

Modifying a Table

This lesson covers two Required Tasks for the Skill Area Modifying a Table for the Expert User level.

In this lesson you learn two of the Required Tasks for the "Modify a Database" Skill Area:

- ▶ Modify field layout
- ▶ Modify field properties

Moving a Field

Being able to select an entire field column in Datasheet view makes it very easy to change the layout of your table and move the field to a different position. For example, if you have a Customers table in which the First Name field appears before the Last Name field, you might want to rearrange the table so that the Last Name field appears before the First Name field. You will find this layout especially useful if you want to sort a table by Last Name and First Name, which is covered in Lesson 7, "Sorting Records."

To move a field, complete the following steps:

1. Place the mouse pointer at the top of a field column and point at the field heading (the column heading). The mouse pointer turns into a down-pointing arrow, which is a column-selection tool. Click once to select the entire column.

2. Press the left mouse button and drag the column to its new position, as shown in Figure 6.1. In effect, you are dropping the field column on top of the field that you want to shift to the right.

Figure 6.1

You can drag a field column to a new location in a table.

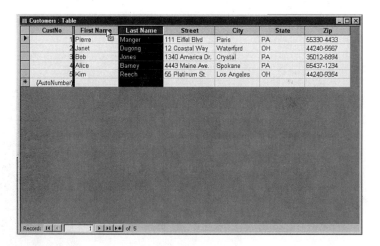

CustNo	First Name	Last Name	Street	City	State	Zip
1	Pierre	Manger	111 Eiffel Blvd	Paris	PA	55330-4433
2	Janet	Dugong	12 Coastal Way	Waterford	OH	44240-5567
3	Bob	Jones	1340 America Dr.	Crystal	PA	35012-6894
4	Alice	Barney	4443 Maine Ave.	Spokane	PA	65437-1234
5	Kim	Reech	55 Platinum St.	Los Angeles	OH	44240-9354
*	(AutoNumber)					

Being able to move a particular field is very useful if you want to view two field columns side by side. For instance, if you need to make phone calls to customers and the Phone field is one of the last fields in a very wide table, you can drag the field so that it appears next to the customers' names.

When you move a field in a table, Access considers it a change of table structure. All changes to a table's structure must be saved before closing the table. Click the **Save** button on the toolbar to save the new structure.

Using Drag and Drop The technique that you used to move the column is called *drag and drop*. You can use this feature to move columns, fields, text, and even graphics. Drag and drop is the easiest way to move or copy a selection a short distance.

Switching Between Datasheet View and Design View

You can also change the position of a field in Design view. To switch to Design view, click the **View** button on the Table toolbar (see Figure 6.2).

In Design view, the fields are arranged in rows in the Field Grid pane. Each field has a field selection button (the gray box) just to the left of the field's name.

To move a field in Design view, follow these steps:

1. Click the **Row Selector** button for the field. The entire field row is selected.

2. Drag the field to the new location. Place it on top of the field that currently holds the position you want it to occupy, as shown in Figure 6.2. The field currently in the position moves down one row.

Figure 6.2

In Design view, you can select a field and drag it to a new position.

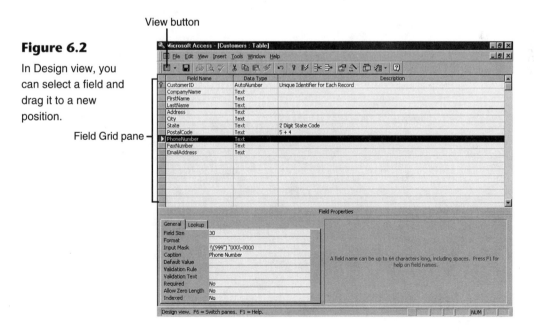

3. Click the **Save** button on the toolbar to save this layout change.

4. To return to the Datasheet view of the table, click the **View** button on the Table Design toolbar (the first button on the toolbar).

The field's new position in the table will be reflected in the table's Datasheet view.

Changing Field Column Widths

The default column width for the Datasheet view of your tables is approximately 1 inch. Some of the data you enter may be too wide to fit within the default column width; the data will appear truncated. You can alter the field column width in two ways: using the mouse and using menus. The following sections explain both methods.

Changing Column Widths with the Mouse

Changing column widths in Datasheet view is extremely simple. Follow these steps:

1. Place your mouse pointer on the dividing line between two fields that is to the right of the field column that you want to adjust. The mouse pointer becomes a Column Sizing tool, as shown in Figure 6.3.

Figure 6.3

The Column Sizing tool enables you to change the width of your columns.

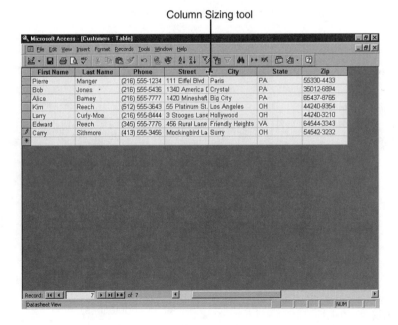

Column Sizing tool

2. Click and hold the left mouse button. Use the Column Sizing tool to drag the column border to the right until the new width accommodates the widest entry in the field column.

You can also change a column width to *best fit*. Best fit changes the column width to accommodate the widest entry in the field. To set the width to best fit, place the mouse pointer on the column border to the right of the field you want to widen. Double-click the **Column Sizing** tool when it appears. The column width will adjust to the widest entry. You can also select several contiguous columns and then double-click one of the field's borders to apply the same best-fit width to all the selected columns.

Changing Column Widths with Menus

You can also change the widths of the field columns via the Format menu. Complete the following steps:

1. Click anywhere in the field column you want to adjust.

2. Select **Format**, **Column Width**. The Column Width dialog box appears, as shown in Figure 6.4.

Figure 6.4

The Column Width dialog box enables you to set a column width for a particular column in a table.

 Setting a New Global Width   You can change the default setting for your datasheet column widths. Select the **Tools** menu, and then click **Options**. Click the **Datasheet** tab and then put the new column width in the **Default Column Width** box. Changing this setting does not override changes that you make to individual field columns in your tables using the mouse.

Remember to save the layout changes (column widths) that you have made to the table.

 Access Warnings   If you try to exit a table you have made structural changes to (such as column width changes or field deletions), Access prompts you to save the table.

Changing Table Row Height

Widening a column is not the only way to view all the data that appears in a particular field. You can also increase the row height of your tables. Changing the row height for one row in the table changes the default for all the rows in the Datasheet view. Changing the row height actually allows the data in the fields to wrap in the field, making more of the data visible.

To change the row height of the rows, place the mouse pointer on the divider line between any rows. A Height-Sizing tool appears. Drag the **Height-Sizing** tool to increase the height of the row. All row heights increase as well.

 No Best Fit for Row Heights   You cannot set a best fit for the row heights by double-clicking a row divider with the sizing tool.

You can also change the row heights more precisely by using the Row Height dialog box. Select **Format**, **Row Height**, or select a row and right-click. Both actions open the Row Height dialog box. Type the new row height and then click **OK**. The new height takes effect in the table.

Changing the Font for the Table

You can change the font for the data in the table. Any change in font affects the entire table, including the field column headings.

Font changes made in Datasheet view do not affect any other objects (forms and reports) in the database that work with the data in the table.

To change the font for the table, follow these steps:

1. Select the **Format** menu, and then select **Font**. The Font dialog box appears, as shown in Figure 6.5.

2. Choose a new font from the **Font** list box.

3. Choose a style from the **Font style** list box.

4. Choose a size from the **Size** list box.

5. Choose a color from the **Color** drop-down list.

A sample of your changes appears in the Sample area. When you have selected the font changes you want to make, click **OK**.

Figure 6.5

The Font dialog box enables you to change the font style and size for the table.

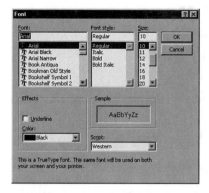

Hiding a Field

You can hide fields that you aren't using at the moment or that you are considering deleting from the table. Hiding a field preserves the data that you have entered in your records and maintains any field properties that you have set. For instance, you may have an Employee table that contains a field for salaries. You may want to hide this field when you are working on the table because of the data's "sensitive" nature.

Datasheet view is the only view in which you can hide an entire field. To do so, complete the following steps:

1. In Datasheet view, select the field you want to hide.

2. Select **Format**, **Hide Columns**. The selected column or columns disappear.

When you want to unhide the column or columns, follow these steps:

1. Select **Format**, **Unhide Columns**. The Unhide Columns dialog box shown in Figure 6.6 appears, with a list of all the columns in the table.

Figure 6.6

Remove the check marks next to the field names to hide the fields.

2. The fields with a check mark beside them are unhidden; hidden fields do not have a check mark. Click the check box of any field that you want to change. Clicking a box changes the status of the field from hidden to unhidden or vice versa.

When you have made your selections, click the **Close** (**x**) button.

Adding New Fields to a Table

You can add new fields to a table in both Datasheet and Design views.

Adding a field to a table in Datasheet view is just a matter of adding a new column. Access adds the column to the left of any column you select.

To add a new field to a table using Datasheet view, complete the following steps:

1. Select a column and then click **Insert**, **Column**. Access places a new column in your table.

2. Access assigns a generic name (Field1) to the new column. To give the field column a name, double-click the **column heading** and type in a field name.

3. Size the column to an appropriate width and enter data for the new field in the records.

Alternatively, you can add a field in Design view by the following these steps:

1. Select a row in the **Field Grid** pane. The new field will be entered above the selected row.

2. Select **Insert**, **Row** or click the **Insert Rows** button on the Design toolbar. A blank field appears, and the selected row moves down, as shown in Figure 6.7.

3. Enter a name, data type, and description for the field.

Changing Field Properties

Whether you create a table from scratch or use the Table Wizard, you will probably need to edit the field properties for some of the fields in the table. Field properties are changed in Design view.

To change the field properties for a particular field, click anywhere in the field's row. The field properties for the field appear in the Field Properties pane at the bottom of the Table Design View window, as shown in Figure 6.8.

Figure 6.7

Adding a row in Design view enables you to select the data type and other field properties for the new field.

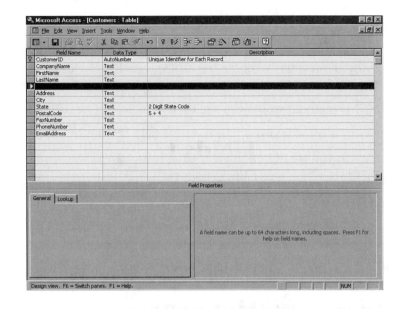

Figure 6.8

The Field Properties pane in the Design window enables you to change the properties of a particular field.

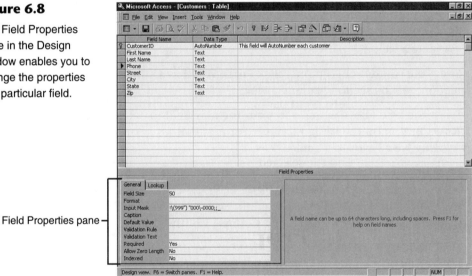

Field Properties pane –

Field properties range from field size to field format to whether or not the field is required. (Access demands that data be entered in fields that have been set as Required.) Using the field properties available can help you cut down on data entry errors. Lesson 10, "Maintaining Data Integrity in Tables," covers field properties and how they can help maintain data integrity.

Review Questions

The Certified Microsoft Office User Exams are task oriented. The following types of questions are not representative of the test. These questions are designed to help you understand the required tasks and methods of performing those tasks prior to taking the test.

1. What methods would you use to move a field in Datasheet view?

2. What steps would you take to hide a field column in Datasheet view?

3. When you are in Design view, what is the easiest way to add a new field?

4. When you are in Datasheet view, how do you change a column's width using the mouse?

5. In which view can you edit the field properties for the table?

Review Question Answers

1. Select the **field column** and drag it onto the field column that you want to appear to the right of the moved field. For more information, see the section "Moving a Field."

2. Select the column or columns; click **Format**, **Hide Columns**. For more information, see the section "Hiding a Field."

3. Select the field above which you want the new field to appear. Click the **Insert Rows** button on the Design toolbar. For more information, see the section "Adding New Fields to a Table."

4. Place the mouse pointer on the column divider between the column you want to resize and the field column to its right. Drag the **Column Sizing** tool to resize the column or double-click the Column Sizing tool for best fit. For more information, see the section "Changing Column Widths with the Mouse."

5. Design view gives you access to the field properties. For more information, see the section "Changing Field Properties."

Practice Lab

The Microsoft Access Expert User Exam lists modify field layout and modify field properties as Required Tasks for the "Modify a Database" Skill Area. The following practice lab covers these required skills.

Required Tasks Two of the Required Tasks for this Skill Area are modify field layout and modify field properties.

Modify Field Layout

Copy the **lesson6.mdb** database from the CD that accompanies this book to a folder on your computer using Windows Explorer. Open the database. Open the **Customers** table and modify the data as follows:

▶ Resize the Company Name field column to accommodate all the entries in the field.

▶ Use best fit to resize the Address field column.

▶ In Datasheet view, add a new field to the left of the Address field column.

▶ Switch to Design view and name the new field **Available Credit**. Set the data type for the field as Currency.

▶ Switch to Datasheet view and move the Available Credit field column to the left of the Phone Number field column.

▶ Hide the Email Address field column.

Modify Field Properties

Edit the following field Properties for the Customers table:

▶ Change the field size of the State field to 2.

▶ Change the name of the Email Address field to **Email**.

▶ Change the field size of the City field to 35.

Save the changes that you made to the table structure. Open the database **lesson6a.mdb** on the CD to see a completed version of the Customers table you worked with in this lab.

Sorting Records

This lesson covers Organize Information skills for the Expert User level.

In this lesson you learn the following Required Tasks for your exam:

▶ Sort data on single fields

▶ Sort data on multiple fields

Sorting Records in a Table

The records in a table are initially ordered as you enter them—the first record entered appears before the second record entered. (If you are using AutoNumber for the primary key field, the records are ordered by the key field, such as Customer Number.) Access provides a sort feature that enables you to reorder the records in a table by the information in a particular field. An application of this feature is sorting an employee table by start date or alphabetically by last name, and then by first name. Access enables you to perform simple as well as complex sorts.

The sort feature can sort the records in ascending or descending order. You can also create a sort to sort table records by more than one field.

Sorting by a Single Field

To sort by a single field, click anywhere in the field column you want to sort by. The table toolbar contains two buttons for sorting: Sort Ascending and Sort Descending (see Figure 7.1). Alternatively, you can access the Sort commands by using the Records, Sort menus.

An example of a single-field sort is a Products table sorted by the units (of product) currently in stock. Knowing which items you have the most of can help you fulfill your customers' orders. To sort descending (from large to small), complete the following steps:

1. Click in the field column you want to sort by (in this case Units In Stock).

2. Click the **Sort Descending** button on the toolbar. Access sorts all the records in the table by the field that you chose in the sort order (ascending or descending) you chose.

 Shortcut for Sorting by One Field   Right-click a field; then choose **Sort Ascending** or **Sort Descending** from the shortcut menu.

If you are sorting the records in a Products table by the units you have in stock, you may also want to sort the records in ascending order (from small to large) to determine which products you need to reorder.

To sort ascending complete the preceding steps, but in step 2 click the **Sort Ascending** button on the toolbar instead of **Sort Descending**.

 Sorting in the Form View   You can also use the sort feature when you are in the Form view of a particular table. Place the insertion point in the field you want to sort by, and then click the appropriate sort button.

Sort Ascending button Sort Descending button

Figure 7.1

Click in a field and
then click either the
Sort Ascending button
or the Sort Descending
button on the toolbar
to sort the records by
the field.

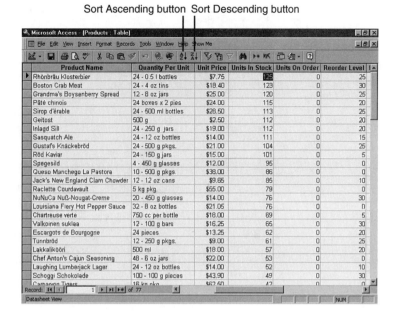

Sorting by Multiple Fields

To sort by multiple fields using the **Sort Ascending** and **Sort Descending** commands,
the fields must be adjacent to each other in the table. For example, you may want to sort a
Customer table by Last Name and then by First Name, as shown in Figure 7.2. Access determines the order of the sort (which field to sort by first) by reading the field columns selected for the sort from left to right. To sort a table by last name, and then first name, the
Last Name field column must be to the left and adjacent to the First Name field column.

To sort by more than one field, complete the following steps:

1. Click the field name to select the first field column for the sort; then **Shift-click**
    to select other fields for the sort (they must be directly to the right of the field
    that will be the primary sort parameter). You can also click and drag across the
    two field column selectors to select the fields.

2. Click the **Sort Ascending** or **Sort Descending** button to do the sort.

3. The table is sorted by the primary sort field first (the first selected field) and then
    by any subsequent fields to the right.

4. Click anywhere in the table to deselect the selected field columns.

Figure 7.2

A table can be sorted by two adjacent fields, such as this Customers table sorted by Last Name and then by First Name.

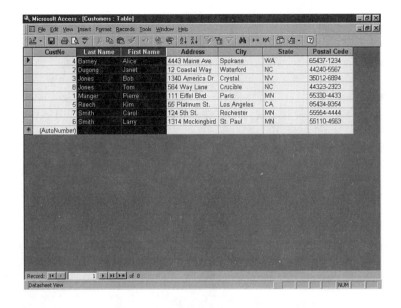

 Moving Fields for Sorts You can move a field column to a new position so that it is positioned appropriately for a multiple-field sort. For more information on moving a field see Lesson 6, "Modifying a Table."

When you have completed a sort and you want to return the records in the table to their previous order, click **Records**, click **Remove Filter/Sort**.

Creating Advanced Sorts

You may find that the simple sorts provided by the **Sort Ascending** and **Sort Descending** commands do not meet all your sorting needs. If so, Access enables you to create a more advanced sort based on nonadjacent multiple fields. With an advanced sort, you can sort by as many as 15 fields.

The Advanced Sort feature is accessed using the **Filter** command on the **Records** menu. A *filter* is a list of certain criteria (such as Customers in Germany) that gives you a subset of the records in your table. Filters are covered in Lesson 8, "Finding and Filtering Records in a Table."

An example of an advanced sort is a situation in which you have clients all over the world and you want to sort them by country, city, and the name of the company. When you sort by more than one field, you need to assign a primary sort field (in this example, Country) and at least a secondary sort field (in this case, City) and determine which direction (ascending or descending) you want the sort to follow. When you give Access all these instructions for your advanced sort, you're setting up the *sort parameters*.

To conduct an advanced sort, complete the following steps:

1. Open the table you want to sort.

2. Click **Records** and then point at **Filter**; click **Advanced Filter/Sort** to open the Filter window.

The Filter window is where you select the fields you want to sort by (see Figure 7.3). You also select the direction of the sorts, such as ascending or descending.

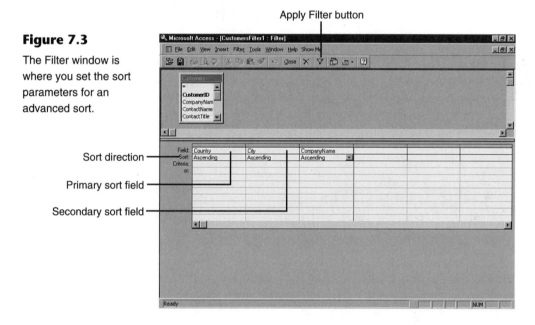

Figure 7.3

The Filter window is where you set the sort parameters for an advanced sort.

The Filter window has two parts. The upper half of the window shows the current table and the fields that it contains, and the lower half is divided into several rows and columns. For designing a sort, the first two rows are used; the first one is marked Field, and the one below it is marked Sort.

When you sort by more than one field, you should place the field names in the Filter window in the order that you want the sort to take place.

To enter the primary sort field, click in the first field column next to Field; a drop-down arrow appears. Click the drop-down arrow, and a list of the fields in the table appears. Select the field you want to sort by. Click the **Sort** box and choose the sort direction (either **Ascending** or **Descending**) from the drop-down list.

Add Fields to the Filter Window with a Double-Click You can also add fields to the field columns in the Filter window via the **Field Name** box that appears in the top half of the Filter window. Click the field column you want to place the field in and then double-click the field name in the **Field Name** box.

To add a secondary sort field, click in the second field column. Select a **field name** via the drop-down list and click the **Sort** box to select the direction of the sort.

When you have completed your selection of fields for the sort, click the **Apply Filter** button on the toolbar. You return to the Table window.

The records in the table are sorted first (in the appropriate order) by the primary sort field and then sorted as needed by any subsequent sort fields.

 Saving Sorts as Queries You can save advance sorts as queries by clicking the **Save** button; enter a name for the query in the **Name** box and then click **OK**. Queries are covered in depth in Lessons 13, "Designing Queries," and 14, "Working with Advanced Queries."

Freezing Columns

The main purpose of the sort feature is to help you view your records in a particular order. However, a sort only orders the records by a particular field or fields; it does not guarantee that field columns will appear in an order that helps you to cross-reference information.

For example, after sorting the records you may want to view the information in a particular field at the same time you view the information in another field column, such as the Product Name field and the Units in Stock field in a Product table. This may be impossible in Table view if these two fields are located on opposite ends of a table that contains many fields. You could move the field columns, but you may not want to reorder the fields.

Fortunately, Access enables you to freeze one or more field columns. *Freezing a field column* means that when you scroll to the right and the left in the table, the frozen field remains onscreen. This feature enables you to place two field columns side by side that are normally on opposite ends of the table.

To freeze a field column, complete the following steps:

1. Click the field name to select the field column you want to freeze.

2. Click **Format**, and then click **Freeze Columns**.

3. Click anywhere in the table to deselect the field column. A solid line appears on the right border of the field column, letting you know that the particular field is frozen.

4. Scroll to the right and the frozen column remains onscreen, as shown in Figure 7.4.

To freeze multiple field columns, the fields must be adjacent to each other in the table. Select the first field column you want to freeze and then **Shift-click** any additional adjacent field columns you want to also freeze.

Figure 7.4

You can freeze a column so that it stays onscreen when you scroll horizontally in your table.

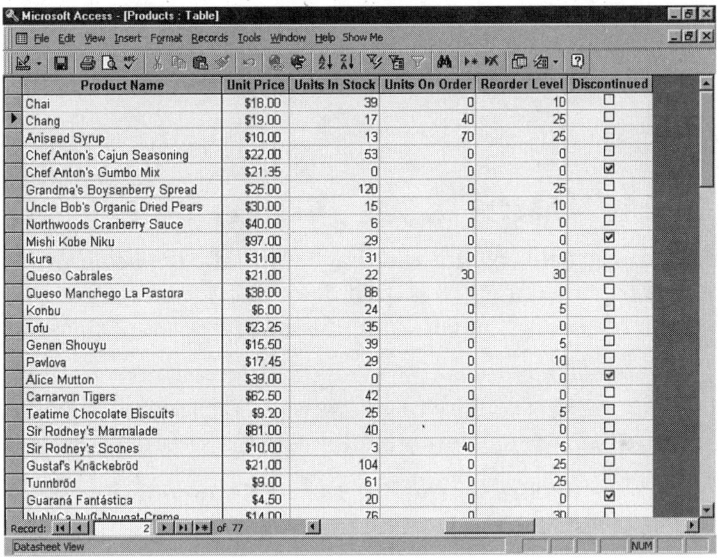

Review Questions

The Certified Microsoft Office User Exams are task oriented. The following types of questions are not representative of the test. These questions are designed to help you understand the required tasks and methods of performing those tasks prior to taking the test.

1. How do you sort a table by one field when you are in Table Datasheet view?

2. How do you sort by more than one field when you are in Table Datasheet view?

3. How do you place the records in their previous order after you run a sort?

4. How do you create an advanced sort in Access?

5. How do you freeze a field column in an Access table?

Review Question Answers

1. Select the field column and drag it onto the field column that you want to appear to the right of the moved field; then click the **Sort** button or select **Sort** from the Records menu. For more information, see the section "Sorting by Multiple Fields."

2. Select the field column or columns; then click **Sort Ascending** or **Sort Descending**. For more information, see the section "Sorting by Multiple Fields."

3. Click the **Records** menu; then select **Remove Filter/Sort**. For more information, see the section "Sorting by a Single Field."

4. Click the **Records** menu; then select **Filter**. Click **Advanced Filter/Sort**. Select the fields for the Sort in the Filter window. For more information, see the section "Creating Advanced Sorts."

5. Select the Field column or columns and then click **Format**, **Freeze Columns**. For more information, see the section "Freezing Columns."

Practice Lab

The Microsoft Access Expert User Exam lists sort data on single fields and sort data on multiple fields as Required Tasks for the Skill Area "Organize Information." The following practice lab covers these Required Tasks.

Required Tasks   The two Required Tasks for this Skill Area are sort data on single fields and sort data on multiple fields.

Sort Data on Single Fields

Copy the **lesson7.mdb** database from the CD that accompanies this book to a folder on your computer using Windows Explorer. Open the database. Open the **Customers** table and sort the data as follows:

▶ Open the **Suppliers** table and sort the records by the Supply Type field in ascending order.

▶ Open the **Expenses** table and sort the records by the Amount Spent field in descending order.

Sort Data on Multiple Fields

▶ Open the **Customers** table and in Datasheet view sort by the LastName and FirstName fields in ascending order. (You may have to move one of the field columns.)

▶ Open the **Employees** table. Use the Advanced Sort feature to sort the table in ascending order by Start Date, Last Name, and then First Name.

Open the database **lesson7a.mdb** on the CD to see the various tables sorted as requested in the preceding exercise.

Finding and Filtering Records in a Table

This lesson covers Locate Information skills for the Expert User level.

In this lesson, you learn the following Required Tasks for your exam

- ▶ Find a specific record
- ▶ Add filters (selection and form)
- ▶ Remove filters

Using the Find Command

The Find feature is useful for locating a particular record in a database table. In a table of customers, for example, you can use this feature to quickly find the record for a customer who has a question about a recent purchase.

Find is really useful only if you are looking for one particular record. A tool for finding groups of records based on the information they hold is the filter. Filters are covered in the section "Filtering Records."

To find a particular record in a table, complete the following steps:

1. In Datasheet view, click the field that contains the data you want to search for. For instance, if you want to find a customer by his or her last name, click the Last Name field. If you're not sure which field holds the data you want, click any field.

2. Click the **Find** button on the toolbar; then select **Edit**, **Find** or press **Ctrl+F**. The Find in Field dialog box appears (see Figure 8.1).

Figure 8.1

The Find in Field dialog box is where you set the parameters for your search.

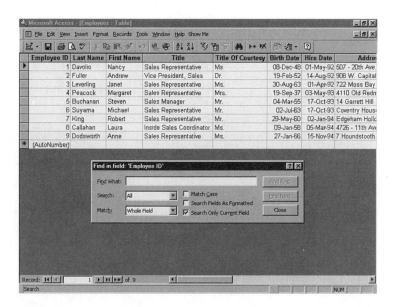

3. Type the text or numbers that you want to find into the **Find What** text box.

Setting Search Parameters

After you enter the data that you want the Find command to search for, you can set several options to control how the search is conducted. You can specify how the search matches potential items to be found with the text or numerical entry in the Find dialog box, as well as the direction of the search. To set the search parameters in the Find in Field dialog box, complete the following steps:

1. Open the **Match** drop-down list and select one of the following:

   Whole Field   Finds fields in which the specified text is the only thing in that field. For example, "Smith" would not find Smithsonian.

   Start of Field   Finds fields that begin with the specified text. For instance, "Smith" would find Smith and Smithsonian, but not Joe Smith.

   Any Part of Field   Finds fields that contain the specified text in any way. "Smith" would find Smith, Smithsonian, and Joe Smith.

2. To search only forward from the current record, open the **Search** drop-down list and select **Down**. To search backward, select **Up**. The default is **All**, which searches all the records from the currently selected field.

3. To limit the match to entries that are the same case as the information you type in the text box (upper or lower), select the **Match Case** check box. After doing so, "Smith" would not find SMITH or smith.

4. To find only the fields with the same formatting as the text you type, select **Search Fields As Formatted**. With this option selected, "3/3/98" would not find 3-3-98; even though the entries refer to the same date, they are formatted differently. The **Search Fields As Formatted** option is available only if you select **Search Only Current Field**.

5. To limit the search to the field where you placed the insertion point at the beginning of these steps, select the **Search Only Current Field** check box (selecting this parameter speeds up the search). If you are not sure which field holds the data, do not check this option.

After you enter the data you want to search for and set the various options in the Find dialog box, you are ready to actually run the search.

To begin the search process, follow these steps:

1. In the Find in Field dialog box, click the **Find First** button to find the first match for the search. You may have to move the Search dialog box out of the way if you cannot see the found field. Access highlights the first field that matches your search entry, as shown in Figure 8.2.

2. To find the next match, click the **Find Next** button. If Access cannot find any more matches, it tells you the search item was not found. Click **OK** to clear the message.

3. When you have completed the search, click the **Close** button to close the Find in Field dialog box.

Figure 8.2

The Find feature highlights the field that matches the data you entered in the Find in Field dialog box.

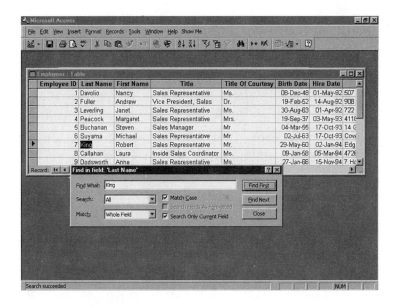

Using Wildcards with Find

Access can also search for parts of words or a particular pattern of alphanumeric or numeric characters if you use wildcard characters as placeholders. *Wildcards* can represent one character, several characters, a list of characters, or even a numeral. Some of the most commonly used wildcard characters and their usage follow:

* The asterisk can take the place of any number of characters. You can use it at the beginning, middle, or end of a character string. For example, a search for the text string **C*a** in a field column of countries would return countries that begin with a capital *C* and end with *a*, such as *Canada* and *Cambodia*. The number of characters represented by the asterisk can vary.

? The question mark can be used anywhere in your search string to represent a single alphanumeric character. Suppose you use the Find feature to search for the text string **f?ll**. Some of the possible matches you could get in a search like this are words that differ by just one character, such as *fill*, *fall*, *full*, and *fell*.

[] Brackets specify a list of possible matches for a single character found in the items you are searching for. For instance, you could set up the Find feature to look for the text string **Jo[ah]n**. Matches to this text string would be limited to *Joan* and *John*.

The number sign represents a single numeric character in a search string. It works very much like the question mark wildcard. Suppose you have a product number field that contains data in the form of three-digit codes (for example, 142 or 333). Your supplier calls and tells you all the products ending in 22 are going to be discontinued. No problem—you can do a search using **#22** to find them.

Wildcards can be quite useful when you are using the Find feature and are not completely sure of the field data that you are searching for. Wildcards can also help you make a search much more precise so that you can find matches for only a portion of a text or numerical entry.

Using Replace

Another Access feature that operates very much like the Find feature is Replace. The Replace feature enables you to not only find certain data entries, but also to replace them with different data. For example, if you misspelled a certain brand name in your inventory table (something that the Spell Checker will not help you with), you can use the Replace feature to find the misspelled entry and replace it with the correctly spelled data.

To find and replace data, complete the following steps:

1. Select **Edit**, **Replace** or press **Ctrl+H**. The Replace in Field dialog box appears (see Figure 8.3).

2. Type the text you want to find in the **Find What** text box. Type the text you want to replace it with in the **Replace With** text box.

Figure 8.3

The Replace feature enables you to locate data and then replace it with new data.

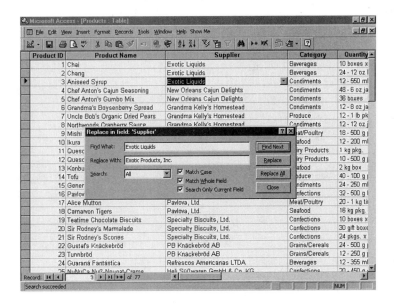

3. Select any search option you want to set (see "Setting Search Parameters" earlier in this chapter for help).

4. Click **Find Next**. Access finds the first occurrence of the **Find What** data and selects it. To replace the data, click the **Replace** button.

5. Click the **Find Next** button to continue and replace the data one instance at a time.

 Replace All   If you are sure you want to replace every occurrence of the data that you are searching for, you can click the **Replace All** button in the Replace in Field dialog box.

You have a couple of options if you find that you inadvertently replaced an item that should not have been replaced. Close the Replace dialog box and immediately click the **Undo** button on the toolbar to undo your last replacement action. If you used Replace All and inadvertently replaced items that you did not want to replace, again close the Replace in Field dialog box and click the **Undo** button. This action reverts all the replaced items to their original value.

Filtering Records

You've already seen that the Find feature enables you to move through a table and locate records that meet your search criteria. However, all the records, even those that don't match your criteria, still appear onscreen and make it more difficult to concentrate on the records that do match the search criteria.

Filters also use criteria to operate. However, filters are superior to the Find feature in that they display only the records that match the filter criteria. The other records in the table are hidden. Filtering makes working with the records easier.

 Find Versus Filters   Use Find to quickly locate records that have a field matching certain criteria. Use filters when you really need to take a hard look at a subset of your table—the records matching the filter criteria.

A *filter* is a selected criterion that returns a subset of the records in your table. There are two ways of filtering tables so that you can view a subset of your records: filter by selection and filter by form. Both methods provide the same results.

Filtering by Selection

An incredibly straightforward way to filter records is filtering by selection. You give Access an example of the field data you want to filter the table by, and Access shows you only the records that match. For example, a Products table usually contains a field for Suppliers. To display a subset of the table that shows only the products that are supplied by a particular supplier, select the supplier and then invoke the **Filter** command.

To filter by selection, complete the following steps:

1. Locate the data in a field column that you want to use to filter the table.

2. Select the value for the filter as follows:

    ▶ To find all records where the field value is identical to the selected value, select the entire field entry.

    ▶ To find all records where the field begins with the selected value, select part of the field entry beginning with the first character.

    ▶ To find all records where the field contains the selected value at any point, select part of the field entry beginning after the first character.

3. Click the **Filter by Selection** button on the toolbar or select **Records**, **Filter**, **Filter by Selection**. The records that match the criteria appear in the table, as you can see in the example in Figure 8.4.

4. To cancel the filter and return all the records in the table to the screen, click the **Remove Filter** button on the toolbar.

Figure 8.4

Filter by selection enables you to quickly view a subset of the records in a table.

Filter by Selection button

Remove Filter button

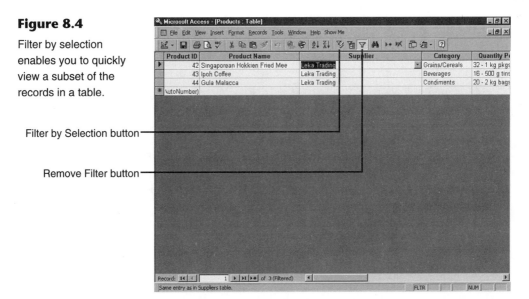

Filtering by Form

When you filter by form, a blank datasheet row appears with all the appropriate Field columns found in your table. Then all you have to do is pick the field or fields you want involved in the filtering. A drop-down arrow appears in each field box; click it and select the data to serve as the filter criteria. The data that appears in the particular field (data from every record in the table) is listed as a potential criterion.

The major difference between filtering by form and filtering by selection is the number of criteria that you can set. Filtering by form enables you to set criteria in multiple fields, whereas filtering by selection allows you to select only one criterion in one field.

 Filtering by Form in the Form View   If you are in the Form view and you want to filter by form, Access provides you with a Form view of a blank record rather than the blank datasheet record that you get when you filter by form in Datasheet view.

To filter by form, complete the following steps:

1. In Datasheet view, click the **Filter by Form** button on the toolbar or select **Records**, **Filter**, **Filter by Form**. A blank datasheet row appears.

2. Click in the field or fields for which you want to set criteria; a drop-down list arrow appears. Click the arrow to select the filter information for that field (or you can type a value in the text box if you want).

3. Enter all the criteria for the filter (see Figure 8.5) and click the **Apply Filter** button on the toolbar.

4. The records that meet your filter criteria appear in the table.

 Clearing the Field with Delete   To clear field data that already appears in the Filter by Form datasheet row, select the entry and press the **Delete** key to remove it.

Filtering by form also enables you to set up conditional criteria for a field. Suppose you want to find the products in your Product table that have fallen below a certain stocking level in your warehouse (for example, items that have fallen below 6 in stock). You could type the logical expression **<6** in the In Stock field on the Filter form. When you apply the filter, only the records for products whose In Stock value is less than 6 would appear in the filter results.

Figure 8.5

Filter by form enables you to set a number of criteria to filter the table by including logical expressions.

Apply Filter button

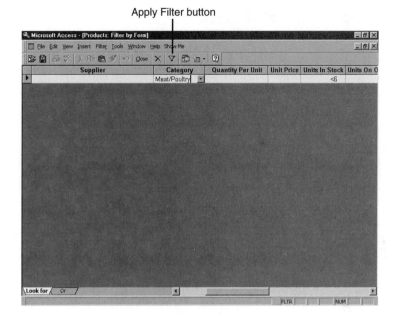

Although filtering by form enables you to create complex filters for your database tables, these kinds of record manipulations may be better served by queries, which are covered in Lessons 13, "Designing Queries," and 14, "Working with Advanced Queries."

Review Questions

The Certified Microsoft Office User Exams are task oriented. The following types of questions are not representative of the test. These questions are designed to help you understand the required tasks and methods of performing those tasks prior to taking the test.

1. Describe how to use the Find feature.

2. How do you filter a table by form?

3. How do you remove a filter from a table?

4. How do you filter a table by selection?

5. True or False: Filtering by form enables you to set filter criteria in more than one field.

Review Question Answers

1. Click somewhere in the field column you want to search by. Click the **Find** button. Type the find value in the **Find What** text box. Select appropriate search criteria and then click **Find First**. The first match will be highlighted. Click **Find Next** to continue the search. For more information, see the section "Using the Find Command."

2. Click the **Filter by Form** button on the toolbar. Set the criteria in the Datasheet form's field columns. Click the **Apply Filter** button to view the results of the filter. For more information, see the section "Filtering by Form."

3. Click the **Remove Filter** button on the toolbar. For more information, see the section "Filtering by Selection."

4. Select all or a portion of the data in a field in a particular record. Click the **Filter by Selection** button on the toolbar to view the results of the filter. For more information, see the section "Filtering Records."

5. True—this is the major difference between filtering by form and filtering by selection. For more information, see the sections "Using the Find Command" and "Filtering Records."

Practice Lab

The Microsoft Access Expert User Exam lists three Required Tasks for the "Locate Information" Skill Area. The following Practice Lab covers each Required Task.

 Required Tasks   The three Required Tasks for this Skill Area are find a specific record, add filters (selection and form), and remove filters.

Copy the **lesson8.mdb** database from the CD that accompanies this book to a folder on your computer using Windows Explorer. Open the database.

Find a Specific Record

1. Open the **Suppliers** table. Use the Find feature to locate the Supplier who has Gordon Mill as the contact person.

2. Open the **Customers** table. Use the Find feature to locate the record for the customer who lives in California.

3. Open the **Employees** table and use the Replace feature to replace the last name of Smith with Johnson. (You are looking for Alice Smith's record.)

Add and Remove Filters

1. Open the **Employees** table and use filter by selection to view the records for the employees who work in the Porches and Decks department.

2. Remove the current filter, and then close the table.

3. Open the **Customers** table and use filter by form to determine which customers live in Minnesota

4. Open the **Employees** table and use filter by form to determine which employees started after 8/8/96. Remove the filter after viewing the results.

Find a Specific Record

1. Open the **Suppliers** table and click the Contact Person field column. Click the **Find** button. In the **Find What** text box, type **Gordon Mill**.

2. Open the **Customers** table and click the State field. Click the **Find** button. Type **CA** in the **Find What** text box.

3. Open the **Employees** table and click the Last Name field. Click **Edit**, **Replace**. Type **Smith** in the **Find What** text box and type **Johnson** in the **Replace With** text box.

Add and Remove Filters

1. Open the **Employees** table; in the Department field column, select the first entry of Porches and Decks. Click the **Filter by Selection** button to filter the table.

2. Click the **Remove Filter** button.

3. Open the **Customers** table and click the **Filter by Form** button. In the State field column on the form, use the drop-down arrow to select **MN**. Click the **Apply Filter** button.

4. Open the **Employees** table and click the **Filter by Form** button. Click the Start Date field and type **>8/8/96**. Click the **Apply Filter** button. The results of this filter appear in Figure 8.6.

Figure 8.6

The results of the filter by start date.

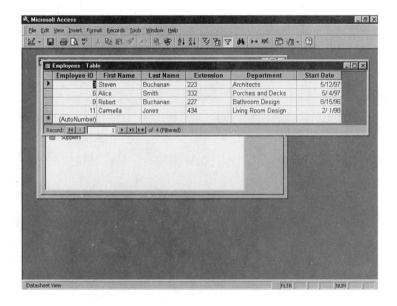

Building a Relational Database

This lesson covers Build a Relational Database skills for the Expert User level.

In this lesson, you learn the following Required Tasks for your exam:

▶ Identify relationships

▶ Relate tables

Understanding Table Relationships

One of the strengths of Access as a relational database is its capability to relate tables together via a common field. For example, you may have a Customers table that contains all the information on your customers, including a separate customer number for each record. (This customer number would be the primary key field for this table.)

Another table in your database may be an Orders table that details every order you've taken. The Orders table would obviously need to reference the customer who made the order. You can establish this relationship by entering the customer number in the Orders table. The data in these two tables is then linked (that is, related) by a common field: CustNo (see Figure 9.1).

Figure 9.1

Related tables share a common field (CustNo) that links the information in the two tables.

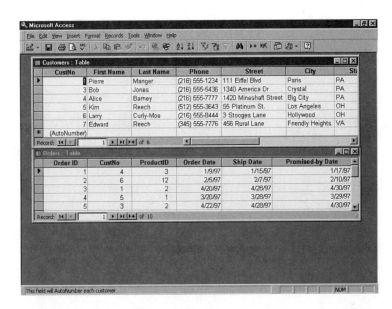

Relating the tables in a database gives you a great deal of analytical power over the information that the database holds. As you create your tables and the fields that they contain, you should identify and include fields that can potentially link two tables. Both tables must have the field in their table structure. The shared field is usually the primary key for one of the tables in the relationship. In the other table, the shared field is referred to as the *foreign key*.

 Relating Tables with a Nonprimary Key Field If you plan to relate two tables with a shared field that does not serve as the primary key for either table, the field must be indexed in one of the tables. See Lesson 14, "Working with Advanced Queries," for information on indexing fields.

The ideal relational database is made up of simple tables that hold subsets of the complete data (all the information). Then, by relating the various tables by common fields, you can integrate the information in the different tables together in your queries, forms, and reports.

Creating Table Relationships

New relationships are created in the Relationships window. Open the database for which you want to create the relationship or relationships and complete the following steps:

1. Select **Relationships** from the Tools menu or click the **Relationships** button on the Database toolbar. The Relationships window appears.

2. In the Relationships window, the Show Table dialog box displays a list of the tables in your database, as shown in Figure 9.2.

Show Table button

Figure 9.2

The Show Table dialog box enables you to add tables to the Relationships window.

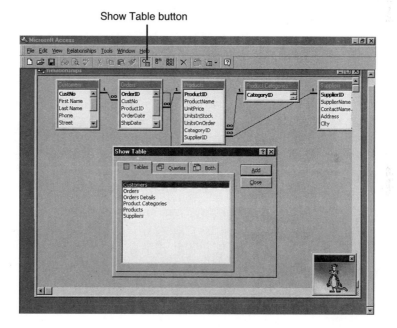

3. Select the tables for which you want to create relationships; select a table and then click the **Add** button. Repeat this step until you have added all the tables you need.

4. Click the **Close** button to close the Add Tables dialog box.

Reopen the Show Table Dialog Box If you inadvertently close the Show Table dialog box or have already created some relationships between tables and open the Relationships window to add more, you can open the Show Table dialog box by clicking the **Show Table** button on the Relationship toolbar.

 Ready-Made Relationships When you use the Table Wizard, the tables you create with the sample fields often have shared fields. Access knows that you will eventually want to relate the tables, so the sample fields overlap between the different sample table types. The Table Wizard even offers you the option of relating the table that you are building to any of the current tables in the database during the creation process. It also asks you whether there is a shared field.

Working in the Relationships Window

After the appropriate tables are in the Relationships window, you are ready to create the actual relationships between the tables.

As you prepare to create your relationships, you should keep two things in mind: The related fields do not have to have the same names; and the fields must have the same data type (with two exceptions). When the matching fields are Number fields, they must also have the same FieldSize property setting. For example, one table may have a field called Customer Number and the other table may have a field named CustomerID. As long as these two fields hold the same kind of data, you can relate them.

The two exceptions to matching data types are that you can match an AutoNumber field with a Number field whose FieldSize property is set to Long Integer, and you can match an AutoNumber field with a Number field if both fields have their FieldSize property set to Replication ID. Field Properties are covered in more detail in Lesson 10, "Maintaining Data Integrity in a Table."

To create relationships between two fields in the Relationships window, complete the following steps:

1. Make sure the two tables that you want to create the relationships between appear in the Relationships window.

2. Select the shared field in the table in which the field serves as the primary key (or is indexed)—the field name will be in bold. Drag the field (a small field box appears) and drop it on the shared field in the other table. The Relationships dialog box appears, as shown in Figure 9.3.

Figure 9.3

The Relationships
dialog box is where
you set the various
parameters for the join
between the two
tables.

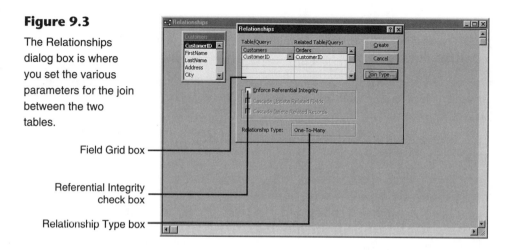

Field Grid box

Referential Integrity
check box

Relationship Type box

The Relationships dialog box has three areas: the Field Grid box, the Referential Integrity area, and the Relationship Type box. The Field Grid box at the top of the dialog box displays the current relationship. Drop-down arrows enable you to change the fields that have been selected in the relationships. You can use the Join Type button to select the type of join you want to create between the two tables.

Referential Integrity

In the middle of the dialog box is a check box labeled **Enforce Referential Integrity**. *Referential integrity* means that a value entered in a field must be in the same pool of data that is found in its related field. For example, if the CustomerID field relates a Customers and Orders table, the values entered in the CustomerID field in the Orders table must exist in the CustomerID field in the Customers table. You could not enter CutomerID 100 in the Orders table if a customer with the CustomerID 100 did not exist in the Customers table.

Another benefit of referential integrity is that you cannot delete any data from a customer's record in the Customers table if that particular customer had orders that were recorded in the Orders table. Access will not allow orders that are not "owned" by a particular customer.

Referential integrity is one of the strategies that can be used to maintain the integrity and validity of the data in your tables. Using referential integrity to maintain your data's integrity is covered in detail in Lesson 10.

Relationship Type

At the bottom of the dialog box is the Relationship Type box. Access categorizes each common field link that you create between tables as a certain type of relationship. The relationship can be a one-to-many relationship, a one-to-one relationship, or a many-to-many relationship. (The relationship types are described in more detail in the section, "Differentiating Relationship Types.")

Access determines the relationship type based on the data that it finds in the tables that you are relating. If Access cannot determine the type of relationship, it places *Indeterminate* in the **Relationship Type** box.

Join Type

The **Join Type** button in the Relationships dialog box enables you to select the type of join that exists between the two related tables. When you click the **Join Type** button, the Join Properties dialog box appears. The default join type for table relationships is Only Include Rows Where the Joined Fields for Both Tables Are Equal. This type of join allows Access queries to display only the records that have matching field data in the related field. Join types are discussed more fully in Lessons 13, "Designing Queries," and 14, which cover the query-creation process.

To select a new join type, complete the following steps:

1. Click the **Join Type** button; the Join Properties dialog box appears.

2. Select the radio button for the Join type.

3. Click **OK** to close the Join Type dialog box.

4. To close the Join Type dialog box without changing the join type, click the **Close** button.

Completing the Relationship Creation Process

After you determine that the fields selected for the relationship are correct and whether or not you want to enforce referential integrity, click the **Create** button to complete the relationship creation process. You return to the Relationships window. The new relationship is represented by a line joining the two tables, as shown in Figure 9.4.

 Understanding Relationship Symbols If you chose to enforce referential integrity in the Relationships dialog box, you may notice that the join line between the tables is marked with special symbols. A **1** marks the portion of a join line attached to a table where the joined field is either in a one-to-many or one-to-one relationship (the field is on the one side of the relationship). An infinity sign (∞) on the join line marks fields involved in one-to-many or many-to-many relationships (the field is on the many side of the relationship).

Figure 9.4

A join line depicts the relationship between the tables.

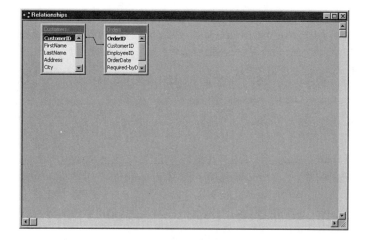

Differentiating Relationship Types

Understanding the types of relationships that can be created between tables can help you identify the shared fields that you will use to join the information in two tables. In a well-designed database, each table typically is related to another table, so in effect all the data in the database can be pulled together in queries, forms, or reports (see Figure 9.5).

Figure 9.5

A well-designed database has joins between all the tables in the database.

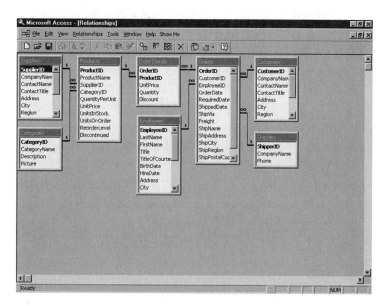

Understanding the type of relationships that can exist between two tables can help you design the tables in your database. In *one-to-many relationships,* Access can match each record of one table to many records of another table. This type of relationship typically occurs between a Customers table and an Orders table. For example, a unique customer number identifies each customer. This uniquely identified customer can place any number of orders for your products. Therefore, Access can match each record in Customers (one) to an infinite number of records (many) in the Orders table. You will find that most relationships you create for a database are one-to-many relationships.

In a *one-to-one relationship*, a record in one table has only one possible matching record in the second table—for example, a publishing company that lets its authors write only one book. If you had an Author table and a Book table for the situation described, sharing the common author number field, you would have a one-to-one relationship. Each author record would match one book record. One-to-one relationships can also be used for security purposes. You might have a table just for Social Security numbers or birth dates that are linked to the employee table by the person's name or employee ID.

In a *many-to-many relationship,* each record in the first table of the relationship can have many matches in the second table, and each record in the second table can have many matches in the first table. An example is a construction company that hires subcontractors to build houses. The records in the Subcontractor table could potentially have many matching records (different house projects) in the House table. And the House table could have many matches in the Subcontractor table because the construction company uses multiple subcontractors to build an entire house.

Compared to the other two types of relationships, the many-to-many relationship is a little more difficult to understand and create in an Access database. This type of relationship is normally created by using a *Join table* (it is also called a *bridge* table) as an intermediary between the two tables that have the many to many relationship.

In the subcontractor/house example, a third table (the Join table) would include only two fields: the subcontractor ID and the house (project) ID. These fields would be the primary key for their respective tables.

Using the Join table creates a one-to-many relationship between the Subcontractor table and the Join table and a one-to-many relationship between the House table and the Join table. The relationship, then, between the Subcontractor table and the House table (due to the inclusion of the Join table) would be many-to-many.

 NorthWind Database Relationships   The NorthWind database that ships with your Access 97 software is an excellent resource for exploring table relationships. Open this database and view the relationships that have been created between the tables.

Deleting Table Relationships

Deleting relationships between tables is accomplished in the Relationships window. To delete a relationship, complete the following steps:

1. Click the **join line** between the two tables. The line is selected (it will appear darker).

2. Press the **Delete** key. You will be asked whether you want to permanently delete the selected relationship from the Database. Click **Yes** to delete the relationship.

Editing Table Relationships

You can also edit table relationships in the Relationships window. To edit a relationship, complete the following steps:

1. Double-click the **join line** between two tables. The Relationships dialog box appears.

2. Make any necessary changes to the relationship and click **OK** to close the Relationships dialog box.

To remove tables from the Relationships window that are not involved in relationships, click the table and press the **Delete** key. When you finish creating, deleting, or editing table relationships, click the **Save** button on the toolbar to save the changes that you made to the database. Close the Relationships window by clicking its **Close** (**x**) button.

Review Questions

The Certified Microsoft Office User Exams are task oriented. The following types of questions are not representative of the test. These questions are designed to help you understand the required tasks and methods of performing those tasks prior to taking the test.

1. Describe how to create a relationship between two tables.

2. How do you delete a relationship between two tables?

3. Describe a one-to-many relationship.

4. How do you edit a table relationship?

5. True or False: The fields that you use to link two tables do not have to be of the same data type.

Review Question Answers

1. Open the Relationships window and drag the field (the primary key) from the first table onto the shared field (the foreign key) in the second table. The Relationships dialog box opens. After selecting options such as Enforce Referential Integrity, click **Create** to close the Relationships dialog box and create the join between the two tables. For more information, see the section "Creating Table Relationships."

2. In the Relationships window, select the join line between two tables that represents the relationship you want to delete. Press the **Delete** key; click **Yes** to proceed with the relationship deletion. For more information, see the section "Deleting Table Relationships."

3. Each record in the table in which the shared field is the primary key or an indexed field has many potential matches to records in the other table in the relationship where the shared field is the foreign key. For more information, see the section "Differentiating Relationship Types."

4. Open the Relationships window and double-click the join line for the relationship you want to edit. Make necessary changes to the relationship in the Relationships dialog box and then click **OK**. For more information, see the section "Editing Table Relationships."

5. False, with two exceptions: You can match an AutoNumber field with a Number field whose FieldSize property is set to Long Integer, and you can match an AutoNumber field with a Number field if both fields have their FieldSize property set to Replication ID. For more information, see the section "Creating Table Relationships."

Practice Lab

The Microsoft Access Expert User Exam lists two Required Tasks for the "Build a Relational Database" Skill Area. The following practice lab covers each Required Task.

Required Tasks   The two Required Tasks for this Skill Area are identify relationships and relate tables.

Copy the **lesson9.mdb** database from the CD that accompanies this book to a folder on your computer using Windows Explorer. Open the database. Open the Relationships window and complete the following tasks:

1. Add the Customers and Orders table to the Relationships window.

2. Identify the shared field that can be used to relate the Customers and Orders table.

3. Create a relationship between the Customers and Orders table. Enforce Referential Integrity in the relationship.

4. Add the Products table and the Suppliers table to the Relationships window.

5. Create a relationship between the Products table and the Suppliers table using a shared field. Do not enforce referential integrity for the relationship.

6. Delete the relationship between the Order Details and Orders tables.

7. Save the changes you have made to the relationships in the database.

Open the database **lesson9a.mdb** on the CD to see a completed version of the database you worked with in this lab.

LESSON 10

Maintaining Data Integrity in a Table

This lesson covers five of the Maintain Data Integrity skills for the Expert User level.

In this lesson, you learn the following Required Tasks for your exam:

- ▶ Identify criteria for data integrity
- ▶ Validate text
- ▶ Set required properties
- ▶ Set validation rules
- ▶ Set Lookup fields

Strategies That Ensure Data Integrity

As you create an Access database, it's important to carefully build the database objects—such as tables, forms, queries, and reports—that you will use in the database. In the final analysis, however, it is the data held in the database, not the objects, that make the database valuable. Therefore, you need to develop strategies to ensure the data's integrity; that is, whether you or someone else enters the data, you must make sure the right values get into the right fields.

You've already learned that you can use simple features such as the Description box in table Design view to provide information about the field when it is entered during the data entry process. And you can set the field width in the Field Properties box to limit the number of characters that can be entered into the field (see Lesson 3, "Creating Tables"). Access provides several other strategies for ensuring data integrity, which can greatly simplify the data entry process.

Specifying a Default Value in a Field

One strategy for making sure the right data ends up in a particular field is to specify a default value for the field in the table. Setting a default value in a field does not preclude you from entering other values when you enter data in the table. The default value provides a possible entry and should be set as the most likely entry to appear in that field.

For example, if you have a Credit Limit field for your customers that is usually $8,000, then it makes sense to set 8000 as the default value. You can set a default value for a field in table Design view.

In Design view, open the table that holds the field to which you want to assign a default value. To place the table in Design view, you can either select the table in the Database window and click the **Design** button or, if the table is already open, click the **View** button on the toolbar (the View button toggles between Table and Design views).

After the table is open in Design view, follow these steps to assign a default value to a field:

1. In the field grid box, click the field row for the field in which you want to set the default value.

2. Click the **Default Value** box in the Field Properties pane.

3. Enter the default value for the field. You can enter text or numbers in the **Default Value** box. For example, if most of your customers reside in Minnesota, you could set MN as the default value for the State field, or if the typical credit limit is $15,000, you could place 15000 in the **Default Value** box for the Credit Limit field (see Figure 10.1).

4. Click the **Save** button on the Design toolbar to save changes that you make to the table structure.

When you return to Table view and enter new records, the default value appears in the field. To override the default value, select the field information (the default value) and type a new value or text entry.

Figure 10.1

Setting default values for fields helps you get the right values into your fields.

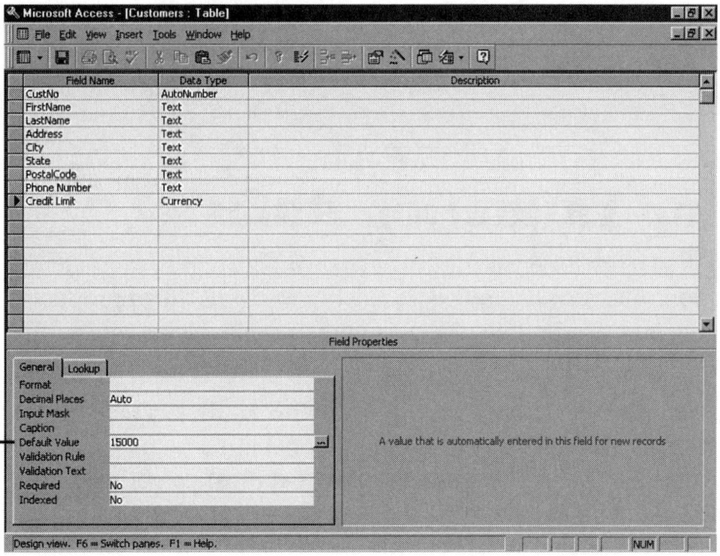

Default Value box

Setting default values for your fields is very straightforward. Table 10.1 gives examples of fields and their data types and shows how a sample default value would appear in the Default Value box.

Table 10.1 Field data types and possible default values.

Field	Data Type	Default Value
Items On Order	Number	50
Credit Limit	Currency	10000
		The Currency data type supplies the dollar sign and decimal places for you.
Region	Text	Midwest

continues

Table 10.1 Continued

Field	Data Type	Default Value
Title	Text	"Secretary, Department of the Interior"
		If a default value has punctuation in it, you must enclose the default value in quotation marks.
Order Date	Date	Date()
		This value enters the current date.

Using Validation Rules

Another strategy for ensuring your data's integrity is to validate text in a field by setting a validation rule. A *validation rule* is a list or range of the appropriate values that can be entered into a particular field. These values are called *legal values*. The validation rule rejects any entry that you try to make in the field that is not a legal entry.

Validation rules can also be accompanied by validation text. *Validation text* appears in the error message box that opens if you enter data in a field that violates the validation rule. Access does not permit you to leave the field until you enter a legal value; therefore, the validation text should describe the parameters for a legal value. This technique will help the person entering the data get the correct information into the particular field.

Entering Validation Rules

Validation rules are set in the Properties pane of the table Design window. To set a validation rule and enter the accompanying validation text, follow these steps:

1. Open the table in Design view. In the **Field Grid** box, click the field row for the field where you want to set the validation rule.

2. Click the **Validation Rule** box in the Properties pane. Enter the validation rule. For example, if you always reorder products that your company sells in amounts of at least 5 and no more than 25, you would enter the validation rule **>=5 And <=25** in the **Validation Rule** box for the Units on Order field, as shown in Figure 10.2. The *And* in the rule means that both conditions must be true for the value to be a legal entry; it can be 5 and above *and* it cannot be more than 25.

3. After you enter the validation rule, you enter the validation text. This text appears in the error message that opens when the validation rule is violated during data entry in the table. Click the **Validation Text** box and enter the text. For the validation rule set in step 2, the validation text might be `Order Amount must be greater than or equal to 5 or less than or equal to 25`.

Figure 10.2

You can use validation rules and validation text to make sure that legal values are entered in your table fields.

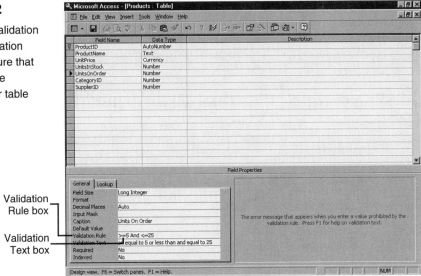

4. Before exiting the Design window or switching to Table view, save the changes you made to the table's structure by clicking the **Save** button on the toolbar.

5. If data has already been entered in the field for which you have created the validation rule, the following message box appears: `Data Integrity Rules have been changed; existing data may not be valid for new rules`. You are given the option of having the existing data checked with the new rule. If you want to check the existing data, click **Yes**; if not, click **No**. If you click **Yes**, Access notifies you if data already in the field violates the rule. However, you are not given details about which record (or records) is violating the new validation rule.

 Use a Filter to Find Records That Violate the Validation Rule   If the message appears that records currently in your table violate the new validation rule, you can set up a filter by form that shows the records with values that fall outside the legal entries (see Lesson 8, "Finding and Filtering Records in a Table," for information on filters).

6. When you return to Table view and enter data, entries in the field that has been assigned a validation rule must be legal values. When you enter a value that is not legal, an error message appears, as shown in Figure 10.3.

Figure 10.3

Validation text appears in the error message box when you violate the validation rule during data entry.

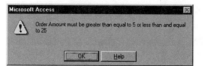

Understanding Validation Rule Operators

Validation rules use a set of operators, whether you are creating rules that contain text or numbers. Table 10.2 lists some of the operators and how you use them.

Table 10.2 Validation rule operators.

Operator	Use in a Validation Rule	Example
And	A rule that validates the data by more than one parameter, or places legal entries within a range of numbers.	>=5 And <=25 The data must be greater than or equal to 5 *and* less than or equal to 25.
Or	A rule that validates the data with a list of possible legal entries.	MN Or WI Or MI Legal entries consist of MN *or* WI *or* MI only.
=	A rule that validates the data by allowing only one legal entry. be 15000. This type of rule could	=15000 The data entered in the field must be used with a default value.
>	A rule that validates data by designating a range of values that must be greater than the specified data.	>07/15/97 The dates entered in the field must be greater than (or after) July 15, 1997.
<	A rule that validates data by designating a range of values that must be less than the specified data.	<50 The numerical data entered must be less than 50.

You can combine the preceding operators to provide more complex rules. Remember that validation text should accompany all the rules that you create. This text tells the person doing the data entry the range of legal values for a particular field.

Using the Expression Builder When you click the **Validation Rule** box, a button containing an ellipsis (three periods) appears. This **Build** button opens the Expression Builder window. You can use the Expression Builder to create mathematical expressions and conditional statements involving your table fields. You can also use the Expression Builder when you design forms, queries, and reports (see Lesson 12, "Advanced Form Design," Lesson 13, "Designing Queries," and Lesson 16, "Modifying Report Design").

Setting Required Fields

Another way to ensure your data integrity is to specify fields as *required*—the field must have data entered into it before you can proceed to another field. Although setting fields as required does not mean that the data in the field is correct, it does mean that an entry must be made in the field; it cannot be left blank. This method is particularly useful when you definitely require the data in a particular field, such as the social security field in an Employees table.

You can use the Required Field parameter along with other data integrity strategies, such as validation rules, to make sure that the field data is entered and entered correctly.

To specify a required field, complete the following steps:

1. Open the table in Design view; click the row of the field you want to make a required field.

2. In the Properties pane, click the **Required** box. A drop-down arrow appears. Click the arrow and select **Yes**. The field is now required (see Figure 10.4).

3. Save changes that you make to the table's structure. The **Data Integrity** message box displays the following message: Data Integrity Rules have been changed; existing data may not be valid for new rules. You are given the option of having the fields currently in the table checked for data in the required field. To check the fields, click **Yes**; to skip this step, click **No**.

If you skip a required field as you enter new records, you receive an error message as you attempt to leave the record stating that the required field cannot contain a null value. Access will not let you leave the record until you place a value in the required field.

Figure 10.4

You can designate fields as required to make sure that data is entered into them.

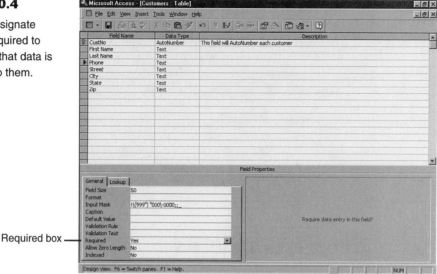

Required box ────

Setting Field Size

Setting the field size for a field can also help you get the appropriate data into a particular field. You learned Lesson 6, "Modifying a Table," that you can use the field size to limit the number of characters entered in a text field. For instance, you might set the field size to 2 for a text field where you enter the state abbreviation (MN, TX, or AZ).

Field size cannot be changed for Time/Date fields or Currency fields. Their field size is handled by their format (see "Specifying a Format and Input Masks" in this lesson).

Setting the field size for number fields can be important, depending on the size of the number you want to enter in the field. The default field size for a number field is Long Integer. This field size can store numbers from –2,147,483,648 to 2,147,483,647 (it does not accept fractions). Five other field sizes exist for numbers; your selection depends on the range of numeric values you want to store in the field:

▶ **Byte**   Stores numbers from 0 to 255 (no fractions).

▶ **Integer**   Stores numbers from –32,768 to 32,767 (no fractions).

▶ **Single**   Stores numbers from –3.402823E38 to –1.401298E–45 for negative values and from 1.401298E–45 to 3.402823E38 for positive values.

▶ **Double**   Stores numbers from –1.79769313486231E308 to –4.94065645841247E–324 for negative values and from 1.79769313486231E308 to 4.94065645841247E–324 for positive values.

▶ **Replication ID** This field size is used only when you have several copies of the database in different locations and the databases are synchronized periodically. Replication IDs play an important part in the synchronization. You will rarely, if ever, use this field size for a table, even in databases that are shared on a network.

AutoNumber fields can have a field size of Long Integer or Replication ID. Long Integer is the default and should remain the field size for the field except when multiple copies of the database must be synchronized.

To select a new field size for a text, number, or AutoNumber field, click the Field Properties pane **Field Size** box. For text, enter a new size (1 to 255). For number and AutoNumber fields, click the drop-down arrow in the **Field Size** box and select the appropriate field size.

Changing Field Sizes If you change a large field size for a Number field to a smaller field size, you stand the risk of losing data. Set the field sizes for your fields when you first build the table. This method precludes the potential for lost data.

Specifying a Format and Input Masks

Two other strategies for ensuring data integrity are specifying a format and using input masks. Although these two features do not verify entries or reject illegal entries, they can help you input the data in the correct format or with the correct number of characters. You can also use these two features to format the case (uppercase or lowercase) of an entry and to enter repeating characters into an entry (such as the hyphens (-) in a social security number).

Specifying a Format

Specifying a format for a particular field simply means that you predetermine the number of characters or how the data should appear when entered into the field. For example, you may want characters entered into the State field to always appear in uppercase letters. By placing the greater than (>) sign in the **Format** box, you assure that entries in the field always appear in uppercase.

You can use several special symbols to format the text entered in text fields. Table 10.3 describes the symbols and gives examples of their use.

Table 10.3 Formatting symbols.

Symbol	Description	Example
@	Text character (either a character or a space) is required.	@@@-@@-@@@@ The entry **555443333** appears as 555-44-3333.
<	Force all characters to lowercase.	< The entry **cat** or **DOG** appears as cat or dog.
>	Force all characters to uppercase.	> The entry **mn** or **oH** appears as MN or OH.

To enter a format for a text field, type the format in the Field Properties pane **Format** box.

The Date, Number, and Currency data types have ready-made formats, which can be selected in the **Format** box. To change the format for the date, number or currency fields, follow these steps:

1. Open the table in Design view and select the field in the Field Grid pane.

2. To change the field format, click the Field Properties pane **Format** box. Select a new format from the drop-down list shown in Figure 10.5.

3. Save changes that you make to the table structure.

Input Masks

Input masks can do a lot of the same things that formats can do, but input masks are actually easier to create because you can use the Input Mask Wizard. This Wizard walks you through the steps of creating an input mask for a particular field.

For example, social security numbers have a hyphen (-) between each sequence of numbers. An input mask can ensure that you enter the right number of characters for a social security number and will automatically enter the hyphens for you. The fact that input masks enter repeating characters for you enables you to concentrate on the data that must be entered in the field.

To create an input mask for a field, complete the following steps:

1. Select the field in the **Field Grid** box for which you want to create the input mask.

Figure 10.5

Formats for Date,
Number, and Currency
fields can help you
enter the appropriate
data in the field.

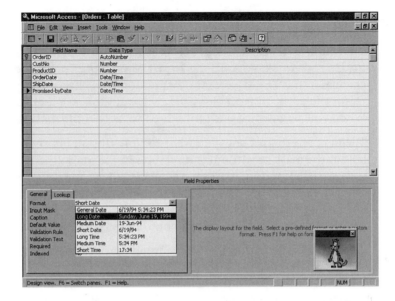

2. In the Field Properties pane, click the **Input Mask** box. A **Mask** button (the gray button with the ellipsis) appears on the right side of the **Input Mask** box.

3. Click the **Mask** button to start the Input Mask Wizard. The Input Mask Wizard window opens. The first screen displays a selection of input masks, including formats for zip codes, social security numbers, phone numbers, and dates.

4. To select a preexisting mask, click **Input Mask** in the scroll box. To try the mask, press the **Tab** key. The insertion point moves to the **Try It** box. Type some sample data into the box to see how the mask works, as shown in Figure 10.6.

Figure 10.6

You can try the various
input masks before
proceeding to the Input
Mask Wizard's next
screen.

5. After you select your input mask, click the **Next** button. The next screen provides you with the option of editing the mask. For example, the standard zip code mask is "5 plus 4" (xxxxx-xxxx). If you want to remove the last four digits for the zip code mask, do so in the **Input Mask** box. You can test your mask changes in the **Try It** box. Another option is to change the placeholder character for the mask. In most cases, you will want to leave it at the default value. When you are satisfied with the edited version of the mask, click **Next**.

6. The next screen asks how you want to store the data in the table: with the symbols in the mask or without the symbols in the mask (the hyphen (-) in the zip code or social security masks is a symbol). A few stored symbols will not really affect the size of your database file (but in the case of very complex masks that enter a large number of symbols, you may to decide not to store them with the data). Select the appropriate radio button and click **Next** to continue.

7. Click the **Finish** button to end the input mask creation process.

Now when you enter data into the field in the table view, the input mask limits the number of characters that can be entered in the field and supplies special symbols such as parentheses and hyphens.

Enforcing Referential Integrity in Table Relationships

Referential Integrity means that a value entered in a field must be in the same pool of data that is found in its related field. For example, if the CustomerID field relates a Customers table and an Orders table, the values entered in the CustomerID field in the Orders table must already exist in the CustomerID field in the Customers table. You cannot enter CustomerID 100 in the Orders table if a customer with the CustomerID 100 does not exist in the Customers table.

Using Referential Integrity as a strategy for ensuring data validity means that you must enter the data into your tables in a particular order. For example, if CustomerID relates a Customers table and an Orders table as before, you must enter the customer information in the Customers table before you can enter the customer's order in the Orders table.

The situation is not unlike the chicken and the egg paradox. You must be aware of the relationships that you create between your tables and know which relationships are enforcing Referential Integrity. These relationships dictate which table you should enter new data in first.

To enforce Referential Integrity in a relationship, complete the following steps:

1. Click the **Relationships** button on the Database toolbar. The Relationships window appears.

2. In the Relationships window, the Show Table dialog box opens. If necessary, select the tables you want to create relationships for and add them to the Relationships window.

3. When you have added all the tables you need, click the **Close** button to close the Show Tables dialog box.

4. Drag a shared field from the table where it is the primary key to the table where the field is the foreign key. The Relationships dialog box opens.

5. In the middle of the dialog box is a check box labeled **Enforce Referential Integrity**. Click the check box.

6. Click **Create** to create the relationship. The new relationship appears between the tables in the Relationship window. The join line is labeled with symbols that depict the type of relationship that exists between the two tables (see Figure 10.7). For example, in a one-to-many relationship, the join line is marked with a 1 on the one side of the relationship. An infinity sign (∞) on the join line depicts the many side of the relationship (one-to-many relationship).

You can also enforce Referential Integrity on existing relationships. Double-click the relationship join line to open the Relationships dialog box. Click the **Enforce Referential Integrity** check box. Click **OK** to close the Relationships dialog box. The join line is labeled with relationship symbols as shown in Figure 10.7.

Figure 10.7

Relationship symbols appear on join lines where Referential Integrity has been enforced.

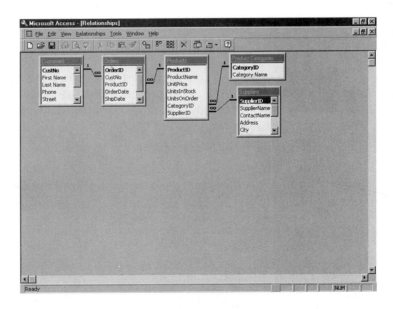

Make sure that you save the changes you make to the database's relationships. For more information on creating (and understanding) database relationships, see Lesson 9, "Building a Relational Database."

Using Lookup Fields

An excellent way to ensure that the correct data is being entered into a field is to use Lookup fields. A Lookup field provides a list of the legal data values during the data entry process. This list of legal values can be derived from information in another table—called a *Lookup list*—or from a list that you create during the creation of the Lookup field—called a *Value list*.

To use a Lookup list for your new Lookup field, another table must share the field that you plan to work with. For example, an Orders table would contain a CustomerID field to identify which customer placed a particular order. You could use the CustomerID field in the Customers table as the Lookup list for your Lookup field (CustomerID in the Orders table). The tables that you have created relationships between supply you with the shared field you need to create Lookup fields. A Lookup field is the foreign key in the relationship and derives its Lookup list from the primary key in the relationship.

Obviously, if you want to create a Lookup field using a field that is not shared between tables, you will have to create a Value list, which provides the legal values for the field.

When you create a new field or plan to edit an existing field to take advantage of the Lookup feature, you select Lookup Wizard from the Data Type drop-down box. The Lookup Wizard walks you through the Lookup creation process.

To create a Lookup field, follow these steps:

1. In the table Design view, create a new field or select the field that you want to make a Lookup field.

2. Click the **Data Type** drop-down arrow and select **Lookup Wizard** from the list. The Lookup Wizard opens. In the first screen, you must determine whether the values will come from an existing field in another table or from a list you create. Click either the **I Want the Lookup Column to Lookup the Values in a Table or Query** option or the **I Will Type in the Values I Want** option. Click **Next** to continue.

3. A list of the tables in your database appears. (You can also select a radio button to show the queries in the database or both the tables and queries.) Select the table that contains the field (the primary key) that you will use for the Lookup list (see Figure 10.8). Click **Next** to continue.

Figure 10.8

The Lookup Wizard asks you to select a table or query that contains the field you will use for your Lookup list.

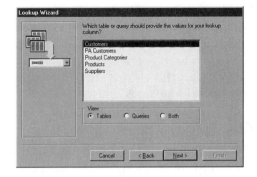

4. The next Lookup Wizard screen asks you to select the fields that should appear in the Lookup list. The list can contain more than one column. For example, in the case of the Orders table, you may want to place the CustomerID in the field for which you are creating the Lookup list. However, it will be easier to select the customer by first and last name from the Lookup list. You can include the CustomerID as a column in the Lookup list as well as the Last Name and First Name for the customer, as shown in Figure 10.9.

Figure 10.9

The Lookup Wizard asks you to select the fields that will be columns in your Lookup List.

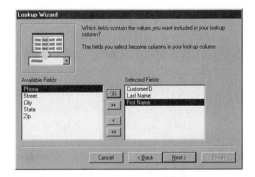

 Lookup List Columns Only the data from the key field in the table that shares the field is placed in the Lookup field in the current table. The other columns that you select during the Lookup list creation process are strictly informational. If Mary Smith places an order and you want to enter her CustomerID into the table, selecting the ID number by seeing her name is easier than trying to remember that she is CustomerID 103.

5. After selecting the field columns, click the **Next** button. The next screen enables you to adjust the widths of the field columns that you have selected for the Lookup list (that is, to make sure that all the data in a particular column will show in the list). A check box is also provided; when checked, it hides the key column in the Lookup list. This checkbox is selected by default. If you hide the key column, the first column in the Lookup list is the data that appears in the field when you enter your data. However, the key field value is actually what is stored in the field. Click **Next** to continue.

6. You are asked to supply a name for the Lookup field. The default name consists of the field name that you gave the field when you created it in the table Design view. Type in a name and click **Finish** to complete the process.

7. Save the changes that you made to the table structures.

 Relationships Will Be Automatically Created—If you create a Lookup field using shared fields in tables that are not currently related, Access automatically creates a relationship between the two tables based on the shared field. You are asked to save this new relationship after you click **Finish** in the Lookup Wizard window. You can view this new relationship in the Relationships window.

When you return to the Datasheet view of the table to enter data, a drop-down button appears when you enter the field for which you created the Lookup list. Select the appropriate value from the list. The data from the first column in the Lookup field is placed in the table. The table actually stores the primary key information in the field even though it displays the first column information from the Lookup list as shown in Figure 10.10.

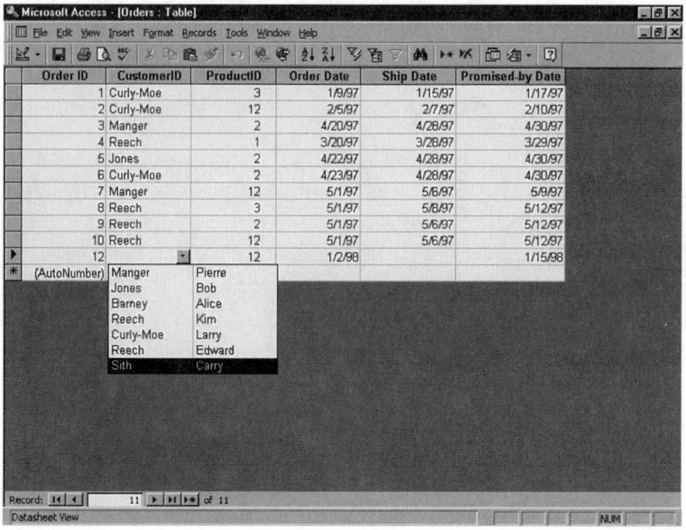

Figure 10.10

The Lookup list provides you with a list of values for the Lookup field.

Review Questions

The Certified Microsoft Office User Exams are task oriented. The following types of questions are not representative of the test. These questions are designed to help you understand the required tasks and methods of performing those tasks prior to taking the test.

1. List four strategies for maintaining data integrity in your tables.

2. How do you enforce Referential Integrity?

3. How do you set a default value for a field?

4. Where does a Lookup field get the list of legal data?

5. How do you enter a validation rule?

Review Question Answers

1. Four strategies for maintaining data integrity are validation rules, default values, Lookup fields, and enforcing Referential Integrity. For more information, see the section "Strategies That Ensure Data Integrity."

2. Open the Relationships window for the database and create a new relationship or edit an existing relationship. In the Relationships dialog box, click the **Enforce Referential Integrity** check box; then click **Create** for a new relationship or **OK** for a relationship that you are editing. Relationship symbols appear on the join line between the tables. For more information, see the section "Enforcing Referential Integrity in Table Relationships."

3. In the table Design view, click the Field Properties pane's **Default Value** box. Enter the default value. Save the changes you made to the table's structure. For more information, see the section "Specifying a Default Value in a Field."

4. The Lookup field gets the list of legal values from either a Lookup list or a Value list. The Lookup list derives its value from fields in the table that shares a common field with the table that contains the Lookup field. A Value list consists of values that you type into a list during the Lookup field creation process. For more information, see the section "Using Lookup Fields."

5. To enter a validation rule, click the Field Properties pane's **Validation Rule** box. Type in a set of values or a range of values for the field using the appropriate operators (And, Or, <, >, and so on). For more information, see the section "Entering Validation Rules."

Practice Lab

The Microsoft Access Expert User Exam lists identify criteria for data integrity, validate text, set required properties, set validation rules, and set Lookup fields as five Required Tasks for the Skill Area "Maintain Data Integrity." The following practice lab covers these skills.

 Required Tasks   Five of the Required Tasks for this Skill Area are identify criteria for data integrity, validate text, set required properties, set validation rules, and set Lookup fields.

Copy the **lesson10.mdb** database from the CD that accompanies this book to a folder on your computer using Windows Explorer. Open the database and complete the following tasks:

Validate Text

1. Open the **Suppliers** table in Design view. Set the Field Size for the State field to 2. In the **Format** box, place the appropriate symbol to ensure that State field entries appear in uppercase letters.

2. Set the default value for the State field in the Suppliers table to **MN**.

3. Create an input mask for the Postal Code field in the Suppliers table. Save the changes you make to the Suppliers table structure.

Set Required Properties

1. Open the **Expenses** table in Design view. Change the DateSubmitted field format to Medium Date. Make the DateSubmitted field a required field.

2. In the **Project** table, create a default value for the Project Begin field that enters the current date in the field.

Set Validation Rules

1. In the Expenses table, create a validation rule for the Amount Spent field. All entries in the field must be >0 and <$6000.00. For the validation text, enter **Maximum Expense cannot exceed $6000 without approval**.

2. In the Departments table, create a validation rule for the DepartmentName field. The legal values for the validation rule are Bathroom Design, Living Room Design, Kitchen Design, Porches and Decks, Architects, and New Construction. The Validation text should list the legal entries for the field.

3. Create a relationship between the Departments table and the Employees table using a shared field. Enforce Referential Integrity for the relationship.

4. Create a relationship between the Customers table and the Orders table. Enforce Referential Integrity in the relationship.

Set Lookup Fields

1. Create a Lookup field for the EmployeeID in the Expenses table. Use the Employees table as the source for the Lookup list that is created for the field.

2. Create a Lookup field for the Department field in the Project table. Use the Departments table as the source for the Lookup list that is created.

Open the database **lesson10a.mdb** on the CD to see a completed version of the database you worked with in this lab.

Working with Forms

This lesson covers three of the Use Forms and three of the View Information skills for the Expert User level.

In this lesson, you learn the following Required Tasks for your exam:

Use Forms Skill Area:

- ▶ Create a simple form
- ▶ Modify a form
- ▶ Add a record using a form

View Information Skill Area:

- ▶ View information in a form
- ▶ View multiple records
- ▶ Switch between views

Creating Forms

Although tables serve as the repositories for the information in a database, in Access you are not restricted to doing all your data entry directly into the tables. Forms provide a customizable environment for entering your data. Forms enable you to concentrate on the data that must be entered in a particular record. You can create custom forms for entering data into more than one table at a time or providing a pictorial representation of the data—a chart.

Forms can use all or part of the fields from their associated table or tables. Access gives you three ways to create a form:

▶ **AutoForm** The fastest way to create a form for data entry, AutoForm creates a form for the current table using all the fields in the table. With a table open in the Access window, click the **AutoForm** button on the toolbar. (Using AutoForm is covered in Lesson 4, "Entering Data in a Table.")

▶ **Form Wizard** The Wizard walks you through a series of steps to create either simple or complex forms. However, using the Wizard does take away some of the flexibility that you have when you create a form from scratch.

▶ **Design View** Creating a form from scratch is the most difficult of the three methods, but it gives you maximum flexibility and enables you to create custom forms based on your particular needs and your own ideas.

 Explore Form Creation with the Form Wizard When you are beginning your exploration of form use and design, create your forms using the Form Wizard. It gives you quick results and enables you to take a look at how the forms have been designed. As your understanding of form design grows, you will feel more comfortable creating your own forms from scratch.

Using the Form Wizard

Although AutoForm is the fastest and easiest way to generate a form for a table, the Form Wizard provides a great deal of assistance and still enables you to select some aspects of the form's design. To use the Form Wizard to create a new form, complete the following steps:

1. In the Database window, click the **Forms** tab.

2. Click the **New** button. The New Form dialog box appears as shown in Figure 11.1.

3. A drop-down box at the bottom of the New Form dialog box enables you to se-
    lect the table on which you want to base the new form. When using the Form
    Wizard, you can either select the table now or wait until the Form Wizard's first
    screen appears, which again gives you the option of selecting a table. For the
    other form types, such as AutoForm, you first must select a table.

Figure 11.1

The New Form dialog
box is where you
select the type of form
you want to create.

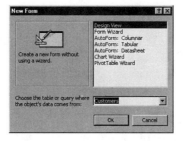

4. Click **Form Wizard**, and then click **OK** to continue.

5. The first screen of the Form Wizard asks you to select the table on which you
    want to base the form from the **Tables/Queries** drop-down box. After you
    select the table, the Wizard lists those fields in the **Available Fields** box (see
    Figure 11.2).

Figure 11.2

The Form Wizard asks
you to select a table or
query on which to
base the form and
then to select the fields
you want to include in
the new form.

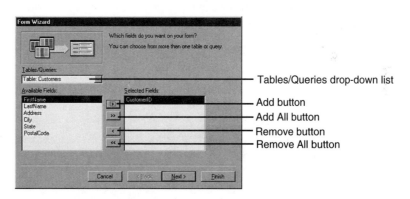

Tables/Queries drop-down list
Add button
Add All button
Remove button
Remove All button

Queries Can Be Used to Build Forms   When you create a new form, you can base
a form on a table or you can base a new form on a query. Also keep in mind that a
form can include fields from more than one table or query.

6. To add fields to the form, select a field in the **Available Fields** box and then click the **Add (>)** button to place the field in the **Selected Fields** box. If you inadvertently add a field, select it in the **Selected Fields** box and click the **Remove (<)** button. (Remove all the fields by clicking the **Remove All (<<)** button.)

 Use Add All to Include all Fields in the New Form   You can quickly include all the fields from a particular table in your new form by clicking the **Add All (>>)** button.

7. After you select the fields that you want to use from the currently selected table, you can return to the **Tables/Queries** drop-down list and select a new table or query. Include additional fields from the new table or query in your form by selecting the appropriate fields and placing them in the **Selected Fields** box.

8. Complete your selection of fields for the new form and then click the **Next** button to continue. The next Wizard screen asks you to select a format for the new form. You have four layout choices: columnar, tabular, datasheet, or justified.

   A *columnar* layout places each field on its own line in a vertically oriented form; this type of form shows only one record at a time. A *tabular* layout places the field names at the top of the form in separate columns and then lists the data records, one to a line, below the column headings. The *datasheet* layout sets up the form to look like a table, using rows and columns. The *justified* layout places the fields in equal rows across the form. These field rows align or are justified on the right and the left.

 Choosing the Correct Layout   The type of layout you choose for your form affects the arrangement of the fields on the screen; therefore, you want to create a form that's easy on the eyes and makes data entry more efficient. The columnar layout is great for creating a form that is based on a table with only a few fields. This layout type also enables you to view records separately. The tabular layout works well when you have a lot of fields and want to view a number of records at a time. The datasheet layout enables you to hide certain fields during data entry (items like a salary field) but still in a datasheet type environment. The justified layout is similar to the columnar layout but places the fields in equal rows.

9. To see a preview of a particular layout, click its radio button; the preview appears in the left half of the Wizard screen. After you decide on a particular layout, make sure its radio button is selected and then click **Next** to continue.

10. The next screen asks you to select a style. Click each style for a preview. Select the style you want to use for the form and click **Next**.

11. The final Form Wizard screen asks you to enter a name for the form in the title box. If you do not supply a name, the Wizard names the form after the table you based it on. This screen also provides options for what you want to do after the form is completed. You can open the form to view or enter data, or you can go directly to the form's Design view to modify its design.

12. In most cases, it makes sense to view the new form with data in it before you begin any redesign work. Make sure the **Open the Form to view or enter information** option button is selected and click **Finish**.

The new form appears, ready for data entry, as shown in Figure 11.3. Notice that the form has the same kind of navigation buttons that your tables have. You can move forward and backward through the records using these buttons. The New Record button (an advance button (>) followed by an asterisk) moves you to a blank record ready for data input.

To enter data in the form, you can click in a particular field and enter the information. You can also use the **Tab** key to advance forward (from field to field) in the form, or use the **Shift+Tab** key combination to move backward through the form.

Figure 11.3

The Form Wizard creates a simple but usable form; in Form view, the form shows the first record found in the associated table.

Switching Between Views

Form view is where you enter and view the data that resides in the table (or tables) on which the new form was based. Design view is where you change the design of the form. To switch to Form Design view, click the **Design View** button on the Forms toolbar. The Form Design window opens, as shown in Figure 11.4.

 View the Form Header and Footer Areas If the form's header and footer areas are not showing when you enter Form Design view, click **View, Form Header/Footer**.

Figure 11.4

Form Design view
enables you to change
the layout of your
forms.

Form Header area ⏌

Form Detail area ⏤

Form Toolbox ⏤

Form Footer area ⏤

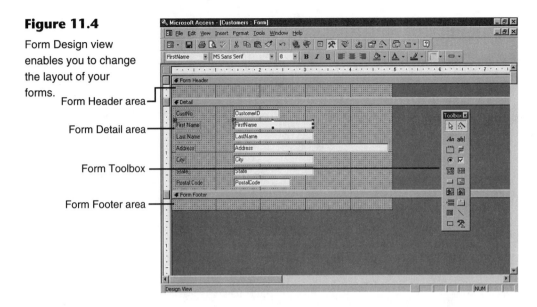

The Form Design window has three parts: Form Header, Detail, and Form Footer. The *Form Header* area is where you display the name of the form and any other information or items that you want repeated on each form as you view the records in Form view. These items can include special command buttons that you create to open related forms or perform special tasks such as printing the form.

The *Detail* area contains all the fields that appear on the form when you are in Form view or on the printed form. The Detail area is of special importance because it holds the fields that you use to enter and view data.

In Design view, the fields are broken down into two boxes: labels and controls. The *labels* are the field names and were derived from the table fields that you used to create the form. The *controls* are where the actual data is entered. Controls also can dictate how the data is input into the form. For example, a control can accept an entry from the keyboard or display a list of data (a list box) from which you must select. You work with different types of controls in Lesson 12, "Advanced Form Design."

The *Form Footer* area is at the bottom of the Form window, and you can use it for items that you want to display on each form as the records are viewed or entered. Footer information can include the date or short directions on how to use the form.

Another item that appears in the Form Design window is the *Form Toolbox*. The Toolbox provides you with all the tools that you need to customize your forms.

Important Form Design Tools   When you work in Form Design view, you may want to have the ruler, grid, and Toolbox showing. To see each of these items, click their respective menu choice on the View menu.

Customizing Forms

Customizing a form in Form Design view consists of adding, deleting, and editing the various labels and controls found on the form. You can also change the layout of the form by moving labels and controls. Areas of the form, such as the Form Header, Detail, and Form Footer, can be expanded or reduced to accommodate your design changes.

Creating a Form Title

One of the most straightforward edits to make on a form in Design view is editing the form's title. Because the title needs to appear on each form as you move from record to record, form titles are placed in the Form Header area.

To place a title in the Form Header area, complete the following steps:

1. If necessary, click the **View** menu; then click **Form Header/Footer**. The Form Header and Form Footer appear in the Design window.

2. Place the mouse pointer on the line that divides the Form Header area from the Detail area. A Sizing tool appears. Hold down the mouse button and drag the Form Header border downward about a half inch (use the ruler to help you estimate) as shown in Figure 11.5.

Using the Forms Toolbox

After you expand the Form Header area, you can place a new label in the Form Header that will serve as the tile for the form. To add an item to a form such as a label or control, you use the tools on the Toolbox. You can drag the Toolbox to any position in the Form Design window by clicking and dragging it by the title bar.

To add a new label to the form, click the **Label** button on the Toolbox. The mouse pointer becomes a cross shape above a capital **A**. This pointer is used as a drawing tool.

Place the mouse pointer where you want to create the new label (in this case in the Form Header area of your form). Hold down the mouse button and drag the mouse pointer to draw a rectangle in the Form Header area. When you release the mouse button, the rectangle becomes opaque and an insertion point appears in the upper-left corner (see Figure 11.6).

Figure 11.5

You can expand or contract the areas of the form in Design view.

Sizing tool ———

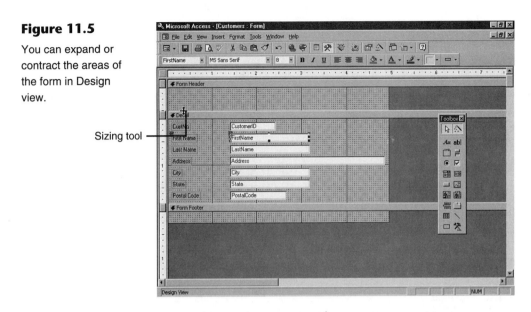

Figure 11.6

The Label tool enables you to add text to the form.

New label ———

Label button ———

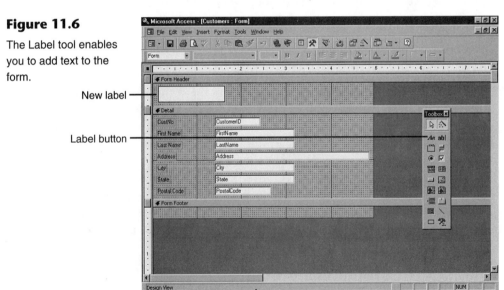

Type the text that you want to appear in the label. When you have finished typing the label text, click outside the **Label** box. Your new label appears in the Form Header.

The method used for inserting a new label into the form is also used to insert other items into the form. Select the appropriate button from the Toolbox and then place the new item in the appropriate area of the form.

 Form Toolbox The Toolbox can help you add a number of items to your form design. You can add new field labels and controls, text boxes, command buttons, check boxes, and graphics. A number of Toolbox tools are examined in Lesson 12.

To move a new label or other item that you place in the form, click the item; a frame with sizing handles appears. Place the mouse pointer on the frame (do not place the pointer on the sizing handles). A hand pointer appears; drag the frame to a new position. To size the frame, place the mouse pointer on a sizing handle. A sizing tool appears. Change the size of the frame as appropriate.

Formatting Text and Borders

After you add a new label (or control) to a form, you can format the text using the buttons on the Form Design formatting toolbar. To change the text format, complete the following steps:

1. Click the label to select it (see Figure 11.7).

2. To increase or decrease the font size, click the **Font Size** drop-down arrow on the formatting toolbar and select a new size.

3. To change the font style, click the **Font** drop-down arrow on the formatting toolbar and select a new font.

4. To change the font to bold, click the **Bold** button on the formatting toolbar.

5. To change the font color, click the **Font/Fore Color** drop-down arrow on the formatting toolbar. Select a new color from the color palette.

6. To color the background of the items box, click the **Fill/Back Color** drop-down arrow and select a new color from the color palette.

7. You can also place a border around a label (or any other item) you place in your form. Select the item and then click the **Line/Border Width** button.

8. The **Line/Border Color** button enables you to change the color of the border.

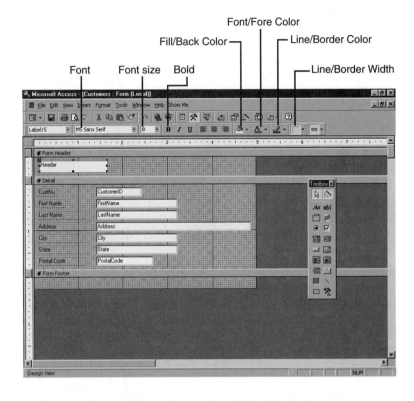

Figure 11.7

The Form Design formatting tools enables you to format the text.

Forms are meant to be used onscreen, and their design should facilitate viewing and entering data. When editing or designing forms, make them easy on the eyes and accommodating for data entry. Don't pack the labels and controls together on the form. The human eye enters a page starting on the left and moves to the right, so don't leave a lot of dead space on the left side of the form.

Creating a Form from Scratch

Creating a form from scratch in Design view provides you with the greatest design control. This method is, however, the most time-consuming of the new form creation methods.

You may want to edit the design of forms that you create with AutoForm or the Form Wizard to get a feel for how a proper form should be built. To explore the creation of a form in Design view, follow these steps:

1. In the Database window, click the **Forms** tab.

2. Click the **New** button. The New Form dialog box appears. Select **Design View**.

3. Use the **Tables/Queries** drop-down list to select a table or query on which to base the form; then click **OK**. The Form Design window opens, as shown in Figure 11.8.

Figure 11.8

Form Design view
provides a blank
palette for a new form.

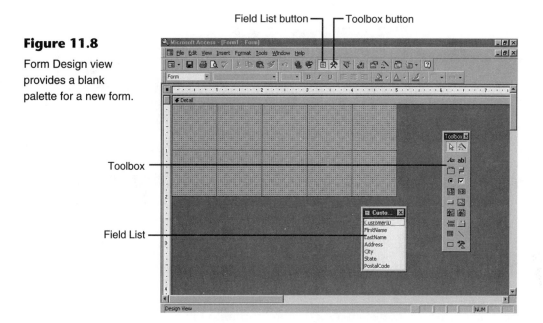

Field List button ——— ┌— Toolbox button

Toolbox ———

Field List ———

4. On the Form Design standard toolbar, click the **Field List** button. A list of the
   fields in the associated table appears, which makes it easy for you to add controls
   for these fields to the form.

Adding Fields to the Form

The easiest way to add fields to the new form is via the Field list. Click the **Field List** button if the Field list is not showing. The fields will be placed in the form's Detail area. Complete the following steps:

1. Drag a field from the Field list onto the Detail area of the form. A label and a
   control are created for the form, as shown in Figure 11.9.

2. From the Field list, drag the other fields that you want to place on the form.

You can move more than one field into the Detail area at a time. The options are described
as follows:

▶ To select a series of fields, click the first field you want and then **Shift+click**
   the last field.

▶ To select nonadjacent fields, click the first field and then **Ctrl+click** additional
   fields.

▶ To select all the fields in the Field list box, double-click the Field list title bar.

Figure 11.9

Fields can be placed onto the new form using the Field list box.

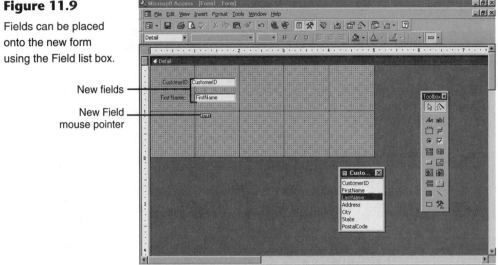

New fields —

New Field — mouse pointer

After selecting fields as outlined above, drag the fields onto the Detail area of the form.

 Using Snap to Grid Click **Format**, and then click **Snap to Grid.** This feature makes it easier to align the fields that you place in the form's Detail area.

Moving a Field

The fields that you place in the form consist of two parts: the label and the control. The label supplies the name of the field, and the control is where the data is placed. When you move a field in Design view, the label and the control move together.

To move a field to a new position, click the field's control or label; drag the label or control to a new position. The label moves with the control.

 Expanding the Detail Area To expand the width and the height of the Detail area, place your mouse on any of the area's borders; a sizing tool appears. Drag the border to a new location to change the size. Lesson 12 explains other strategies to change the look of your form's design.

Adjusting Field Label and Control Sizes

Depending on where you place the new fields on the Detail area, you may need to resize the label or the control. Click the label or control of the field and use the sizing handles to change the size as needed. You can use this technique to resize any item you add to a form.

Saving the Form

When your form design is complete, you must save the form. Click the **Save** button on the Design toolbar.

The Save As dialog box opens. Type a name into the **Form Name** box. Click **OK** to save the form. Whenever you make changes to a form in Design view, make sure to save the changes before you close the form or switch to Form view. (In both cases, Access prompts you to save the changes.)

Entering Data in a New Form

When you are satisfied with your form's design, you are ready to enter data into it. Complete the following steps:

1. Open the form from the Database window (click the **Form** tab), or if you are in Form Design view, click the **Form View** button.

2. Click the **New Record** button (the button with the asterisk on the bottom left of the form). Enter the data in the first field. Use the **Tab** key to advance to the next field. Use **Shift+Tab** to move back a field. Enter all the data for the record.

3. Repeat step 2 to add as many new records as needed.

4. To move backward or forward through the records you enter, use the directional buttons at the bottom left of the Form window: the right-pointing triangle moves to the next record, and the left-pointing triangle moves to the previous record.

Working with one record at a time enables you to concentrate on the data that needs to be entered. You don't have to deal with the informational clutter that is inherent in a datasheet.

Viewing Multiple Records in a Form

The default view for your forms in Form view is *Single Form*, which means only one record is displayed onscreen at a time. Complete the following steps to view multiple records in a form:

1. Open the form in Design view.

2. Double-click the form selector to open the Form property sheet shown in Figure 11.10.

3. In the Default View property box, click one of the following settings:

   ▶ **Single Form** Displays one record at a time.

   ▶ **Continuous Forms** Displays as many complete records as can be displayed on the form in the Form View window.

   ▶ **Datasheet** Displays the records in rows and columns much the same as a table.

Figure 11.10

You can set the forms properties so that multiple records appear in Form view.

Form selector

Properties dialog box

Default View property box

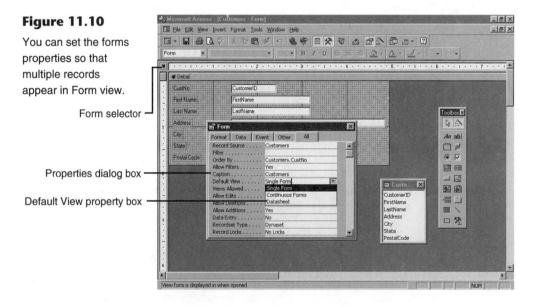

You work with other form and control properties in Lesson 12, which describes a number of property boxes found in the Properties dialog box.

Review Questions

The Certified Microsoft Office User Exams are task oriented. The following types of questions are not representative of the test. These questions are designed to help you understand the required tasks and methods of performing those tasks prior to taking the test.

1. Describe how to use the Form Wizard to create a form.

2. How do you create a new form from scratch?

3. How do you switch between form views?

4. How do you add a new record using a form?

5. How do you change the number of records displayed in Form view?

Review Question Answers

1. On the **Forms** tab, click the **New** button. Select Form Wizard in the New Form dialog box and click **OK**. Select the table or query you want to use to create the form from the Form Wizard's **Tables/Queries** drop-down box. Select and include the fields you want to include in the table. Continue the Form Wizard process by selecting a layout and a style for your new form. Name the form and complete the form creation process. For more information, see the section "Using the Form Wizard."

2. On the **Forms** tab, click the **New** button. Select **Design View** and select the table or query you want to use to create the form from the **Tables/Queries** drop-down box. Click **OK**. In Form Design view, use the Field list box to add fields to the form's Detail area. When you have added all the fields, save the form. For more information, see the section "Creating a Form from Scratch."

3. Click the **View** button on the Form toolbar to toggle between Form view and Form Design view. For more information, see the section "Switching Between Views."

4. In Form view, click the **New Record** button (an advance button (>) followed by an asterisk) on the lower-left of the form. Type the appropriate data in the form's fields. For more information, see the section "Entering Data in a New Form."

5. In Form Design view, double-click the form selector to open the form's property sheet. In the Default View box, select **Single Form**, **Continuous Forms**, or **Datasheet**. Close the Form Properties dialog box. Save the changes to the form. Switch to Form view to view records in the new form format. For more information, see the section "Viewing Multiple Records in a Form."

Practice Lab

The Microsoft Access Expert User Exam lists create a simple form, modify a form, and add a record using a form as Required Tasks for the "Use Forms" Skill Area and view information in a form, view multiple records, and switch between views for the "View Information" Skill Area. The following practice lab covers these tasks.

 Required Tasks   The three Required Tasks for the "Use Forms" Skill Area are create a simple form, modify a form, and add a record using a form. The three Required Tasks for the "View Information" Skill Area are view information in a form, view multiple records, and switch between views.

Copy the **lesson11.mdb** database from the CD that accompanies this book to a folder on your computer using Windows Explorer. Open the database.

Create a Simple Form

1. Use the Form Wizard to create a form for the Suppliers table in this database. Use all the fields in the table for the form. Save the form as **Dairy Suppliers**.

2. Create a new form for the Customers table in the database (use Design view). Include all the fields from the table for the form. Arrange the fields in Design view in a left-justified column (the field labels should all line up on the left). Save the form as **Retail Customers**.

Modify a Form and Switch Between Views

1. Open the **Suppliers** form in Form view. Switch to Design view. Add a title label to the Form Header area of the form that reads **Dairy Suppliers**. Format the text in the label as bold, italic, 16 point, Arial.

2. Move and realign the SupplierName and ContactName fields so that they are on the same line of the form (you may have to widen the Detail area). Save the changes to the form.

Add a Record Using a Form

Add the following record to the Supplier's table using your Dairy Suppliers form:

Field	Data
Supplier ID	N/A
Supplier Name	United Process Cheeses
Contact Name	Alyson Stevens
Address	1435 Wayside Lane
City	Kansas City
Postal Code	22240-4342
State/Province	MO
Phone Number	(530)555-7171
Fax Number	(520)555-7172
Email Address	Cheese@united.com
Notes	Carries seasonal drinks, such as eggnog, and cheeses.

View Information in a Form

Open the **Retail Customers** form and use it to view all the customer records (use the navigation buttons) in the Customers table.

View Multiple Forms

Open the **Customers** table and switch to Design view. Open the form's property sheet and in the Default View box select Continuous Forms. Switch back to Form view and view the multiple records. After you complete the viewing, return to Design view and set the Default View to Single Form. Make sure to save any changes you make to the form design.

Open the database **lesson11a.mdb** on the CD to see completed version of the forms you worked with in this lab.

LESSON 12

Advanced Form Design

This lesson covers Use Forms, Create Subforms, Build a Form for Other Users, and Print skills for the Expert User level.

In this lesson, you learn the following Required Tasks for your exam:

Use Forms Skill Area:

- ▶ Create controls on a form
- ▶ Modify controls
- ▶ Show related records on a form

Create Subforms Skill Area:

- ▶ Identify appropriate uses for subforms
- ▶ Add a record with a main form
- ▶ Add records with subforms
- ▶ Merge two tables into a form

Build a Form for Other Users Skill Area:

▶ Modify form design

▶ Improve accuracy in forms

▶ Enhance design of a form

Print Skill Area:

▶ Print a form

Creating Controls on a Form

In Lesson 11, "Working with Forms," you used the Form Wizard to create forms from scratch in Form Design view. You also had the opportunity to add and format a label to a Form Header area in Design view. In this lesson, you work primarily in the Form Design view, exploring advanced form design techniques and working with controls.

When you use the Form Wizard to create a form or create a form from scratch, you select fields from a particular table or tables to include in the form. In Form Design view these fields appear to be made up of two parts: a label that contains the name of the field and a second box that contains the actual data (or allows data to be entered) in the field in the table. This data-holding box is called the *control*.

Understanding Form Controls

The fields in your forms are really made up of two parts: a label that denotes what kind of data will be found in the control (a label for the State control might be State) and the control itself, which holds the data. Most of the controls in a form are associated with fields in a particular table or tables. However, controls can also contain data that comes from a calculation or some other source such as a linked or embedded object.

The controls in a form that are associated with a particular field in a table are called *bound controls*. Controls not associated with a particular field in a table are called *unbound controls*. Whenever you use a Wizard to create a form, all the controls created will be bound to their respective fields in the table or tables you told the Wizard to use in the form creation process.

Unbound controls can take the form of *calculated controls*, and you can use the Access Expression Builder to create a formula that provides the information that actually appears in the control. An example of a simple unbound calculated control is a control that returns the current date. An excellent place for a calculated control, such as the current date, is the Form Footer area.

Entering a New Control in the Form Footer

The Form Header and Form Footer areas of the form provide places to insert information that is repeated on the form as you move from record to record. In Lesson 11 you had the opportunity to place a label in the Form Header, which provided the form with a title. You can also place information in the Form Footer in labels or controls.

To place a Current Date control in the Form Footer, follow these steps:

1. Open an existing form in Form Design view. If necessary, click the **View** menu and then click **Form Header/Footer**. The form's Header and Footer appear in the Design window.

2. Place the mouse pointer on the bottom border of the Form Footer. A Sizing tool appears; drag the Form Footer area down slightly to provide more room for your Date control.

3. Click the **Text Box** tool in the Form Toolbox. Drag the control mouse pointer to create a small rectangle on the left side of the Footer area (about 1 inch from the left border of the Footer area). A new control is created. Notice that the control consists of an empty control label (it does have a Label box number in it) and the Control box. Place the mouse pointer in the Label box until the pointer turns to an I-beam. Double-click the current text in the Label box to select it and then type **Date**. You can widen the Label box if necessary to accommodate the text entry.

 Controls Consist of Two Separate Boxes   When you create a new control using the Text Box tool, the control consists of a new Label box (to name the control) and the control itself, where you either place an expression or designate a field from which the control gets its data. The label part of the control appears on the form as text. The control itself returns a value based on its control source (a field or expression).

4. Double-click the edge of your new Control box. The control Properties dialog box opens. This box enables you to choose the format and the source of the information that appears in the control. Click the **Data** tab in the dialog box. You want to attach an expression to this control that provides the current date. Click the **Control Source** box (see Figure 12.1).

 Bound Versus Calculated Controls   You can associate an unbound control with a particular field in a table, making the control a bound control, or you can place an expression in the unbound control, making it a calculated control.

Figure 12.1

The control Properties dialog box enables you to specify the source for the data in the control.

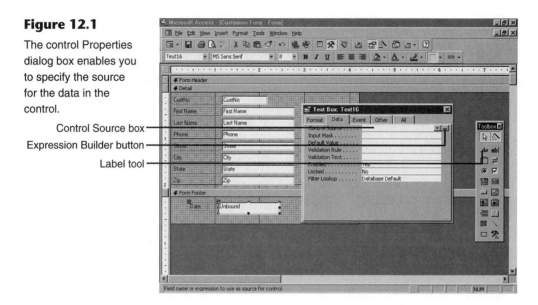

Control Source box

Expression Builder button

Label tool

5. The Control Source box contains a drop-down arrow and a button marked with an ellipsis. When you click the drop-down arrow, it displays a list of the fields contained in the table associated with this form. To make this control a bound control, select a field from the list. To create a calculated control, click the button marked with the ellipsis, which opens the Expression Builder dialog box. Click the **Expression Builder** button.

Using the Expression Builder to Create Calculated Controls

The Expression Builder enables you to build calculated controls. These can be as simple as a control that places the First Name and Last Name field side by side in the new control. Or you may want to build a control that returns the answer to a mathematical calculation. Calculated controls can, obviously, be quite complex, or as simple as a control that displays the current date.

The first column of the Expression Builder dialog box contains a list of possible items that you can use to build an expression for your control (see Figure 12.2). These items include Tables, Queries, Forms, and Reports as well as Functions, Constants, Operators, and Common Expressions.

Figure 12.2

The Expression
Builder helps you
create expressions for
calculated controls.

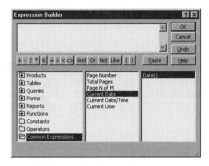

To create an expression that places the current date in a control, follow these steps:

1. In the Expression folder box, click the **Common Expressions** folder. The second column displays a list of ready-made expressions; double-click the **Current Date** expression.

2. The Date() expression appears in the Expression box at the top of the Expression Builder dialog box. Click **OK** to close the Expression Builder dialog box and return to the Properties dialog box. Your expression appears in the Control Source box.

3. Click the **Close** (x) button on the Properties dialog box. The expression, in this case Date(), appears in the form control in the Form Footer.

To view the calculated result of the expression in the control (the current date), switch to the Form view of the form. This view shows the data in the various fields of the current record and the current date in the Form Footer (see Figure 12.3).

Figure 12.3

The results of the
calculated control
appear in the Form
Footer area in Form
View.

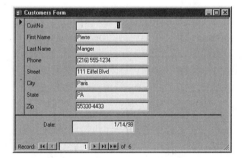

Calculations in a Form

You can also create controls containing expressions that provide a calculated result for your forms; for example, you may want to keep track of the total value of the products in your warehouse (unit price multiplied by (*) the units in stock). You can use the Expression Builder to create the control that multiplies the data found in other controls (UnitsInStock and UnitPrice) in the form and returns a result. Complete the following steps:

1. Switch to Design view and open the form into which you want to place the calculated control. Drag the right border of the Detail area if necessary to provide room for the new control (or arrange the current controls in the form to find the ideal spot for your new control).

2. Use the Text Box tool on the Toolbox to create a new control in the Detail area.

3. In the control label, double-click and type a name for the control (in this case, type **Total Value**). Double-click the **Control** box. The Properties dialog box appears.

 Right-click to Open a Control's Properties Dialog Box You can also open the Properties dialog box for a particular control by placing the mouse on the control and clicking the right mouse button. Choose **Properties** from the shortcut menu.

4. On the **Data** tab of the Properties dialog box, click the **Control Source** box. Click the **Expression Builder** button to open the Expression Builder dialog box.

5. In the first column of the Expression Builder, click the **Form1 folder** (the first folder in the box), or if you've already saved and named the form, click the appropriate folder. The controls and control labels in the form appear in the middle column at the bottom of the Expression Builder dialog box. Double-click the name of the first control that you want to include in the new control's expression. The control appears in the Expression box.

6. Click the appropriate operator, such as the multiplication sign (*), division sign (/), or other operator from the Expression Builder's Operator toolbar. Then double-click the other controls that you want to include in the expression. In Figure 12.4, the expression in the Expression box multiples the values in the two controls.

Understanding the Expression Builder's Operators   The operators that appear in the Expression Builder window create the various expressions that you place in your calculated controls. Many of these operators are typical math symbols such as +, -, and * characters that serve as the addition, subtraction, and multiplication symbols. You use these symbols to build expressions that perform mathematical calculations on a field or group of fields. For example, you can build an expression that multiplies a field containing the number of items sold by the price of the items, which appears in another field. Other operators are also available—for example, And, Or, Not, and Like. These operators can build conditional statements that return data that meet certain criteria.

Figure 12.4

The Expression Builder dialog box contains the tools you need to build simple and complex expressions for your form controls.

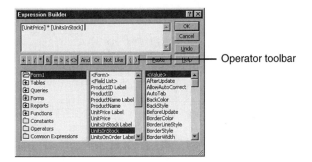

— Operator toolbar

After completing your expression, click **OK** to close the Expression Builder dialog box and then close the Properties dialog box for the control. The new expression appears in the control. To view the results of the expression, switch to Form view of the form. Remember to save any changes that you've made to the form design before closing the form.

 Format the Control   If you build an expression for a control that deals with currency, dates, or numbers that need to be formatted in a particular way, open the control's Properties dialog box. On the **Format** tab, click the **Format** box and then click the drop-down arrow. A list of formats including Currency, various date formats, and several number formats are available for the formatting of the control.

Improving Data Accuracy Using Combo and List Boxes on Forms

The options in Form Design view enable you to create well-designed forms that make viewing and entering data a much more agreeable task. Each record can be viewed separately, different form layouts give you a choice of how the controls are arranged on the form, and new controls can be created that can place a date or the result of a math expression into your form.

Three special data entry controls help you get the correct data into a particular field on the form. These three special controls are the List, Combo, and Option boxes:

▶ The List box presents a list of the data that should be placed in the field associated with the control.

▶ The Combo box is the same as the List box; however, it also gives you the options of entering an item into the field that does not appear on the list.

▶ The Option box provides a set of options from which you must select one. These options can take the form of buttons, toggle buttons, or check boxes.

Access provides a Wizard to help you build these controls. Make sure that the Control **Wizards** button on the Form Toolbox is selected before you begin to create one of these special controls.

Creating a Combo Box

List boxes and combo boxes are very useful when you have a defined number of data possibilities for a certain field in a table. The list box or the combo box can provide a list of these data values, and you can place them on the form by selecting from the list.

For example, if all your customers live in a four-state region, there will be only four possible values for the State field in your Customers table (and any forms used to enter data into the Customers table). The combo box gives you the added benefit of being able to enter values that are not on the list.

Follow these steps to create a combo box (creating a list box is very similar) in Form Design view:

1. Make sure the **Control Wizards** button is selected on the Toolbox.

2. Click the **Combo Box** button in the Toolbox. The mouse pointer changes to a combo box pointer (see Figure 12.5).

3. In the form's Detail area, drag your mouse to draw a box where you want to place the new control. When you release the mouse, the Wizard for the combo box control type starts.

4. The first screen of the Combo Box Wizard asks you to select how your Combo box will get the values that it lists. Three choices are provided (see Figure 12.6).

Figure 12.5

Use the combo box pointer to place the new Combo Box control on a form.

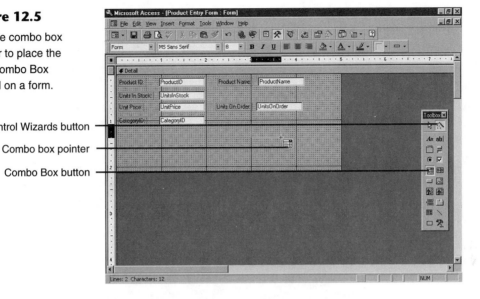

Control Wizards button

Combo box pointer

Combo Box button

Figure 12.6

The first screen of the Combo Box Wizard asks you how the combo box should derive its list.

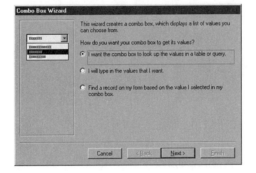

You can have the combo box look up the list values from a table or query. You can type in the values for the list. Or you can have the Wizard find a record in the current form based on the value in the combo box.

The first choice, a combo box that lists values found in a table or query, is the best choice because the values are based on data that exists in another table. For example, if the combo box provides a list of your Suppliers, you can easily enter them into your Products form. If the combo box pulls its list from the Suppliers table, every time you add a new Supplier to the table, the combo list in the Products form provides an updated list of Suppliers.

The second choice, typing in the values, gives you a usable list of possibilities, but you have to manually update the list if the available choices change.

The third possibility, using the control to find records in the current form, does not give you a bound control. (Remember, a bound control is tied to a specific field in the table related to that form.) This type of combo box can find records that contain data that matches the combo box list.

Select one of the radio buttons and then click **Next** to continue. If you opt to type the values for the combo box, the next screen provides an area in which you can type the values. If you opt to have the list derived from an existing table or query, the next screen asks you to select the table or query that contains the values.

Again, probably the best choice is to derive the list from an existing table or query. After selecting the table or query on the Wizard's second screen, click **Next** to continue.

Select the fields that will supply the combo box list from an Available Fields box, as shown in Figure 12.7. Add the fields to the Selected Fields box.

Figure 12.7

Select the fields that you want to appear as columns in the combo box list.

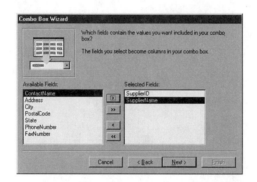

In many cases, you will be using combo boxes (or list boxes) to add SupplierID numbers to Products tables or CustomerID numbers to Orders tables. The reason is that you usually use the primary key from one table (such as the CustomerID in the Customers table) to create a relationship with a table that shares the particular field as a foreign key (such as an Orders table). Therefore, by design you must enter this redundant data (the CustomerID in the Customers and Orders table).

Setting up your combo box list to show only the CustomerID does not really help you select the correct number from the list. You still have to memorize which CustomerID belongs to a particular customer. So, by placing the CustomerID, the First Name, and the Last Name fields in the combo box list, the name you are entering into the form via the list is obvious (see Figure 12.7). Each field you choose appears as a separate column in the combo box list.

After you select the fields for the list, click the **Next** button. The next screen gives you the option of not displaying the key field information in the combo box list. This option is a recommended default—only the name of your customer or your supplier appears in the combo box list, even though the key field information will be entered into the table that is tied to the form you are building. Click **Next** to continue.

The next screen gives you the choice of having Access remember the values in your combo box for later use or having it store the values in a particular field. Normally, you select the latter. The primary purpose of the combo box is to help you enter data into the form, which in turn enters the data into the associated table.

Now, you may ask, when do I have Access remember the values in the combo box for later use? You may have a situation in which the value in the control is used in a mathematical calculation. The result of the calculation is much more important than the value you choose from the combo list. Access then remembers the value so that the calculation takes place and returns the result in the appropriate field. Selecting this radio button creates an unbound control. Access does not store the data in a field in a associated table; it does however, list the data that appears in that field.

Select the **Store That Value in This Field** radio button and then use the drop-down arrow and accompanying list to select the appropriate field. Click **Next** to continue.

The final screen asks you to type a name for your new combo box. You may want to give the combo box a name that reflects the information that will appear in it. Give it a name and then click the **Finish** button. The new Combo Box control appears on the form.

Using a Combo Box

After you create a combo box, you are returned to your form in Design view. The new Combo Box control is bound to the field that you selected during the control creation process (the field that provides the list of values). To use the combo box, switch to Form view. Click the drop-down arrow and select the appropriate value from the drop-down list, as shown in Figure 12.8.

Combo and list boxes work well in forms that you design for other users. This method gives them a list of the possible values for a particular field. You can also add toggle buttons, options buttons, or check boxes to your forms. These special control types enable you to choose from a group of options, click a selection in a check box, or toggle a particular field on the form between two possible values (such as Yes and No).

Each of these special control types has a wizard that helps you create the control. Creating one of these special controls is very similar to creating a combo or list box. Make sure the **Control Wizards** button is selected on the Toolbox before selecting any of these special controls in the Toolbox.

Figure 12.8

Select the value from combo box list to enter the data on the form.

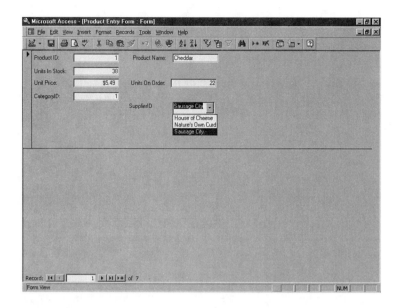

Creating Subforms

Access provides a way to build a form that displays the fields from two different tables; this method enables you to view data from two different tables and enter data into the two tables using the same form. To create a form that shows the fields in two different tables, you add a subform to an existing form (or a form that you are currently creating). A *subform* is really just like any other form and can be associated with a particular table. The original form (the form to which you added the subform) is now referred to as the *main* form. Don't forget that the tables with which these two forms are associated must have a relationship; that is, they must share a common field.

For example, if you add a subform based on your Orders table to a form based on your Products table, you can use just one compound form to view the orders associated with a particular product (the two forms will be in sync when you move from record to record) and to add new data to either table.

The most straightforward way to create a main form containing a subform is to create the two forms separately, either in Design view or by using the Form Wizard. When you have the main form and the subform, merging them into a compound form is really quite easy.

 Use Tabular Format for Subform When you create a form that you will use as a subform, you may want to create it in a tabular format. This particular format (controls laid out left to right horizontally) works well in the compound form setting.

To add a subform to a main form, follow these steps:

1. Open the main form (this could be any form you've previously created or a form in process) in Form Design view.

2. Expand the Detail area of the form (move the current controls if necessary), using the mouse to drag the various borders to new positions. Now you have enough room on the main form to place the subform. Figure 12.9 shows an expanded main form.

3. Make sure that the **Wizard** button is selected on the Form Toolbox. A wizard walks you through the creation of the subform on the current form. Click the **Subform/Subreport** button on the Toolbox. A subform pointer replaces your mouse pointer; drag out a rectangle on the current form (you may want to place it below the current controls in the main form). Make the rectangle large enough to accommodate the size of the form you plan on using as the subform. (You can always size the subform control later to accommodate all its fields.)

Figure 12.9

Make space in the Detail area of the main form to accommodate the control for the subform.

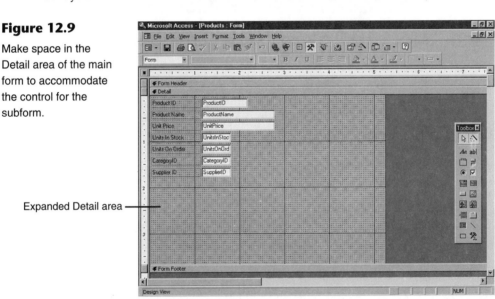

Expanded Detail area

4. As soon as you release the mouse, the first screen of the Subform/Subreport Wizard appears.

5. Decide whether to use an existing form to create your subform or to build a new form based on a table or query. Click the appropriate radio button. In the accompanying drop-down box, select a form from the list if you want to use an existing form; alternatively, select a table or query to build a new form. Click **Next** to continue.

The next screen asks you to select the field that will link the two forms. Because the forms are based on tables that are already related, the Subform/Subreport Wizard can usually pick the field for you. For example, if a Products table and an Orders table are related by the ProductID field, their forms also share this field. The Wizard provides a list of possible links as shown in Figure 12.10; one option is Show Orders for Each Record in Products Using ProductID.

Figure 12.10

The Subform Wizard helps you select the field that will link the main form and subform.

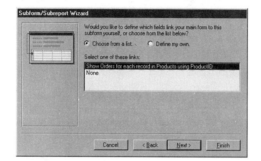

6. Select the field that links the forms or define it yourself; then click the **Next** button to continue.

7. The Wizard's final screen asks you to supply a name for your subform. Use the default name (it will be the same as the name you used when you created the form that you are using as the subform) or type a new name in the **Name** box. Click **Finish** to complete the process.

Make sure that you save the changes that you make to the main form (such as adding the subform control).

 A main form and subform must share a common field that synchronizes their records. Normally, this synchronizing field is the shared field that relates the two tables that the main form and subform were based on (such as CustomerID, which can link a Customers table to an Orders table by appearing in both tables). If the forms were not created using related tables, you must specify the field that links the forms. The field does not need the same name in the two forms, but it must have the same data type.

To specify the linking field between the two forms, double-click the subform control. Its Properties box opens. On the **Data** tab of the Properties box, specify the field in the **Link Child Fields** box (this is the linking field in the subform). In the **Link Master Fields** box, specify the field contained in the master form that links to the field in the **Child Fields** box (they can have the same or different names). When the main form and subform are based on related tables, the Link Child and Link Master field information is entered automatically for you in the subform Properties dialog box.

Viewing Related Records

The great thing about placing a subform on a main form is that you will be able to view related records. For example, when you move to a record for a particular product in the Products portion of the compound form (main form portion of the compound form), the orders for that product appear in the subform portion of the compound form (see Figure 12.11).

Figure 12.11

The records in the main form and the subform are synchronized by the shared field.

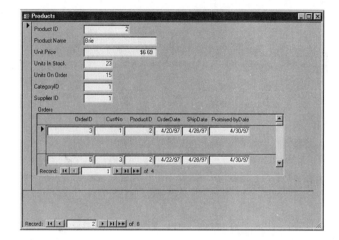

The records in both the main form (in this case, Products) and the subform (in this case, Orders) are synchronized by the shared field (ProductID).

Adding New Records to a Compound Form

Another bonus of creating forms that contain a subform is that you can use the same form to enter data into two different tables. For example, if you decide to stock a new product, you can add the new product record to the Products portion of the form. Then when new orders come in for that particular product, you can enter them in the Orders subform.

The main form and the subform have their own set of form navigation buttons. To enter a new record in the main form, click the **New Record** button at the bottom of the Form window. A blank form appears in the main part of the form. Because you are entering a new product for which you do not yet have any orders, the Orders area of the form also shows a new record. (Remember, the records that you see in the two forms are linked by the shared field.)

Click the first field of the main form that requires data entry. As you enter the new record, move from field to field in the main form using the **Tab** key.

After you enter the new product in the main part of the form, you can then add any orders associated with this new product in the subform. Enter data in the subform as you would any other form. The subform has a set of navigation buttons and its own **New Record** button. Again use the **Tab** key to move from field to field as you enter the data.

Keep in mind that as you enter information into a compound form, you are actually entering data into two different tables. Forms that contain subforms really do provide a very good way to look at related information (in the related records) and to enter data that is logically related (such as products and orders).

Modifying Controls

You can modify your controls by sizing them or formatting them with special text attributes and colors. You can also move the controls to different positions in the Detail area of the form.

You've already worked with ways to enhance the design of a form by adding special controls such as calculated controls, combo boxes, and subforms. You can further enhance a form by adding graphics. The following sections discuss some of the techniques you can use to modify your controls and enhance the design of your forms.

Changing Tab Order

When you enter data on a form, you press the **Tab** key to move from field to field. This *tab order* is dictated when you first create your form either in Design view or by using the Form Wizard. When you rearrange the fields in a new order on the form (in Design view), the tab order remains the same—that is, pressing the **Tab** key when in Form view takes you from field 1 to field 2, even if they are no longer in their original positions.

When you rearrange the fields, you should also adjust the tab order so that it reflects the new structure of the form. To change the tab order, follow these steps:

1. In Design View, select **View**, **Tab Order**. Figure 12.12 shows the Tab Order dialog box.

2. The fields appear in their original tab order. To change the order, click a **field** and then drag it up or down in the list.

3. To quickly change the tab order based on the current position of the controls in your form (from top to bottom), click the **Auto Order** button. When you have completed your changes to the tab order, click the **OK** button.

Figure 12.12

The Tab Order dialog box is where you adjust the tab order to reflect the control order in your form.

Formatting Control Text and Colors

After you place all the controls on a form in Form Design view, you can format both the label and control text and even change the fill and text colors.

Figure 12.13 shows the Formatting toolbar; it provides all the tools you need to format the controls. To change the text font, size, or color in a control or label, select the text and then click the appropriate button on the toolbar.

Figure 12.13

The Formatting toolbar provides all the tools you need to format your form controls and labels.

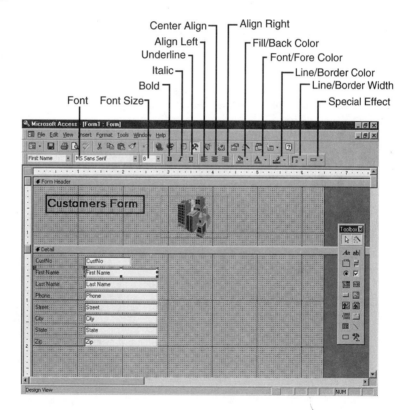

Adding Graphics

Another way to enhance a form is to add graphics, such as a scanned company logo or clip art, that is provided with a particular software package.

 Microsoft Office Clip Art Microsoft Office comes with a fairly large collection of clip art that you can use on your Access forms. However, if you purchased Access as a standalone product, it does not include a clip art collection.

As you already know, all objects placed on a form reside in a control. You place a graphic on an Access form as it would any other linked or embedded object. To add a picture to an Access form, follow these steps:

1. In Design view, expand the area in which you want to place the graphic. Give yourself enough room to draw the box that will contain the graphic. If you want the graphic to appear on each record in Form view, place the graphic in the Form Header or Form Footer.

2. Click the **Image** button on the Toolbox. Drag to create a box for the image. When you release the mouse, the Insert Picture dialog box opens (see Figure 12.14). Locate the picture you want to use by selecting the appropriate drive and folder on your computer. To see a preview of the graphic files, click the **Preview** button in the Insert Picture dialog box.

Figure 12.14

The Insert Picture dialog box enables you to locate and preview the image you want to place on your form.

Image button ——

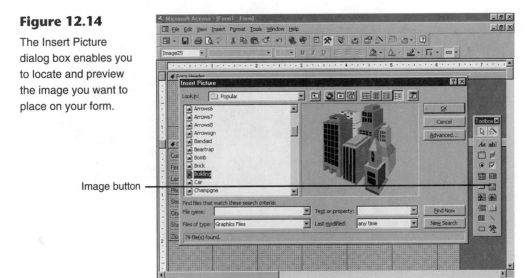

3. Select the graphic file you want to insert and click the **OK** button. The graphic is placed in the Image box.

4. In most cases, the image appears to be too large for the Image box. Right-click the **Image** box. Select **Properties** on the shortcut menu that appears.

5. In the Properties dialog box, select the **Format** tab. Click the **Size Mode** box on the **Format** tab. A drop-down arrow appears. Click the arrow and select **Zoom**. Zoom resizes the image so that it appears properly in the box you created.

6. Close the Properties dialog box. Figure 12.15 shows how the image appears in the Image box.

Figure 12.15

You can enhance your form by adding graphics.

After the graphic is in place on the form, you can always move it or size it. When Zoom is set as the Size mode for the graphic, enlarging the frame around the graphic also enlarges the image.

When you move the graphic from one area to another (such as from the Form Footer to the Form Header), the graphic automatically enlarges the area receiving the image to accommodate the size of the image. You can undo your last change to the graphics size or position by clicking the **Undo** button on the toolbar.

Printing a Form

Although forms are basically designed to be onscreen database objects, you can also print them. The easiest way to print all the record forms for a particular table is to open the form in the Access window. Click the **Print** button on the Form View toolbar. All the records in the associated table are printed as continuous forms. To print a particular record, select **File**, **Print**. The Print dialog box appears. In the Print dialog box, select the **Selected Record(s)** radio button to print the current form (that is, the one with the insertion point).

You can also use Print Preview to see how a form will look in a printed format. Go to the record you want to print and click the **Print Preview** button on the Form toolbar.

Review Questions

The Certified Microsoft Office User Exams are task-oriented. The following types of questions are not representative of the test. These questions are designed to help you understand the required tasks and methods of performing those tasks prior to taking the test.

1. Name the two general types of controls that can be placed on a form.

2. What is the purpose of a combo or list box?

3. What are some of the ways that you can modify and enhance the design of a form?

4. What must you do to a form to see related records from more than one table?

5. Which Access tool do you use to design expressions for calculated controls in a form?

Review Question Answers

1. A new control can be bound (tied to a particular field in a table) or unbound. Unbound controls are often set up as calculated controls. For more information, see the section "Creating Controls on a Form."

2. Both of these control types provide a list of the valid values for a field in the form. The list can be created by you or derived from a particular field in a table. For more information, see the section "Creating a Combo Box."

3. You can rearrange the controls on the form; add controls to the Detail, Header, or Footer areas; expand areas of the form; and add graphics. You can also change the font and colors of the controls in the form. For more information, see the sections "Formatting Control Text and Colors" and "Adding Graphics."

4. You can add a subform to a form. The original form displays the records in one table, and the subform shows records in a related table. The two forms that make up the compound form are synchronized by a shared field. For more information, see the section "Creating Subforms."

5. The Expression Builder assists you in building expressions for calculated controls. For more information, see the section "Calculations in a Form."

Practice Lab

The Microsoft Access Expert User Exam lists use forms, create subforms, build a form for other users, and print skills for the Expert User level. The following practice lab covers these skills.

Required Tasks Three Required Tasks for the "Use Forms" Skill Area are create controls on a form, modify controls, and show related records on a form. Four Required Tasks for the "Create Subforms" Skill Area are identify appropriate uses for subforms, add a record with a main form, add records with subforms, and merge two tables into a form. Three Required Task for the "Build a Form for Other Users" Skill Area are modify form design, improve accuracy in forms, and enhance design of a form. One task for the "Print" Skill Area is print a form.

Copy the **lesson12.mdb** database from the CD that accompanies this book to a folder on your computer using Windows Explorer.

Create and Modify Controls

1. Create a new form in Design view for the Products table. Add a calculated control that displays the current date to the Form Footer. Save the form.

2. Create a new control in the Detail area of the form you just created. Use the Expression Builder to modify the control so that it is a calculated control that multiplies the UnitPrice control times the UnitsInStock control. Save the form.

Improve Accuracy in Forms

1. Open the form you created in steps 1 and 2 in Design view. Delete the controls for the CategoryID and the SupplierID. Replace these two controls with combo boxes that get their list of values from the CategoryID in the Product Categories table and the SupplierID in the Suppliers table.

2. Create a new form for the Orders table (use the Form Wizard or create the form in Design view). Create combo or list boxes for the CustNo and ProductID fields (delete the current controls for these fields). The CustNo combo box should derive its values from the Customers table, and the ProductID combo box should derive its values from the Products table.

Merge Two Tables into a Form

Use the Products table as the main form and add the Orders table to it as a subform. Save the compound form.

Add Records with a Main Form and Subform

1. Add the following record to the main form of the compound form you just created:

Product ID	Product Name	Unit Price	Units In Stock	Units On Order	Supplier ID	CategoryID
9	Sausage	$7.49	40	0	2	2

2. Add the following record to the subform of the compound form:

Order ID	CustNo	Product ID	Order Date	Ship Date	Promised-by Date
11	4	2	1/9/98	1/15/98	1/17/98

Modify and Enhance Form Design

1. Open the **Customers** form. Change the font of the control labels to Arial 10 point, bold. Add red borders to the controls.

2. Insert the **Logo.bmp** graphic file (from the CD) into an Image box in the Header area of the Customers form.

Print a Form

Open the **Customers** form in Form view and print the first record.

Open the database **lesson12a.mdb** on the CD to see completed versions of the forms you created in this the lab.

Designing Queries

This lesson covers two of the Required Tasks for the Expert User "Locate Information" Skill Area and six of the Required Tasks for the "Refine Results of a Query" Skill Area.

In this lesson, you learn the following Required Tasks for your exam:

Locate Information Skill Area:

- ▶ Create a simple query

- ▶ Create a query with multiple criteria

Refine Results of a Query Skill Area:

- ▶ Add fields to a query

- ▶ Remove fields from a query

- ▶ Sort a query

- ▶ Save a query

- ▶ Join tables in a query

- ▶ Remove joins in a query

Understanding Queries

A *query* is a question that you pose to your database table or tables; in simplest terms, a query provides you with a more sophisticated way to sort and filter data than the sort and filter features do. You might want to know which of your salespeople have reached their sales goal for the year, or you may want to see a list of customers who live in a certain state. Both of these questions can be answered using a query.

The query type that you will most often work with is the Select query. A *Select query* finds and lists the records that satisfy the criteria that you set. The data that satisfies the criteria and appears when you run the query (the Select query results are in a table format) is called the *dynaset.*

You can also design queries that actually do something to a table— Action queries. *Action queries* can delete records in a table or move records to another table. Action queries always result in some kind of change to the table or tables involved in the query.

You can even create queries that display their results in a crosstab format that looks a lot like a spreadsheet. These tables, called *Crosstab queries,* provide a very unique way to look at the information that results from the query.

 Saving a Filter as a Query If a new query is needed to filter data in a table, you can use the Access Filter feature and then save the filter as a query. With the filter displayed in the Filter By Form window or the Advanced Filter/Sort window, click **Save As Query** on the Filter/Sort toolbar. For more about filters, see Lesson 8, "Finding and Filtering Records in a Table."

Access provides two basic methods for creating queries (as was the case for tables and forms). You can create a query from scratch in Query Design view, or you can use the Query Wizard. The easiest way to create a query for one table is through Query Design view. A third way to create queries is to write the SQL code for the query, using the Microsoft Visual Basic language for applications. This technique of query creation is mostly used by programmers and developers who build high-end custom databases.

Creating a Simple Query for One Table

If you create a query for one table, you probably expect to set criteria for a field or fields to limit the records that are displayed when you run the query. To create a simple query for one table, you can use Query Design view, which looks a great deal like the Advanced Filter/Sort window.

To use Query Design view to create a simple query, follow these steps:

1. Open the database in which you want to create the query. Click the **Query** tab; then in the Database window, click the **New** button. The New Query dialog box, shown in Figure 13.1, opens. Double-click **Design View**.

Figure 13.1

The New Query dialog box is where you select the type of new query you want to create.

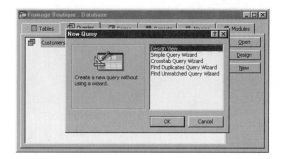

2. The Query Design View window opens, and the Show Table dialog box opens on top of it. To select the table (or tables) that you want to include in the query, select the table and click **Add**. Add all the tables that you want to use for the query (in this case, one table only—Customers), click the **Close** button to close the Show Table dialog box.

3. The Query Design View window is divided into two panes (see Figure 13.2). The upper pane displays the tables that you selected for inclusion in the query. The bottom pane consists of the Query Design grid, where you will set the criteria for your query.

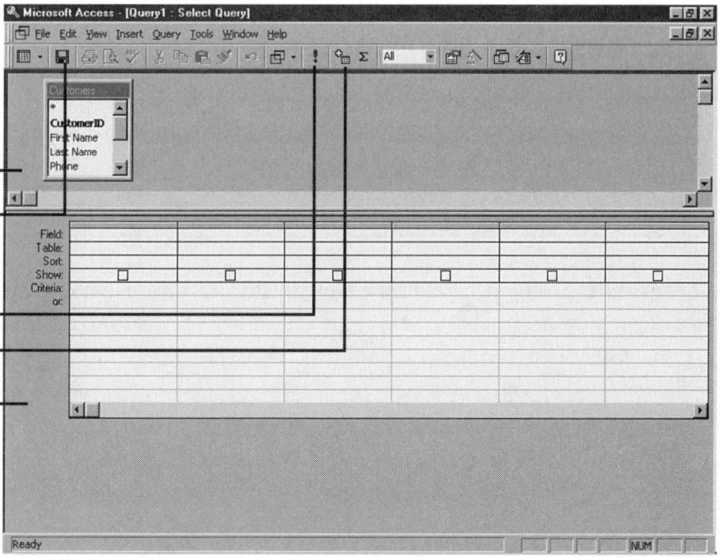

Figure 13.2

The Query Design View window is where you build your query.

Table pane
Save button
Run button
Show Table button
Query Design grid

After you open the Query Design View window and select the tables to use for the query, you are ready to specify the fields that should appear in the query. The field names are placed in a design grid. Access offers two ways to specify a field in a particular grid column.

 Understanding Query by Example   The way that you design queries in Query Design view in Access is called *query by example*. In other words, you use a graphical interface to designate the fields and the query parameters for a query. The other method of designing a query is to type the query expression at a prompt. Query by example (often abbreviated as QBE) is obviously a much easier approach to designing both simple and complex queries.

Adding Fields to a Query

The first row of the Query Design grid is where you designate the field names of the fields you want to include in the query. (Select only the fields that will appear in the query.) To select the fields that you want to include in the query, follow these steps:

1. To place the first field in the design grid, click the first grid column in the **Field row**. A drop-down arrow appears. Click the drop-down arrow. All the fields in the table or tables selected for the query appear in the list. Select the appropriate field name from the list.

2. Continue to add fields to the subsequent columns in the design grid until you have selected all the fields that you want to include in the query.

 Dragging Fields into the Design Grid   You can also select fields in the tables displayed in Query Design view and drag them onto the design grid for inclusion in the query. To include all the fields in a table, double-click the title bar of the table and then drag all the selected fields onto the design grid. You can also select contiguous field names by clicking the first field name and then Shift+clicking the last field name. Use the Ctrl+click method to select noncontiguous fields.

You can also add fields to the Query Design grid by double-clicking a field name in one of the tables that you included in the Query Design View window. Each table provides a scroll box to help you locate a particular field in the field list.

Removing Fields

You may end up with fields in the design grid that you do not want to include in the query. To delete a field from the query, click the grid column that the field occupies and then select **Edit**, **Delete Column**.

You can also select the field column by placing the mouse pointer directly above the column. The mouse pointer becomes a column selection tool. Click to select the column and then press the **Delete** key.

Rather than delete an entire column in the grid, you can replace an unwanted field with a field that you do want to include in the query. Simply click the appropriate column's Field row and use the drop-down arrow to select a different field from the field list.

Hiding or Showing a Field

On some occasions, you may need to include a field in the query, but you do not want to see the particular field's data in the query results. For example, you may want to set up a query that limits the records to a certain date range, but you do not want to see the date field in the query results.

To exclude a field from the query results, deselect the check box in the Show row. To include the field again, click the check box again.

Adding Criteria to the Query

After you select the fields that you want to include in the query, you will want to add criteria to choose the records that appear in the query results. The criteria are meant to place restrictions on the query. For instance, you may want to restrict the query to show only the customers in your Customer table who live in Minnesota or the products in your Product table that are stocked at a certain level or have a particular per unit price.

The criteria that you place in your query can be very simple expressions such as `"MN"`, which would select only the customers in Minnesota, or more complex expressions that use operators such as And or Or. For example, you may want to view only the customer records that have a credit limit `"Between 8000 and 15000"`. You can even create criteria that perform calculations; for example, you may want to design a query that multiplies the number of items you have in stock by the cost of each item so that you can calculate the total value of the stock that you have on hand.

To add criteria for a field, follow these steps:

1. In Query Design view, click the **Criteria row** in the desired field's column.

2. Type the criteria you want to use. The example in Figure 13.3 selects from the Products table only the UnitsInStock that are less than or equal to 10.

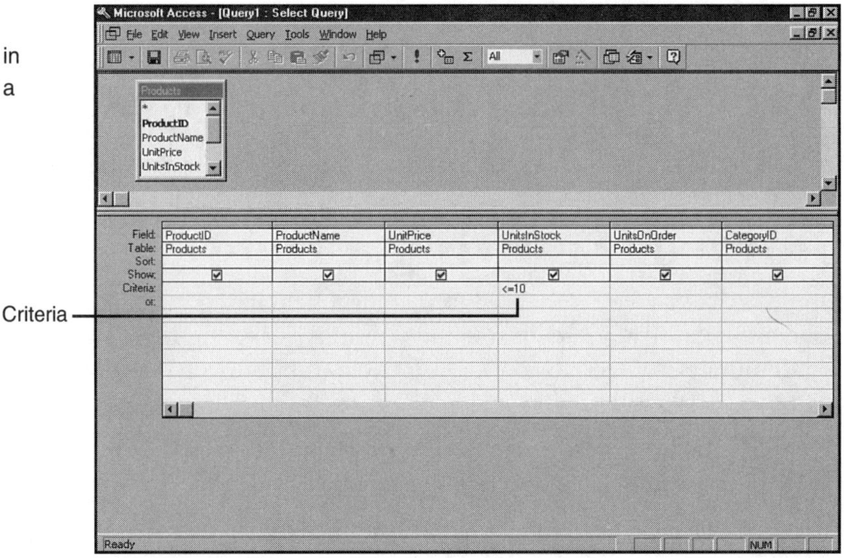

Figure 13.3

Enter your criteria in the Criteria row of a particular field.

A number of operators are available to help you define the criteria for your queries. Table 13.1 lists some of these operators and their uses.

Table 13.1 Criteria operators.

Operator	Description	Example
And	Enables you to set compound criteria in which both values must be met for a return.	Not Sales and Not Marketing Returns records in which employees are in neither of the listed departments.
Or	Enables you to set criteria that can be either one of two or more values.	OH Or MN Returns records that have *OH* or *MN* in the State field.
Like	Enables you to use wildcards in criteria.	Like Sm* Returns records that have *Smith* or *Smythe* in the Last Name field.

Operator	Description	Example
Between	Enables you to set criteria that select values that fall into a range.	`Between 01/01/98 and 03/01/98` Returns records in which the date in the Date field is after January 1, 1998 and before March 1, 1998.
Not	Enables you to set criteria that select values that are not the criteria value.	`Not >10` Returns records in which the number is not more than 10 in the specified field.

You can combine operators to build more complex criteria. You can also use operators such as greater than (>), less than (<), and equal to (=) when you set criteria for number and date fields. Another way to build complex criteria is to use the Expression Builder, which is discussed in Lesson 14, "Working with Advanced Queries."

 Clearing the Design Grid If you start to build a query and then decide that you want to start over, you can clear the QBE design grid. Click **Edit**, **Clear Grid** to clear all the fields, sort parameters, and criteria from the design grid.

Designing Queries with Multiple Criteria

Designing queries with multiple or compound criteria means that the data that appears in the query results has to satisfy more than one condition. For example, you may want to determine which items in stock fall in a particular price range and are stocked at a certain level. You would set criteria for both the UnitPrice field and the UnitsInStock field.

Multiple criteria can be tricky, however, and there are actually two types of multiple, or compound, criteria: "and" criteria and "or" criteria.

When you use "and" criteria, each individual condition must be true or met before the compound condition can be true. For example, if you use "and" criteria, you can find customers in Ohio (OH) who purchased a product from your company on a particular date, such as 01/02/98. Both of the criteria must be met for the particular customer to appear in the query results.

When you use "or" criteria, only one of the multiple conditions must be met. For example, you may design a query to find employees who have been with the company since a particular date *or* have sold a certain amount of product in the last year. The employee appears in the query results if he or she meets either condition.

To create "and" criteria, place the criteria in the same row of the query grid (the Criteria row). To create "or" criteria, place the first criteria in the first Criteria row and subsequent criteria in the second ("or") row of the grid. Figure 13.4 shows a query with an "and" criteria.

Figure 13.4

Multiple criteria on the same line are "and" criteria and all conditions must be met for a record to appear in the query results.

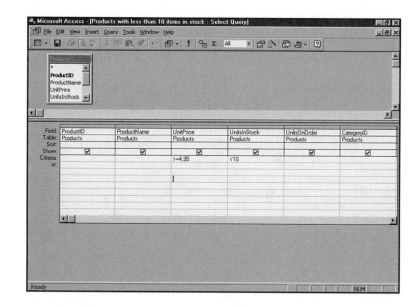

When you build queries using fields from more than one table, you will find multiple criteria a common occurrence.

Sorting Records in a Query

Queries also have the capability to sort the records that appear in the query results. You can sort by one or a number of fields. To sort by a field or fields, switch to Query Design view and follow these steps:

1. In the query grid box, click the **Sort row** for the field you want to sort. A drop-down arrow appears.

2. Click the drop-down arrow and select **Ascending** or **Descending** from the list.

If you want to sort by more than one field, the location of the fields in the grid box becomes important. To have a query sort its results by the Last Name field and then by the First Name field, the Last Name field has to appear before (from left to right) the First Name field in the grid box.

If you decide you no longer want to sort the query results by a particular field, click the **Sort** drop-down arrow for the field and select **(not sorted)**.

Saving a Query

After you select the fields for the query, set the criteria, and select any sort parameters, you may want to save the query. Click the **Save** button on the Query Design toolbar. The Save As dialog box appears; type a name for the query and click **OK**.

You actually don't have to save the query before you run it. You can run the query, and if the results appear to be what you want, click the **Save** button on the Query Design toolbar and assign a name to the query.

Your saved queries appear on the Query tab of the Database window. To open an existing query, double-click the query's icon. This will display the query's results. To open the query in Design view, select the query and then click the **Design** button.

Running the Query

After you design your query, you will want to run it to see the results. To run the query, click the **Run** button on the Query Design toolbar.

The results of the query appear in the Query window. Notice that the query looks exactly like a table. The records shown in the query are the records that met the criteria you set in the query. The fields shown in the query are the fields that you selected during the query creation process.

You can also run the query by switching from Design view to Datasheet view. The **View** button on the toolbar enables you to switch between the two views. When you switch from Design view to Datasheet view you are, in effect, running the query and the results of the query appear in a datasheet.

Using the Simple Query Wizard

An alternative to creating a query in Design view is to use the Simple Query Wizard, which helps you create a query that retrieves data from the fields in one or more tables or existing queries. The Wizard does not allow you to limit the information that appears for a particular field by setting criteria as you can do in Design view. You also cannot set any sort parameters for the fields in the query. The Wizard can, however, sum, count, average, and calculate the maximum or minimum value for a field. The Simple Query Wizard is very good at helping you combine field information from several tables.

If you do use the Simple Query Wizard to create a query and then determine that you want to limit the information retrieved for a particular field or sort the results of the query by a particular field, you can save the query and then edit it in Query Design view. To use the Simple Query Wizard, follow these steps:

1. Open the database you want to work with and click the **Queries** tab on the Database window.

2. Click the **New** button (in the Database window); the New Query dialog box appears. The New Query dialog box offers you several different possibilities for creating new queries.

3. Click **Simple Query Wizard**; then click **OK**. The Simple Query Wizard appears.

4. The first screen of the Simple Query Wizard asks you to select the table or query—queries can be based on other queries—that you want to use as the source for the fields that will be used in the query. Select the table in the **Tables/Queries** drop-down box. The fields in the table appear in the Available Fields box, as shown in Figure 13.5.

Figure 13.5

The Simple Query Wizard helps you select the fields for your query.

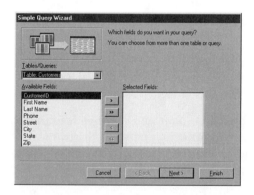

5. Select a field in the **Available Fields** list box; to include the field in the Selected Fields box (and in your query), click the **Add** (>) button. If you inadvertently add a field and want to remove it, select the field in the **Selected Fields** box and click the **Remove** (<) button. (The **Add All** (>>) button adds all the fields in the Available Field box, and the **Remove All** (<<) button removes all the fields in the Selected Fields box.)

6. You can select fields from more than one table. After you add the fields from the first table, select a second table in the **Tables/Queries** drop-down box. If you use more than one table for the fields that will appear in the query, the tables must be related. (Creating a join between tables in Query Design view is discussed in the section "Creating Queries Involving Multiple Tables.")

7. After you select all the fields that you want to include in the query, click the **Next** button.

 Selecting More Than One Table When Using the Simple Query Wizard When you want to run a query that includes fields from two (or more tables), the tables must be related. If they are not, Access closes the Simple Query Wizard and takes you to the Relationships window so that you may create the necessary relationships. For information on table relationships, see Lesson 9, "Building a Relational Database."

8. The next screen asks you which type of simple query you want to run: a Detail query or Summary query. A *Detail query* shows all the data in every field of every record. A *Summary query* enables you to calculate summary values for numerical or currency data found in the fields you include in the query. Select either the **Detail** or **Summary** radio button.

9. If you select the **Summary** radio button, click the **Summary Options** button. The Summary Options dialog box opens (see Figure 13.6). This dialog box displays the numerical and currency fields that you included in the query. You can total (Sum), average (Avg), or determine the minimum (Min) or maximum (Max) for the data in the field or fields. For example, a query for a Products table can take a currency field, such as the UnitPrice of the products, and average the information or find the minimum or maximum value. The query can also calculate more than one of these values. Select the **Sum**, **Avg**, **Min** and/or **Max** check box and then click **OK**.

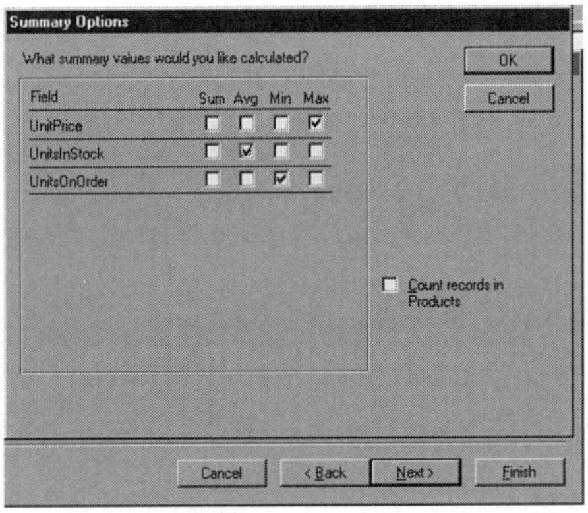

Figure 13.6

The Simple Query Wizard can help you add Summary calculations to your query.

If you select the fields for your query from only one table and none of the fields that you've selected for your query are either Number or Currency data types, the Query Wizard takes you directly from the Field Selection screen to the Wizard Finish screen. The default query is the Detail query, meaning that all the fields selected will display the data that is currently in the table or tables you selected. A Detail query for one table is really nothing more than a duplicate of the table (minus any of the fields that you did not include in the query) and provides practically the same information as the table does.

10. After you determine the type of query—Detail or Summary—click the **Next** button. If you've included a date field in your query and you selected the Summary query, the next screen asks you how to group the data in the date field or fields. You can group it by a Unique Date/Time, Day, Month, Quarter, or Year. For instance, if you choose Month, the month and year of the field information are displayed. If you want the data to appear as it appears in the table field itself, you must select Date/Time. Choose the appropriate radio button and click the **Next** button.

11. The final screen of the Simple Query Wizard prompts you to type a name for your query in the **What Title Do You Want for Your Query** box. (The Wizard supplies a default name based on the table that you used to select the fields for the query.) Type in a new name. You are have the option of opening the query and viewing its results or opening the query in Design view so that you can modify it. Select either radio button. Click the **Finish** button to complete the query creation process. When you use the Simple Query Wizard, the new query is automatically saved for you.

If you chose to run the query and view the results, the query appears in a datasheet showing the field data (and summary information) that you selected in the query creation process. Figure 13.7 shows a simple query created using the Wizard to combine field information from more than one table.

Figure 13.7

You can use the Simple Query Wizard to build simple or summary query.

First Name	Last Name	Phone	Promised-by Date	Product Name
Alice	Barney	(216) 555-7777	1/17/97	Swiss
Larry	Curly-Moe	(216) 555-8444	2/10/97	Gouda
Pierre	Manger	(216) 555-1234	4/30/97	Brie
Kim	Reech	(512) 555-3643	3/29/97	Cheddar
Bob	Jones	(216) 555-5436	4/30/97	Brie
Larry	Curly-Moe	(216) 555-8444	4/30/97	Brie
Pierre	Manger	(216) 555-1234	5/9/97	Gouda
Edward	Reech	(345) 555-7776	5/12/97	Swiss
Edward	Reech	(345) 555-7776	5/12/97	Brie
Edward	Reech	(345) 555-7776	5/12/97	Gouda

Customer Orders : Select Query

Record: 1 of 10

Creating Queries Involving Multiple Tables

Queries involving multiple tables can be built in Design view or by using the Simple Query Wizard. Query Design view, however, offers you the greatest flexibility for setting criteria and sorting options.

The only real difference between creating a query involving more than one table and building a query for one table is that the tables involved in a multitable query must be related. (For information on how to create a join in Query Design view, see "Joining Tables in a Query.")

To build a query using more than one table in Design view, follow these steps:

1. Open the database for which you want to create the query. Click the **Queries** tab, and then in the Database window, click the **New** button. The New Query dialog box appears.

2. Double-click **Design View**. The Query Design View and the Show Table dialog box open. Add each table that you want to include in the query; then click the **Close** button.

 Add Tables to the Query Design Window   If you want to add tables to the Design window after you close the Show Table dialog box, you can reopen it by clicking the **Show Table** button on the Query Design toolbar. You can also toggle the **Show Table Names row** in the grid box, using the View menu. Click **View**, **Table Names**. A check mark by Table Names means that the row is visible. Remove the check mark to hide the Table Name row.

3. Add the fields that you want to include in the query into the grid box columns from the tables that appear in the table pane of the Design window.

4. Set criteria and sort parameters for the fields.

5. Save the query design by clicking the **Save** button on the toolbar. The query in Figure 13.8 contains fields from multiple tables, will be sorted by Last Name and First Name, and contains multiple criteria.

There will probably be occasions when you want to create a multitable query, but you have not established any relationships between the tables you want to include in the query. You can create relationships between tables in the Query Design window.

Figure 13.8

You can design queries from fields that are contained in more than one table.

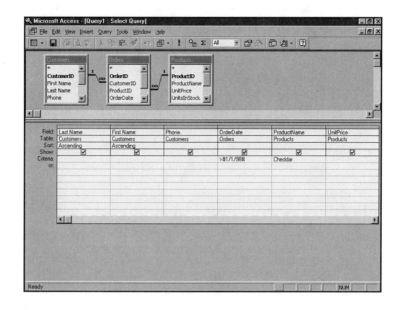

Joining Tables in a Query

Joining tables in the Query Design window can happen in two different ways: automatically or manually (meaning you have to do it). When you add two tables to the Query window using the Add Table box and each table contains the same field with the same name and holding the same data (in effect a shared field), join lines automatically appear between the two occurrences of the "shared" field in the two tables. For example, you may add a Customers table and an Orders table to the Query window; both of these tables will probably include a field for CustomerID. As soon as you add the tables to the Query window, Access automatically creates a join line between the shared fields in the two tables. However, for automatic joining to occur, the field shared by the two tables must be the primary key in one of the tables.

To join two tables manually (which is necessary if the shared field that relates the tables does not have the same name in both tables), drag one of the matching fields from a table and drop it on the other matching field in the other table. This step creates a join line between the two tables. Figure 13.9 shows a join that was automatically created by Access (the field names are the same) and a join that was created manually.

Remember that in most cases the field you use to create a relationship between two tables will be the primary key in one of the tables and the foreign key in the other table. For more about table relationships, see Lesson 9.

Enforcing Referential Integrity The relationship joins that you create between tables in the Query Design window cannot be set to enforce Referential Integrity. You must edit the relationship in the Relationships window.

Figure 13.9

You can create relationship join lines between tables in the Query Design window.

Join created by Access

Manual join

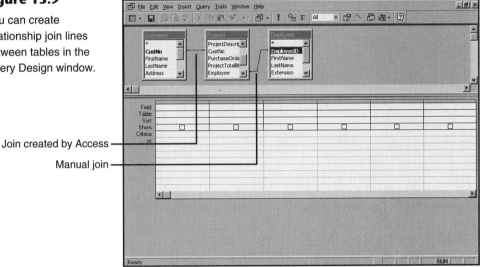

After you create the needed relationships between the tables, you can go ahead and add fields to the query grid box and assign criteria and sort parameters to the query. When you have completed these aspects of query design, you can save the query and then run it.

The joins you create between the tables in your query are saved with the query. They do not become part of the database relationships contained in the Relationships window. Consequently, the relationships you create for one query are not necessarily available for other queries. Therefore, you should consider creating relationships that will be used to create multiple database objects (queries, forms, reports) in the Relationships window.

Removing Joins in a Query

You can also remove the join lines that relate two tables when you are working in the Query Design window. Use the mouse to select a join line and press the **Delete** key.

Deleting a join line in the Query Design window does not delete the relationship between the two tables for other Access objects if the relationship was created in the Relationships window. Only the query in which you deleted the join line will no longer recognize the relationship.

Review Questions

The Certified Microsoft Office User Exams are task oriented. The following types of questions are not representative of the test. These questions are designed to help you understand the required tasks and methods of performing those tasks prior to taking the test.

1. What are two ways that you can create simple queries in Access?

2. What does it mean to have a query with multiple criteria?

3. Which view do you use to add and delete fields from a query?

4. How do you set sort parameters for the fields in a query in Design view?

5. What is the fastest way to save a query in the Query Design window?

6. In which part of the Query Design window are joins between tables created and removed?

Review Question Answers

1. You can create simple queries in Query Design view and by using the Simple Query Wizard. See sections "Creating a Simple Query for One Table" and "Using the Simple Query Wizard" for more information.

2. A query with multiple criteria selects the records from the table or tables included in the query by more than one selection criterion. For example, you may design a query that selects all the customers living in Ohio (OH) who ordered a certain product. Two criteria, state and product name, would have to be met for a record to appear in the query results. For more information, see the section "Designing Queries with Multiple Criteria."

3. You add and delete fields from a query in Query Design view. For more information, see the sections "Adding Fields to a Query" and "Removing Fields."

4. To set the sort criteria for a field or fields in the Query Design window, click the grid's **Sort row** for the field and select **Ascending** or **Descending** from the drop-down box. For more information, see the section "Sorting Records in a Query."

5. Click the **Save** button on the Query Design toolbar and then provide a name for the new query. Click **OK** to complete the process. For more information, see the section "Saving a Query."

6. Joins are created and removed in the upper pane of the Query Design window. For more information, see the sections "Joining Tables in a Query" and "Removing Joins in a Query."

Practice Lab

The Microsoft Access Expert User Exam lists two of the Required Tasks for the Expert User "Locate Information" Skill Area and six of the Required Tasks for the "Refine Results of a Query" Skill Area. The following practice lab covers many of these tasks.

 Required Tasks Two Required Tasks for the "Locate Information" Skill Area are create a simple query and create a query with multiple criteria. Six Required Tasks for the "Refine Results of a Query" Skill Area are add fields to a query, remove fields from a query, sort a query, save a query, join tables in a query, and remove joins in a query.

Copy the **lesson13.mdb** database from the CD that accompanies this book to a folder on your computer using the Windows Explorer. Open the database. Make sure to run each query after you finish designing the query or making changes to the query. The save a query skill is practiced in each lab.

Create a Simple Query

Start a new query in Design view. Add the **Products** table to the Design window. Add all the fields from the table to the design grid. Set criteria for the UnitsInStock field so that the query selects the records for items that are stocked at less than or equal to 15. Save the query as Low Stock Query.

Create a Query with Multiple Criteria

Start a new query in Design view. Add the **Customers**, **Orders**, and **Products** table to the Design window. In the design grid add the First Name, Last Name, and State fields from the Customers table and the Product Name from the Products table. Set criteria for the State field that will select records for customers in PA. For the Product Name field, set criteria that will select for the products Swiss or Brie. Save the query as **PA Swiss Brie Query**.

Sort a Query

Open the query **Sort Query** in Design view. Sort the table by the Last Name field and the First Name field in ascending order. Save the changes you make to the query.

Add Fields to a Query

Open the **PA Swiss Brie Query**; add the OrderDate field from the Orders table to the query and the UnitPrice field from the Products table. Save the query and then run the query.

Join Tables in a Query

Open a new query in Design view. Add the **Products** table and the **Suppliers** table to the Design window. Create a join between the SupplierID field in the Suppliers table and the Supplier field in the Products table. Add the ProductName, and the UnitsOnOrder fields from the Product table to the grid. Add the SupplierName, ContactName, and PhoneNumber fields from the Supplier table to the grid. Save the query as **Add Join Query**.

Remove Joins in a Query

Open the **Remove Join** table. Remove the join between the ProductsID field in the Orders table and the ProductsID field in the Orders Detail table.

Open the database **lesson13a.mdb** on the CD to see completed versions of the queries you created in this the lab.

Working with Advanced Queries

This lesson covers three Required Tasks for the Access 97 Expert User "Analyze Data" Skill Area and one Required Task for the "Print" Skill Area.

In this lesson, you learn the following Required Tasks for your exam:

Analyze Data Skill Area:

- ▶ Build a summary query
- ▶ Calculate fields
- ▶ Set Crosstab queries

Print Skill Area:

- ▶ Print the results of a query

Calculating Fields in Summary Queries

You learned in Lesson 13, "Designing Queries," that queries enable you to sort and select information found in a table or tables (or other queries). Queries also enable you to calculate statistical information using field data. This type of query is called a summary query; it can supply totals, averages, and other statistical calculations for your data fields. In other words, a summary query helps you statistically summarize data from a table or tables.

For example, you can use summary fields to get a total (Sum) of all the products you have in stock or an average (Avg) of the number of support calls that come into your computer help desk in a month. You can also use a query to find the maximum (Max), minimum (Min), or standard deviation (StDev) of a certain field or fields.

To create a summary query for your database, follow these steps:

1. Open the database you want to work with and click the **Queries** tab on the Database window.

2. Click the **New** button (in the Database window); the New Query dialog box appears. Double-click **Design View** to open the Query Design view and the Show Table dialog box.

3. Add the tables that you want to include in the query. Click **OK** to close the Add Table dialog box.

4. Add the fields that you want to include in the query to the query grid.

5. Set any sort parameters or criteria for the fields.

Do not place sort parameters or criteria in the field columns for the fields that will serve as the summary fields. If you do need to set criteria for a field, or include the field in the query results, and also use that field in a summary calculation, then place the field in two grid boxes. For instance, if you want to calculate the total number of items in your warehouse using the UnitsInStock field, the field must appear in a grid box without sort parameters or criteria. If you also want to see the UnitsInStock for each product, you must place the field in another grid box.

Fields that will supply summary information must have a way of calculating a particular statistical value. To add summary information to your queries, you must add another row to the query grid area that will hold the formula.

Using the Totals Section in the Query Grid

To create a summary query, you need to add a row to the query grid; click the **Totals** button on the Query Design toolbar. A Total row appears in the query grid. The new row is below the Table row and above the Sort row, as shown in Figure 14.1.

Figure 14.1

The Totals button adds a Total row to the query grid area that will hold the summary formulas for the fields.

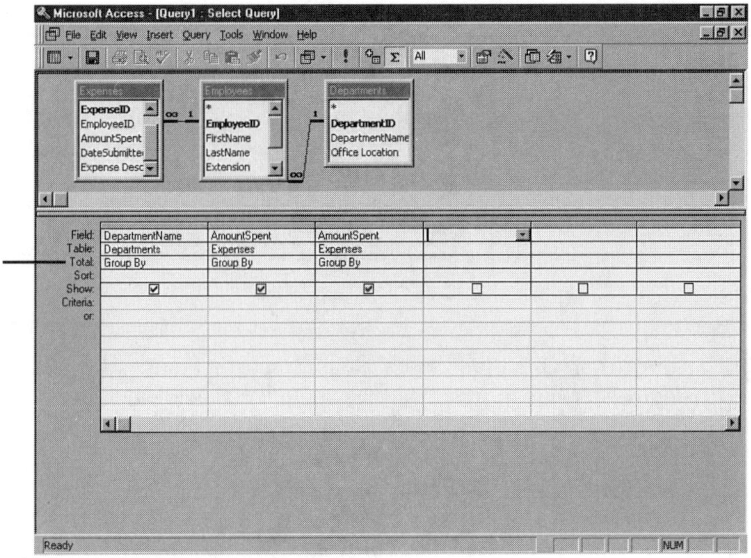

Total row ————

Currently the Total row says **Group By** because a formula has not been chosen for the field. Click any of the **Total** boxes in the Field columns, and a drop-down arrow appears. Click the drop-down arrow, and you will see a list of statistical formulas.

The formulas (they are also called *functions*) in the Total row drop-down box can perform calculations on different kinds of field data types. Table 14.1 describes these formulas and their uses.

Table 14.1   Query summary formulas.

Formula	Description	Field Types Formula Will Work On
Sum	Totals the values in the field	Number, Date/Time, Currency, and AutoNumber
Avg	Averages the values in the field	Number, Date/Time, Currency, and AutoNumber
Min	Gives you the lowest value in a field	Text, Number, Date/Time, Currency, and AutoNumber
Max	Gives you the highest value in a field	Text, Number, Date/Time, Currency, and AutoNumber
Count	Actually counts and gives you the number of values in a field	Text, Memo, Number, Date/Time, Currency, AutoNumber, Yes/No, and OLE object

continues

Table 14.1 Continued

Formula	Description	Field Types Formula Will Work On
StDev	Standard deviation of the values in a field	Number, Date/Time, Currency, and AutoNumber
Var	Variance of the values in a field	Number, Date/Time, Currency, and AutoNumber

 More Than One Statistical Calculation for a Field If you want to perform more than one summary calculation on a particular field, such as finding the sum and the average, place the field in two grid boxes and then choose a different summary expression for each occurrence of the field.

As you can see from Table 14.1, the formulas provided in the Total row summarize the information for a particular field. These formulas can count the number of records in a query that are selected by a certain criteria, and the formulas can give you sums and averages.

Calculating Fields in the Total Row

To actually calculate results in a particular field, you must click the summary formula you want to use. Follow these steps to select a formula in the Total row for a particular field:

1. Click the drop-down arrow that appears in the Total row of the field you want to calculate.

2. Select a **summary formula** from the drop-down list.

3. Repeat steps 1 and 2 as needed for other fields. Figure 14.2 shows fields that will contain summary formulas.

4. Save the query and then run it (click the **Run** button on the toolbar). Figure 14.3 shows the results of a summary query that calculated fields using formulas in the Total row.

The summary query resulting from placing formulas in certain fields contains field columns that provide summary information. The column heading for a field that contains a formula in the query is made up of the formula type that you used and the name of the field. For example, if you summed the UnitsInStock field for a Products table, the heading for the summary column in the query results is **SumOfUnitsInStock**, meaning that Access calculated the total units that you have in stock.

Figure 14.2

Calculated fields contain a summary formula in the Total row.

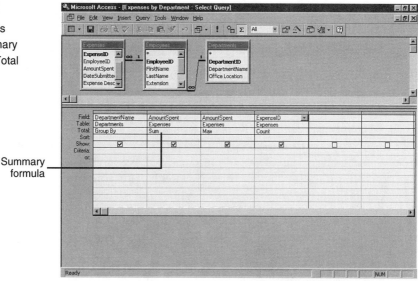

Summary formula

Figure 14.3

A summary query datasheet and its calculated fields.

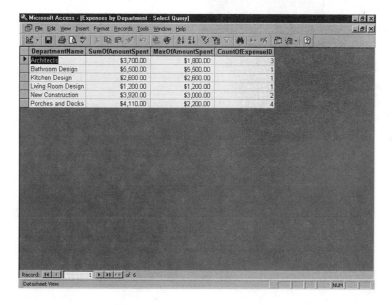

You can use summary queries to calculate statistical information for one or a number of fields. Access also provides another way to perform calculations in queries. The next section discusses performing query calculations with expressions.

Calculating Fields Using Expressions

Another way to summarize or perform calculations on field information in a query is to use expressions. *Expressions* are formulas that you build or use the Access Expression Builder to build. For instance, you may want to set up a formula that multiplies the units you have in stock and the unit price of the products that you have in inventory. This calculation gives the total value of each item that you currently have in stock.

When you design an expression to be used in a query, you place the expression in the Field row of an empty column in the query grid. For example, to multiply two fields such as UnitsInStock and UnitPrice, you would place the expression that actually does the multiplication in a column to the right of these two fields. This column, in effect, becomes your summary field in the query.

To create a query that uses an expression to calculate field information, open the appropriate database and start a new query in Design view. Add the appropriate tables to the Query Design window as shown in Figure 14.4.

To place an expression in a column of the query grid area, click the appropriate **Field row** box; this step places the insertion point where you will enter the expression. The expression that you place in the field column should have two parts: a name for the resulting field and the expression itself. First you will create the expression using the Expression Builder.

Figure 14.4

You can place an expression in a field column of the query grid box that calculates a result using data from other fields in a database table or tables.

Build button

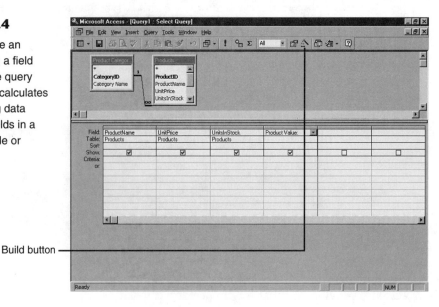

Using the Expression Builder

The Expression Builder provides a work area in which you can design expressions using fields from your database tables. (The Expression Builder can also create expressions for other database objects such as forms and reports.) The Expression Builder also provides various operators for the expressions, such as the multiplication (*) and addition (+) signs.

To open the Expression Builder, click the **Build** button on the Query Design toolbar. The Expression Builder appears as shown in Figure 14.5.

Figure 14.5

The Expression Builder can help you build both simple and complex expressions for use in your data-base objects such as the query.

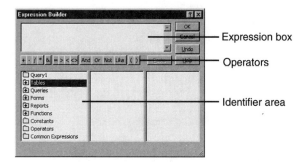

The Expression Builder has two areas: the upper part is the expression box, where you paste your expression, and the lower part is the identifier area where you select the elements for the expression.

All the objects in your database can be accessed via the folders in the identifier area of the Expression Builder window. Additional Functions, Constants, Operators, and Common Expressions are also available in folders in the identifier area.

If you want to create an expression for a query that multiplies two fields together, you must locate those fields in the Tables folder; double-click the **Tables** folder in the identifier area.

All the tables in your database are listed. Double-click the table from which you want to obtain the fields. For example, if you want to include fields for a Product table in the expression, you would double-click the **Products** table. The fields in the table are listed in the second box in the identifier area. Now you can select the fields that will appear in the expression.

Click the first field that you want to include in the expression and then click the **Paste** button. Access pastes the field name into the expression box. You can also paste a field into the expression box by double-clicking the field name.

To place an operator into your expression in the expression box, click an **operator button** on the Operator toolbar below the expression box. For example, if you've placed a field name in the expression and you want to multiply the field values contained in the field by the field values in another field, you would select the multiplication (*) operator.

To complete your expression, add the other fields that will be part of the expression to the expression box. Figure 14.6 shows a completed multiplication formula in the expression box.

 Be Aware of the Natural Order of Math Calculations When Creating Expressions Remember to follow the rules of operator precedence when you create your expressions. Multiplication and division take precedence over addition and subtractions—these operations take place first in a compound expression. You must use parentheses if you want a portion of the expression to be evaluated before another part of the expression that has a higher order operator. For instance, 2*5+6 and 2*(5+6) do not give the same answer. Also, when you have more than one set of parentheses, Access evaluates the parts from left to right. Think your expressions through as you create them.

Figure 14.6

A completed expression appears in the expression box.

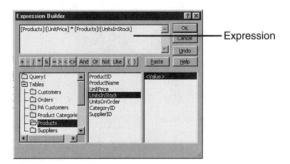

When you have completed your expression, click the **OK** button. You will be returned to the Query Design window. The new expression appears in the appropriate field column.

Now you can add a name to the field box that will appear as the column heading in the query datasheet. Press the **Home** key to place the insertion point before the expression in the field box. Text such as Expr1 will appear before the expression followed by a colon (:). Select the text and type a more appropriate name (such as **Total Product Value**) for the field.

 Use the SQL View to Zoom in on Your Expressions You can enlarge your view of the expression you place in the field box. Click **View**, **SQL View**. This view makes it easier for you to create your own query expressions or to type the text that appears as the field heading in the query results. To return to the Query Design window, click **View**, **Design View**.

The next step is to run the query and see whether the expression actually works. Click the **Run** button. The query results and the results of your expression appear in the query datasheet. Figure 14.7 shows a query datasheet that contains a calculated field.

Figure 14.7

You can use the Expression Builder to build calculated fields for your queries.

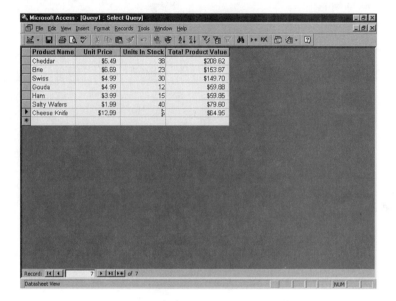

Creating Crosstab Queries

Crosstab queries are summary queries that display their results in a spreadsheet-like format that makes it easier for you to view and compare the data. Crosstab queries are perfect for summarizing numerical data from a particular field and then cross-referencing it to another field that has its data listed in the first column of the Crosstab query.

For example, to see how many orders your customers have placed by product name, you could set up a Crosstab query to list all the customers in the first column and then give a total (number of orders) that they have placed for each product in your inventory. The product names would serve as the column headings in the query's results. Another excellent use for a Crosstab query is calculating total quarterly sales of a particular product or by salesperson. Figure 14.8 depicts quarterly sales by salesperson and product.

Access provides a Crosstab Query Wizard to help you build these special summary queries. However, the Crosstab Query Wizard cannot build a Crosstab query that is based on more than one table or existing query.

To use the Wizard to build a Crosstab query that pulls information from more than one table, you must first build a Select query that incorporates all the table fields (from the multiple tables) that you want to include in the Crosstab query.

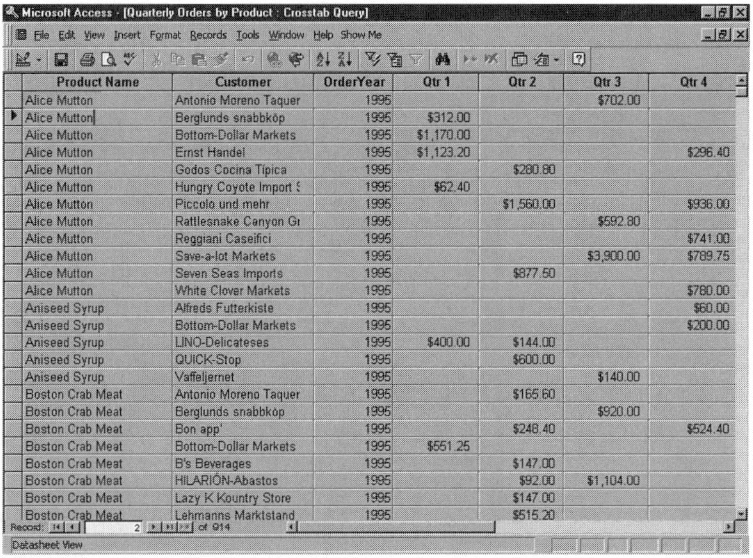

Figure 14.8

Crosstab queries summarize and cross-tabulate information.

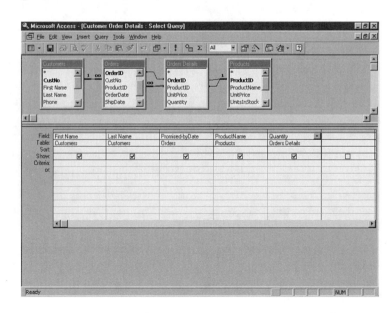

For example, to run a Crosstab query that summarizes product orders by your customers, you must build a simple Select query that incorporates fields from your Customers table, the Orders table, and the Products table. Figure 14.9 shows a simple Select query that incorporates fields from more than one table. The results of this query can then be used to build a Crosstab query using the Crosstab Query Wizard. For information on creating simple queries for multiple tables see Lesson 18, "Access and the Internet."

Figure 14.9

You can use the results of a simple Select query that combines fields from multiple tables as the basis for a Crosstab query created using the Crosstab Query Wizard.

Using the Crosstab Query Wizard

After you create the simple query on which you will base the Crosstab query, you are ready to start the Crosstab Query Wizard; follow these steps:

1. On the **Query** tab, click the **New** button. The New Query dialog box appears.

2. In the New Query dialog box, select **Crosstab Query** and then click **OK**. The first screen of the Crosstab Query Wizard appears.

3. This screen asks you to select the table or query that you want to use to build the Crosstab query. A **View** box contains three radio buttons: **Tables**, **Queries**, and **Both**. Select the appropriate radio button. The tables or queries (or both) in the current database appear in the **Table/Query** box.

4. Select a table or query (for a Crosstab query that uses fields from more than one table, you must use a preexisting query); then click **Next**.

5. Select the fields that will serve as the row headings in the Crosstab query. You can select up to three fields (see Figure 14.10). Select a field in the **Available Fields** box and then click the **Add** button to place the field in the Selected Fields box. When you have completed your field selection, click **Next**.

Figure 14.10

Select the fields that will supply values for the row headings in the Crosstab query.

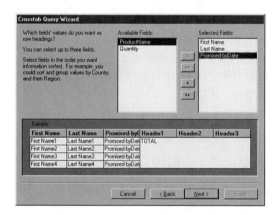

6. Select the field values that will serve as the column headings in the Crosstab query (see Figure 14.11). Product names, employee names, or other fields that contain lists of values make good column headings. Then click **Next**.

7. In the next screen that appears, select the field containing a numerical value that can be calculated (using a statistical formula) and placed at the intersection of each row and column. For instance, you may want to choose an Order Amount field. The amount ordered for each product shown in the Crosstab query results can be totaled (summed) for each customer shown in the query results. Select a

field in the **Fields** box and then select a statistical formula from the **Functions** box. You can choose between a number of formulas including Avg, Count, Min, Max, and Sum. After selecting the field and the function, click **Next** to continue to the last screen of the Crosstab Query Wizard.

Figure 14.11

Select the fields that will supply the values for the column headings in the Cross-tab query.

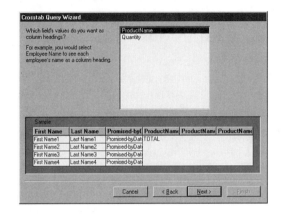

8. Type in a name for the query and then click the **Finish** button. The query re-sults appear in a Crosstab window (see Figure 14.12).

Figure 14.12 shows a Crosstab query that cross-tabulates an order Promised-by Date and customer First Name and Last Name (the row headings) with the number of products or-dered on each occasion (each product serves as a different column heading). The Total of Quantity column sums the amount of all products ordered by a particular customer.

Figure 14.12

The completed Crosstab query sets up the data in a spreadsheet-like format.

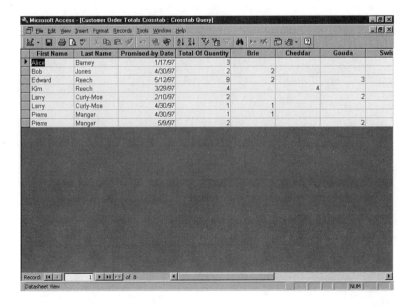

Building Crosstab Queries in Design View

You can also build Crosstab queries in the Query Design view. When you use the **Query Type** button to select Crosstab, an additional row, Crosstab, is added to the query grid box. You use this row to determine which field values will serve as row headings and which will serve as column headings. You can also designate fields that will appear as values in the Crosstab, as the Total of Quantity column did in Figure 14.12. A good strategy for learning how to design Crosstab queries from scratch is to use the Wizard to design a few Crosstab queries and then review how these queries were set up in Query Design view.

Printing Query Results

You can print the results of your queries, but you will find that reports provide the best hard copy representation of the information in your database. (For more about reports, see Lessons 15, "Creating Reports," and 16, "Modifying Report Design.") Queries print as tables do, in the Datasheet view.

To print the entire query datasheet, click the **Print** button on the Query Datasheet toolbar. If you want to print only certain records in the query datasheet, select the records and click **File**, then **Print**. The Print dialog box opens. In the Print dialog box, select the **Selected Record(s)** radio button. Click **OK** to send the selected records to the printer.

Using Append Queries

So far you have worked with simple queries, summary queries, and queries that contain calculated fields. Access offers several other query types, including Append and Delete queries. Both of these queries are Action queries; when you run them they actually change the table or tables that you design them for.

Append queries allow you to copy records from one table and place them in (append them to) another table. For example, you may have an Active Employee table. When an employee leaves the company, it makes sense to remove his or her record from the table. Using an Append query, you can move this data to a Former Employee table. After you copy the data to the Former Employee table, then you can use a Delete query to totally remove the information from the Active Employee table.

To use an Append query you need a table to which you can append the records, and that table should have the same fields as the table from which you are copying the records. The easiest way to create this table is to copy the fields from the original table (the table you want to append from) in Design view and then paste the fields into the Design view of a new table.

To create the Append query, set up a Select query in Query Design view. All the fields that are contained in the table should be placed in the grid box in the Query Design window.

 Use the Simple Query Wizard to Create an Append Query   You can create a Select query using the Simple Query Wizard and then switch to the query's Design view. In Design view, change the query type from Select to Append.

You need to turn this Select query into an Append query. You can change the type of query that you are designing by clicking the **Query Type** button on the Query toolbar. A drop-down list appears, giving you several possibilities. Select **Append Query**; the Append dialog box opens and asks you to designate the table to which you want to append the records. Type in the name of the empty table that you created to accept the appended record and then click **OK**.

A new row, Append To, appears in the query design grid. This row determines the fields in the new table to which you will append the field information. Because the table you are appending to and the current table have exactly the same fields, the Append To row lists the same field names as those listed in the query's Field row (see Figure 14.13).

Figure 14.13

An Append query enables you to copy records from one table to another.

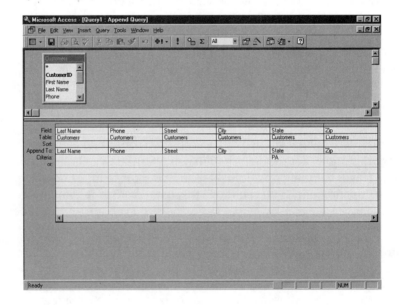

The last step is to insert the criteria into the appropriate field in the grid box that will append records from the current table to the new table. For example, to append records from a current Customers table to a new table that selects only customers who live in Pennsylvania, place **PA** in the State field's Criteria box.

To run the query, click the **Run** button on the toolbar. A dialog box tells you how many records Access will append to the other table (see Figure 14.14). Click **OK** to continue with the process. The query runs and places the appended records based on your query criteria.

Figure 14.14

Access tells you how many records will be appended and asks you to confirm the process.

You will remain in the Query Design window. To view the appended records, you must open the table that contains the appended records. In many cases, you will append the records to a new table and then use a Delete query to remove the records from the current table.

Using Delete Queries

A Delete query is designed in exactly the same way a Select or Append query is designed. Set up the Delete query in Query Design view. Place the appropriate fields from a table or tables in the query grid box. To use an existing Append query as a Delete query, open the Append query in Design view, click the **Query Type** button on the Query toolbar, and select **Delete**.

When you switch a Select or Append query to a Delete query, a new Delete row appears in the query grid box. This row can be designated as **Where** or **From** using a drop-down list that appears in each Delete box in the field columns. When you are setting up a Delete query for a single table, leave the Delete box as Where. When you have multiple tables, you can designate that certain fields from one of the related tables be deleted during the process.

To run the Delete query, click the **Run** button on the toolbar. A dialog box tells you how many records Access will delete from the current table. To continue with the deletion, click **Yes**.

You must close the Query Design window and open the table from which you deleted the records to view the results of the query. When you append or delete records from a table, you cannot use the Undo feature to reverse the process. You may want to run an Append or Delete query as a Select query first to make sure that the appropriate records appear in the query's results.

Other Query Types

Access provides several other important query types: the Make Table query, the Update query, the Find Unmatched query, and the Find Duplicates query.

The *Make Table query* functions like a Select query except that the results of the Make Table query are saved as a new table. The Make Table query can help you normalize a database table that contains fields that should really be in more than one table.

The *Update query* updates information in your Access tables. For example, you may have a credit limit field in a Customers table that currently contains $5,000. To update this data to $8,000 for all (or certain) customers, you can use the Update query. Set criteria as you would for a simple query and then change the query type to Update. A new row appears in the grid box that allows you to enter the Update value for a field or fields. When you run the query, Access tells you that it is about to change field data in the table that you want to update.

The Find Unmatched and Find Duplicate queries are run using the Find Unmatched Query Wizard and the Find Duplicate Query Wizard, respectively. The *Find Unmatched query* enables you to compare two tables and find the records that do not appear in both tables (this comparison is based on certain fields in the tables). The *Find Duplicates query* enables you to find the records that appear in both tables involved in the comparison.

Indexing Fields

Creating indexes for certain fields in your database tables can actually speed up access to the data when you do a search or sort, which means that queries run faster. An indexed field's data is stored in either numeric or alphanumeric order in the index that you create for the field. For example, if you indexed the Last Name field in a Customers table, the field information is stored in the index in alphabetical order. (It does not change the sort order of the information in the table.) A customer named Abbot appears in the index before a customer named Smith. So, in effect, indexed fields are presorted.

Primary Key Fields Are Automatically Indexed When you designate a primary key for a table, the field is automatically indexed.

To create a field index, follow these steps:

1. Open the table in Design view.

2. In the field pane, click the **Field row** of the field you want to index.

3. In the Field Properties box, click the **Indexed** box. A drop-down arrow appears.

4. To index the field, click the drop-down arrow and select either **Yes (Duplicates OK)** or **Yes (No Duplicates)**. In the case of a Last Name field, you should select **Yes (Duplicates OK)** because you are likely to have last names that repeat in the field (such as Smith or Jones). Figure 14.15 shows an index being created for the Last Name field in a table.

You should not plan to create indexes for all the fields in the table; just index the fields that are commonly involved in your queries, particularly those fields that you sort the queries by. Creating too many indexes can actually slow the update performance of your database when you add or append records to a table.

Figure 14.15

You can index fields in your tables to speed up queries.

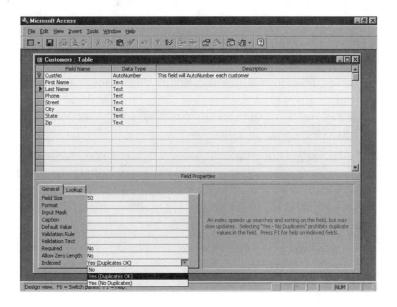

Review Questions

The Certified Microsoft Office User Exams are task oriented. The following types of questions are not representative of the test. These questions are designed to help you understand the Required Tasks and methods of performing those tasks prior to taking the test.

1. What is the main purpose of Summary queries?

2. When calculating fields in the Total row, how do you derive the formulas used?

3. If you want to create a Crosstab query using the Crosstab Query Wizard, how do you ensure that the data will be pulled from more than one table for the query results?

4. If you want to print only certain records in a query's results, how would you accomplish it?

5. If you want to copy records from a particular table to another table and then delete the records from the first table, which query types must you use?

Review Question Answers

1. Summary queries enable you to calculate summary information for a particular field, such as the total, average, maximum, or minimum. For more information, see the section "Calculating Fields in Summary Queries."

2. The Total box for each field contains a drop-down arrow that provides a list of formulas for calculating the field. These formulas are statistical and include Sum, Avg, Max, and Min. For more information, see the section "Calculating Fields in the Total Row."

3. The Crosstab Query Wizard can only create a query based on one table or query. You must create a simple query for multiple tables and then base the Crosstab query created by the Wizard on the simple query (providing a Crosstab query that pulls data for fields from more than one table). For more information, see the section "Creating Crosstab Queries."

4. Select the records in the query results you want to print. Then click **File**, **Print**. In the Print dialog box, select the **Selected Record(s)** radio button; then click **OK** to proceed. For more information, see the section "Printing Query Results."

5. You would use the Append query to copy the records from a particular table to another table (the tables must contain the same fields). After using the Append query to "copy" the records, you can using the Delete query to delete the records from the original table. For more information, see the sections "Using Append Queries" and "Using Delete Queries."

Practice Lab

The Microsoft Access Expert User Exam lists various Required Tasks for the two Skill Areas covered in this lesson. The following practice lab covers many of these tasks.

 Required Tasks Three Required Tasks for the "Analyze Data" Skill Area are build a summary query, calculate fields, and set Crosstab queries. One Required Task for the "Print" Skill Area is print the results of a query.

Build a Summary Query and Calculate Fields

Copy the **lesson14.mdb** database from the CD that accompanies this book to a folder on your computer using Windows Explorer. Open the database.

1. Use the fields in the Customers and Order table to determine the total number of orders placed by each customer. The query should include the First Name and Last Name fields from the Customers table and the OrderDate from the Order table. Save the query as **Total Orders by Customer**. Run the query.

2. Open the **Total Orders by Customer** query in Design view. Add the OrdersDetail table to the tables that appear in the Design window. Add the UnitPrice field to the query. Calculate the total for this field. Use **Save As** to save this query as **Total Owed by Customer**. Run the query.

3. Create a Select query in Design view using the Products table. Include the ProductName and UnitsInStock fields in the query grid. Use the Expression Builder to build a calculated field that determines the total dollar value of each of your products. (Hint: You must build an expression that multiplies two of the fields in the Product table.) Name the calculated field **Total Value**. Name the query **Total Product Value in Stock**.

Set Crosstab Queries

1. Create a simple multitable query using the Customers, Products, Orders, and Orders Detail tables. Include the following fields in the query: First Name, Last Name (from Customers), ProductName (from Products), and Quantity (from OrdersDetails). Save the query as **Customer Order Details**.

2. Use the Crosstab Query Wizard to build a Crosstab query that uses the Customer Order Details query as the source query. Use the First Name and Last Name fields as the row headings in the Crosstab query. Use the ProductName field as the column headings in the Crosstab query. Use the Sum formula to total the Quantity field. Save the Crosstab query as **Customer Order Details_Crosstab**.

Print the Results of a Query

Print the results of the Total Owed by Customer query. Also print Total Product Value in Stock but only the records for Cheddar, Brie, and Swiss.

Open the database **lesson14a.mdb** on the CD to see a completed version the queries you worked with in this lab.

Creating Reports

This lesson covers four Required Tasks for the Expert User "Produce Reports" Skill Area and one Required Task for the "Print" Skill Area.

In this lesson, you learn the following Required Tasks for your exam:

Produce Reports Skill Area:

- ▶ Create a report
- ▶ Modify a report
- ▶ Group data in a report
- ▶ Sort data in a report

Print Skill Area:

- ▶ Print a report

Understanding Access Reports

Although you've already had the opportunity to print tables, forms, and queries, these database objects do not present your data in a format that is ideal for hard copy presentation. Access reports can present the information in your tables and queries in a format that is well designed and easy to read. Reports are designed to be printed and will be the one database object that you will want to share with your colleagues and coworkers.

In Access, you can create reports from single tables or queries or from multiple tables (tables that you have related). You also have the same data and design control in reports as you had when you were working with forms. Consequently, you can create a format that suits your particular needs, and you can add special items to the report such as calculated controls and graphics.

Creating a Report

Access provides several methods for creating a new report. To create a report for one table or query that uses all the fields in the table or query that is currently open in the Access window, you can use the AutoReport feature. Another way to create reports is to use the Report Wizard. The Wizard helps you group and sort data for the report and add calculations.

The third alternative is to build a report from scratch in Report Design view. This method is not unlike building a form from scratch. You add field controls to the Detail area of the report and also create labels and calculated controls for the report.

 Use Design View to Modify Your Reports If you are just learning to create reports, you may prefer using the Report Wizard or AutoReport to build reports and then customize them in Design view, rather than attempting to build reports from scratch.

Using AutoReport

AutoReport provides a quick way put the data from a table or query into a printable format. AutoReport offers two report formats: tabular and columnar. The tabular report resembles a datasheet, and the columnar report resembles a form.

To create a report with AutoReport, follow these steps:

1. Open the database that you want to work with. Open the table or query you want to create the report for. Click the **New Object** drop-down button on the Table or Query toolbar as shown in Figure 15.1. Select **Report** from the New Object list. The New Report dialog box opens.

Figure 15.1

You can quickly build
a new object for the
current table or query
by clicking the New
Object drop-down
button.

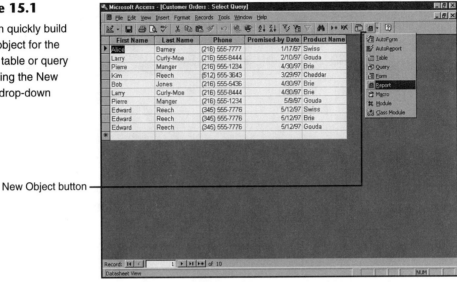

New Object button —

2. In the New Report dialog box, select either **AutoReport: Columnar** or
   AutoReport: Tabular. Click **OK**.

3. The new report appears in the Print Preview window (see Figure 15.2). At this
   point, you can scroll through the report to view the information or send the
   report to the printer by clicking the **Print** button on the toolbar. (Printing reports and working in the Print Preview window are discussed in the section
   "Printing and Viewing Reports in Print Preview.")

4. To close the Print Preview window, click the **Close** button. When you close the
   Print Preview window, you are taken to Report Design view. (Report Design view
   is covered in detail in Lesson 16, "Modifying Report Design.") To save the report,
   click the **Save** button on the toolbar.

5. In the **Save As** box, type a name for the report and then click **OK**. After you
   save the report, you can close the Report Design window.

 Create an AutoReport from the Report Tab You can also use AutoReport to create a new report from the Report tab. Click the **New** button and then select a table or
query for the report in the New Report dialog box. Select either **AutoReport: Columnar** or **AutoReport: Tabular**. Then click **OK**.

Figure 15.2

Your new report appears in the Print Preview window.

Print button
Close button

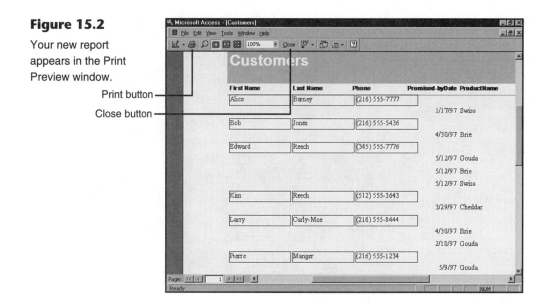

When you use AutoReport to create a report for a typical table, such as a Customers table, you will see the information grouped by CustomerID (the primary key field). For example, CustomerID 1 appears at the top of the report with all the other field data for that particular customer (name, phone number, and so on) detailed.

In the case of a report based on a query, the method AutoReport uses to group the information depends on the fields and information in the query. Figures 15.1 and 15.2, for example, show a query in which customers' orders (some customers had more than one order) are grouped in the report by customer and each order is detailed under the customer's name.

Access reports tend to group information so that it can be printed and easily read and understood. Even AutoReport creates fairly elegant reports without much input from you.

Using the Report Wizard

The Report Wizard is another tool that enables you to create reports in Access. The Wizard offers a fair amount of flexibility and helps you build reports from multiple tables and queries. You have options for the layout or format of the report created.

To use the Report Wizard to create a report, follow these steps:

1. Open the database that you want to create the report in. On the **Report** tab in the Database window, click the **New** button. The New Report dialog box opens.

2. Click **Report Wizard** and then click **OK**. The Report Wizard opens.

3. The first screen of the Report Wizard asks you to select the fields that you want to include in the report. You can select the fields from a table, a query, or multiple tables and queries. Select a table or query in the **Tables/Queries** drop-down list.

4. The fields from the selected table or query appear in the **Available Fields** box. Select a field you want to include in the report and click the **Add** button (see Figure 15.3). Repeat the process until all the fields you want to include in the report appear in the **Selected Fields** box. As mentioned in step 3, you can add fields from multiple tables or queries. When you have finished adding the fields, click **Next**.

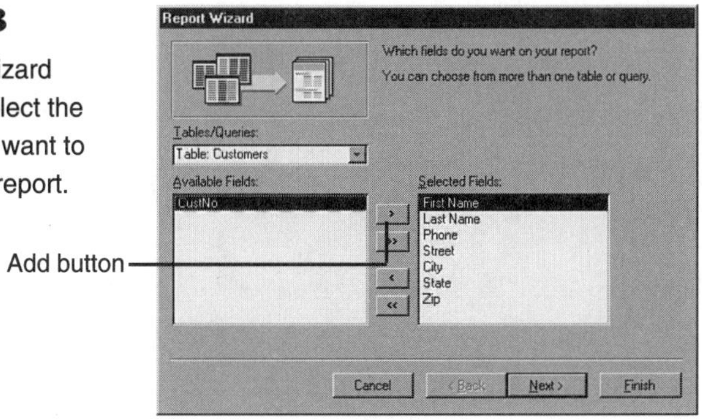

Figure 15.3

The Report Wizard asks you to select the fields that you want to include in the report.

Add button

Grouping Data in a Report

The next screen of the Report Wizard asks you to select fields for grouping the record information that appears in the report. For example, if you were designing the report to list your products by category, you would want to use the Category field as the first grouping level. Additional grouping levels can also be used. For example, you could use multiple grouping levels in a customer report in which you group customers by region first and then by state.

To create grouping levels in the report, select a field in the field box and then click the **Add** button to add the field to the group list. The first field you add provides the first-level grouping in the report. You can add more fields to provide additional grouping levels (see Figure 15.4). When you have completed your selection, click the **Next** button.

Setting Grouping Options The Report Wizard's Grouping screen contains a **Grouping Options** button. Click this button to open the Grouping Intervals dialog box in which you can set the grouping interval for each field by which you will group the data. In most cases, the group interval is Normal (the default setting). However, you can change the interval; for example, for a text field, you could change the interval to 3. This setting means that all values in the particular field that share the first three letters (such as Chai, Chartreuse, and Chang) would be grouped together in the report.

Figure 15.4

The Report Wizard asks you to select the fields that you will use as the grouping levels in the report.

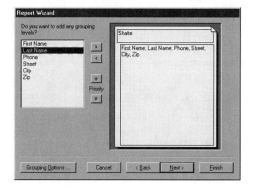

Sorting Data in a Report

The next Report Wizard screen asks whether to sort the records in the report. You can select up to four sort levels. Click the **Level 1 Sort** drop-down box and select the field you want to sort by. Use the other **Sort** drop-down boxes to select additional sort levels.

You can use the **Sort Direction** button to the right of each sort-level box to change the direction of the sort. The default is Ascending. To change to Descending, click the **Sort Direction** button.

If you selected for your report any fields that have a Number, Currency, or Date data type, you can add summary information to the report by clicking the **Summary Options** button. The Summary Options dialog box enables you to specify summary calculations for selected fields in the report, as shown in Figure 15.5.

You can include the Sum, Avg, Min, or Max of each Number, Currency, or Date field, as well as calculate the percent of total for fields that you select to sum. Click the **summary calculation boxes** to specify the summary information you want to include in the report. Click **OK** to return to the Report Wizard's sort order screen.

When you have completed setting the sort order and selecting the summary options (see Figure 15.6), click **Next**.

Figure 15.5

If your report includes Number, Currency, or Date type fields, you can include summary calculations in the report that make use of the data in those fields.

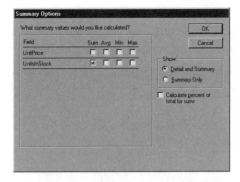

Figure 15.6

Select the fields that you want the Report Wizard to use to sort the records in the report.

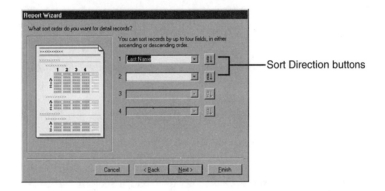

Sort Direction buttons

 Using Sort in the Report If you set up a report that doesn't group the information at different levels, the records appear in the report according to the sort parameters that you set.

Working with Multiple-Table Reports

If you select fields for the report from multiple tables, during the field selection process on the first screen of the Report Wizard an additional Wizard screen appears after you click the **Next** button. This Wizard screen lists the tables that you used to select the fields. For example, if you are creating a report that shows your customer's orders, you may use fields from the Customers table, Orders table, and Product table. The Wizard screen lists the tables that were used to select the fields from (in our example Customers, Orders, and Product tables).

The Wizard screen also asks you to determine how you want to view your data; that is, the Wizard wants you to select one of the tables in its table list. When you select a table, the report groups the records by the fields found in that table. For example, if you select the Customers table, the report groups the information by the customers. If you select the Product table, the report groups the information by the product name, and so on.

Select the table that places the fields in the grouping order you want to use in the report. When you click **Next**, you return to the Report Wizard's field grouping screen (refer to Figure 15.4). This step enables you to modify the grouping further.

Completing the Report

The next Report Wizard screen enables you to choose a layout and page orientation for the report. Several layouts are available. You can print the report stepped, blocked, as an outline (two different layouts) or in left-aligned columns (equally spaced on both the right and the left). When you click the radio button for a particular layout, a preview appears on the left side of the Report Wizard screen.

You can also choose the paper orientation for the report. *Portrait* is a regular sheet of paper in its 8.5-by-11-inch orientation. For *landscape,* you turn the paper 90 degrees for a page with an 11-by-8.5-inch orientation. If your table has only a few fields, use the portrait orientation. If it has a lot of fields, use landscape.

Select the layout and paper orientation for your report as shown in Figure 15.7, and then click **Next**.

The next Report Wizard screen asks you to select a style for your report. Several style types are offered: Bold, Casual, Compact, Corporate, Formal, or Soft Gray. Click a style to see a preview. When you have selected the style you want to use, click the **Next** button.

Figure 15.7

Select a layout and a paper orientation for your report.

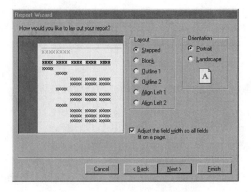

The final screen of the Report Wizard asks you to type a name for your report in the **Report** text box. You also have the option of opening the new report in Print Preview or Design view. Select the appropriate radio button (in this case, **Print Preview**) and click **Finish**.

Printing and Viewing Reports in Print Preview

The new report appears in the Print Preview window. The toolbar along the top of the window contains a number of command buttons (see Figure 15.8). You can click the **Print** button to send your report to the printer, or you can zoom in and out on the page. You can also click a button to exit from Print Preview mode.

Figure 15.8

The Print Preview toolbar provides a number of ways to view a report.

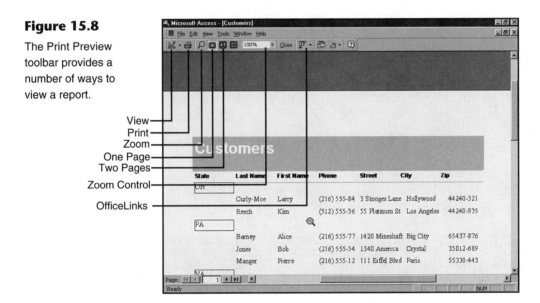

If you move your mouse around when you are in Print Preview mode, you will notice that the mouse pointer has become a zoom controller (it looks like a magnifying glass). When you are zoomed out on your report (you can see the whole page), the zoom controller contains a plus (+) sign. If you click the mouse button now, you zoom in. When you are zoomed in, the zoom controller contains a minus (-) sign. Click, and you zoom out.

You can view one page of the report or multiple pages. If the report layout is satisfactory, you can print the report by clicking **Print**. If the report needs more work, you can switch to Report Design view by clicking the **View** button.

 Export Access Data to Word and Excel   You can also export your Access reports to other members of Microsoft's Office suite of applications. You can send your report to a Microsoft Word document or analyze the data in the report using a Microsoft Excel spreadsheet. Use the **OfficeLinks** button to quickly take advantage of this powerful feature.

Modifying a Report

When you close the Print Preview window or click the **View** button on the Print Preview toolbar, you are taken to Report Design view. This view includes a toolbox that contains the same set of tools that were available when you were working on forms.

Report Design view is very similar to Form Design view. However, some differences should be stressed.

Reports have a Report Header, Report Footer, and Report Detail area similar to the same areas found on forms. The Report Header and Report Footer, respectively, contain information that you want to appear at the top and bottom of the report. In addition, reports have a Page Header and Page Footer for information that you want to repeat at the top or bottom of every page of the report (many reports require multiple pages). For example, you may want to place a control in the Page Footer that adds the page number to the bottom of each page of the report.

When you use the Report Wizard to create a report, a label for the report is placed in the Report Header. A current date control and a page number control are placed in the Page Footer. The Wizard also adds header and footer areas to the report if you selected to group the information by a particular field or fields or if you added any summary formulas during the report creation process (see Figure 15.9).

Figure 15.9

The various header and footer areas in your reports provide places for titles, repeating information, and grouping information.

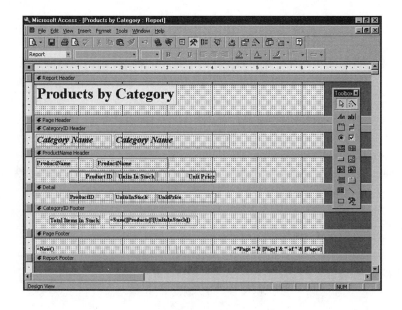

Modifying Report Controls

In Design view you can delete or add field controls and labels to the report. You can also size and move the controls and labels. For example, a report based on a table or query that includes many fields may not provide enough room on the report page for you to view all the data in a particular field (that is, the data in the field is truncated). You can click a field or label and use the sizing boxes to change the width or height of a particular item. You can also adjust the position of controls by dragging them.

You can use the buttons on the Formatting toolbar to format the text items in the labels and control. Select the label or control and then select the button on the toolbar to change the particular text attribute.

Creating a Report in Design View

You can also create a report in Design view. You will be limited, however, to one table or query as the source for the report. Building a report from scratch does give you complete control of the layout of the report and enables you to easily add special controls or labels to the report.

To create a report in Design view, complete the following steps:

1. Open the database you want to work with.

2. On the **Report** tab of the Database window, click the **New** button. The New Report dialog box opens.

3. Choose a table or query in the **Table/Query** drop-down box. Make sure **Design View** is selected and then click **OK**.

4. The Report Design window opens.

Now you can select and modify certain fields, group and sort data, and make any changes to the report.

Selecting Fields for Grouping and Sorting Data

First you need to determine which fields you want to group or sort the data by. If you group data by a particular field or fields, you need to add a header area for the field. Click the **Sorting and Grouping** button on the Design toolbar. The Sorting and Grouping dialog box appears as shown in Figure 15.10.

Figure 15.10

The Sorting and Grouping dialog box is where you select the fields that the report uses to group or sort information.

Sorting and Grouping button

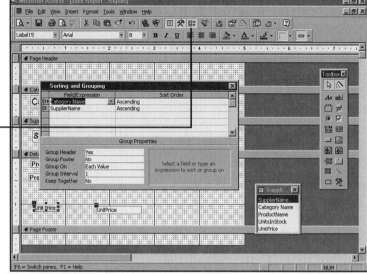

Use the drop-down arrows in the rows provided to select a field you want to group or sort by. If you want to group the information in the report by a field, click the **Group Header** box. Click the drop-down arrow that appears and select **Yes**. A group header for the selected field then appears in the report. Also select any fields you want to sort by. After you make your grouping and sorting field selections, close the Sorting and Grouping dialog box.

Now you have to add the various fields to the report. Click the **Field List** button on the toolbar if necessary. Select any fields by which you are going to group the information in the report and drag them to the appropriate Report Header. Drag the other fields that you want to include in the report to the Detail Area of the report. Make sure to place fields that you have selected to sort by above the other fields in the Detail area. Use text formatting as necessary to highlight fields that you are grouping or sorting the data by.

Moving Labels and Controls

You can move the field labels and controls independently. When you select the label for a control or the control itself, a large handle appears in the upper-left corner of both the label and control. Drag this handle, and the label (or control) moves independently of its partner. This feature enables you to arrange the labels for a control above the control or in a different area than the control. Figure 15.11 shows a report in progress in which the data will be grouped by Category Name and then by Supplier Name.

Figure 15.11

Access gives you complete design license when you work with your reports in Design view.

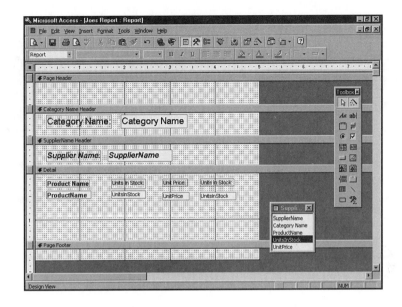

You can switch between Print Preview and Design view by clicking the appropriate view from the **View** button on the toolbar. Make sure you save your report design before closing the Design View window.

Regardless of how you create your report—Design view, AutoReport, or Report Wizard—you will still need to modify the various header and footer areas and add new labels and calculated controls to the report. Lesson 16 covers these report modification techniques.

Review Questions

The Certified Microsoft Office User Exams are task oriented. The following types of questions are not representative of the test. These questions are designed to help you understand the required tasks and methods of performing those tasks prior to taking the test.

1. What are three methods that you can use to create a report in Access?

2. What is the easiest way to create a report that can include fields from multiple tables or queries?

3. In which view would you modify a report?

4. Which dialog box do you use to set grouping levels in Design view?

5. True or False: Can you group and sort data in a report that you build using the Report Wizard?

Review Question Answers

1. You can create a report using AutoReport, using the Report Wizard, or in Design view. For more information see the sections "Using AutoReport," "Using the Report Wizard," and "Creating a Report in Design View."

2. The Report Wizard enables you to select fields from multiple tables or queries when you build a new report. For more information, see the section "Using the Report Wizard."

3. You modify your reports in Design view. For more information, see the section "Modifying a Report."

4. In Design view, click the **Sorting and Grouping** button on the toolbar. Select the fields for sorting and grouping in the Sorting and Grouping dialog box. For more information, see the section "Selecting Fields for Grouping and Sorting Data."

5. True: The Report Wizard enables you to select the fields that you group and sort the report data by. For more information, see the sections "Grouping Data in a Report" and "Sorting Data in a Report."

Practice Lab

The Microsoft Access Expert User Exam lists four Required Tasks for the Expert User "Produce Reports" Skill Area. In addition, the "Print a Report" skill is part of each part of the lab. The following practice lab covers these skills.

> **Required Tasks**   Four Required Tasks for the "Produce Reports" Skill Area are create a report, modify a report, group data in a report, and sort data in a report. One Required Task for the "Print" Skill Area is print a report.

Copy the **lesson15.mdb** database from the CD that accompanies this book to a folder on your computer using Windows Explorer. Open the database. Make sure to run each query after you finish designing the query or making changes to the query. The Print a Report skill is practiced in each of the labs.

Create a Report

Use the AutoReport feature to create a tabular report for the Customers table. Save the table as **Customers** and print the report.

Grouping and Sorting Data

Use the Report Wizard to create a report for multiple tables. Select the following fields for the report: Category Name, ProductName, UnitPrice, UnitsInStock, and the report by ProductName. Use the SupplierName. View the data by Product Categories (which is the grouping field). Sort the records in stepped layout for the report and the Compact style. Name the report **Products by Category**. Print the report.

Modify a Report

Open the **Customers** report you created in Design view. Delete the CustNo label and control from the report. Switch the position of the First Name and Last Name labels and controls. Italicize the text in the control labels in the report. Save the changes you've made to the report and print the report.

Open the database **lesson15a.mdb** on the CD to see completed versions of the reports you created in this the lab.

LESSON 16

Modifying Report Design

This lesson covers five Produce Report skills and one View Information skill for the Expert User level.

In this lesson, you learn the following Required Tasks for your exam:

Produce Reports Skill Area:

- ▶ Modify a report
- ▶ Label a report
- ▶ Customize headers and footers
- ▶ Make a calculation on a report
- ▶ Add custom pages

View Information Skill Area:

- ▶ Present information in a chart

Modifying Reports in Design View

In Lesson 15, "Creating Reports," you worked with various methods of creating Access reports. This lesson continues the study of reports and concentrates on enhancing and modifying reports created using AutoReport, using the Report Wizard, and created from scratch in Design view.

You can add a number of items to your reports in Design view. You can add new controls, labels, graphics, and subreports. You can also create custom pages in your reports by expanding a header or footer area and then placing a page break in the report.

Adding a New Label to a Report

You can add new labels to your report using the Label tool on the Toolbox. Labels that you want to appear at the very top of the report are placed in the Report Header. Any comments or other information that you want to appear at the end of the report can be placed in the Report Footer.

To place a new label in a Report Header, follow these steps:

1. Switch to Design view and open the report that you want to work with.

2. Click **View** and then **Report Header/Footer** to see the Report Header and Report Footer in Design view.

3. Expand the Header or Footer area where you want to place a label.

4. Click the **Label** button on the Toolbox. Drag out the new label box in the appropriate Header or Footer area.

5. Type the text that you want to appear in the label.

6. Click the border of the new label to select the label. Use any of the formatting tools on the Formatting toolbar to enhance the text, border, or fill of the new label.

7. Add any more labels that you want in the report. Figure 16.1 shows new labels that have been placed in a Report Header.

You can also place labels in any of the other report areas if you have a need for additional information. Remember that Report Header and Report Footer information appear at the top and bottom of the report. Page Head and Footer information appear on every page of the report.

Figure 16.1

You can use the Label tool to add labels to your report.

Label button ─────

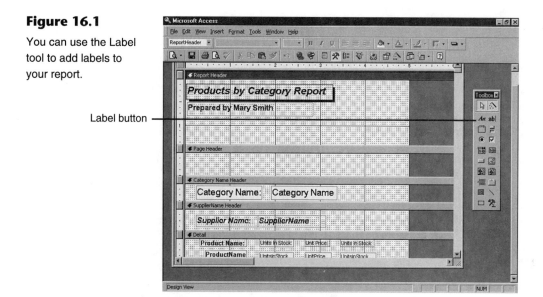

Creating Report Controls

You already know that the report will contain controls related to fields that are contained in an associated table or query. These controls are bound controls. You can also place calculated controls in your reports (as you did with forms) that can return the current date or calculate a result using an expression.

In most cases, the Expression Builder provides the most straightforward method for creating calculated controls in your reports.

Inserting Date and Page Number Controls

You can place controls for the current date and page numbers in the Page Footer of your report so that the date and appropriate page number appear at the bottom of every page of the report.

To place a date control in the report's Page Footer, follow these steps:

1. Make sure the Page Footer is showing in the Design window; click **View**, **Page Header/Footer**.

2. Scroll down in the report window so that the Page Footer appears. Expand the Page Footer if necessary.

3. Click the **Text Box** tool on the Toolbox. Use the mouse to drag out a new control in the Page Footer.

4. Double-click the label box of the new control and type **Date**.

5. Double-click the edge of the new control's control box (it currently says "unbound"). The Text Box Properties dialog box opens (see Figure 16.2).

6. Select the **Data** tab in the Text Box Properties dialog box.

7. Click the **Control Source** box. A drop-down arrow and the Expression Builder button appear. Click the **Expression Builder** button. The Expression Builder window opens.

Figure 16.2

The new controls that contain calculations or that can be bound to fields are created with the Text Box tool.

Text Box control ⎯

Expression Builder button ⎯

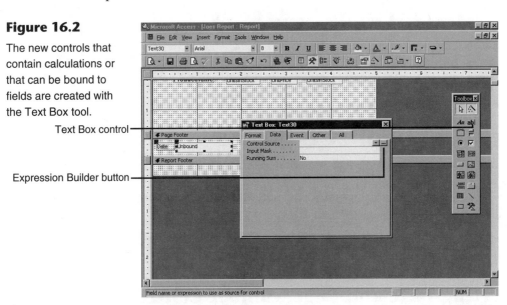

8. In the first column of the Expression Builder, click the **Common Expressions** folder.

9. A list of common expressions such as Page Number and Current Date appears in the second column of the Expression Builder window. Double-click the **Current Date** expression. The expression is placed in the Expression box at the top of the Expression Builder window.

10. Click **OK**. The new expression appears in the Control Source box of the Text Box Properties dialog box. Close the Text Box Properties dialog box. The Date expression now appears in the Date control in the report's Page Footer.

11. To view the new control in Print Preview mode, click the **View** button on the Report Design toolbar.

12. Scroll down to the bottom of the first page of the report to view the new control.

To add a Page Number control to the Page Footer area, repeat this series of steps. You can also add controls containing these types of expressions to other areas of the report.

Making Calculations on a Report

You can also place controls in your reports that use an expression to return a value. For example, you may want to include a totals control at the very bottom of the report that shows the total amount spent from your budget. Or you may want to show the grand total of all the items you have in stock. A "grand total" expression would be placed in the Report Footer so that it appears at the bottom of the report.

You can also place expressions in your reports that provide summary information for a portion of the report. You already know that you can add grouping headers and footers to the report to group the information. (For more information on adding group headers and footers see Lesson 15.) You can also place summary expressions that return a value related to the group in these group headers and footers. For example, you may want to have an expression that gives you a subtotal of the number of items in stock by the categories that you used to group the various items in the report.

Adding a Totals Control

You may have occasion to include a summary calculation at the very end of a report. This new calculated control would be placed in the Report Footer. Follow these steps to place a calculated control at the end of a report:

1. Use the **Text Box** tool to create a new control in the Report Footer. Double-click the label portion of the new control and type the name that you want to give to the control.

2. Double-click the control itself to open the Text Box Properties dialog box. Click the **Control Source** box on the **Data** tab of the Text Box Properties dialog box. Click the **Expression Builder** button to start the Expression Builder.

3. Double-click the **Functions** folder in the first column; a set of subfolders appears in the first column. Double-click the **Built In Functions** folder. The set of folders appear in the second column that categorize the various Access functions. The contents of the selected category appears in the third column. When you select **All** in the second column, all the functions available in Access are listed in the third column in alphabetical order.

4. Select the category of function you want to select from in the second column and then double-click the formula you want to use in the third column.

Choose from Categories of Math Functions The Expression Builder enables you to select subsets of functions by categories (the second column of functions in the Builder). After you select a category of functions, the specific formulas appear in the third column of the Expression Builder.

5. The expression appears in the Expression box. In the case of formulas like Sum, the expression appears in the Expression box with a set parentheses to the right of the expression itself. The parentheses contain «expr». Select this text with the mouse by clicking the Expression box (do not disturb the parentheses).

6. Designate the field that the formula will act on. The field name replaces «expr» in the expression. In the first column of the Expression Builder, click the folder for the current report. (It has the name of the report or Report1 as its label if you have not saved the report.) The labels and controls in the report appear in the second column of the Expression Builder.

7. Double-click the control that you want to place in the expression (see Figure 16.3).

Figure 16.3

After you place the formula in the Expression box, you must designate the field that the expression will act on.

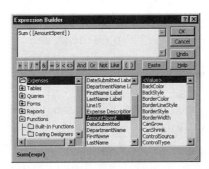

8. Click **OK** to close the Expression Builder. Then close the Text Box Properties box (the expression appears in the Control Source box).

The new expression appears in the control in the Report Footer. To view the results of the new calculated control, switch to the Print Preview window. The total (or result of the formula you built) appears at the end of the report.

To format the results of the expression for Currency or another special Number or Date format, return to Design view and double-click the control to open its Properties box. Click the **Format** tab. Choose a format for the control from the drop-down list in the Format box. Close the Properties dialog box after formatting the control.

Create Custom Expressions for Your Controls   You can also use the Expression Builder to create expressions that include more than one field in the calculations. For example, you may want to multiply two field's data to return a value in a calculated control. See Lesson 12, "Advanced Form Design," for more information on calculated controls involving more than one field.

Adding a Group Subtotal

Your reports can also contain expressions that act on certain groups of information. For example, you may want to see your company's expenses broken down by department. It makes sense to also include a group subtotal that provides the sum of all the expenses by department.

To add calculated controls that act on a certain grouping in your report, you may have to add a new report section. You can add Group Headers and Group Footers to your report using the **Sorting and Grouping** button on the Design toolbar. (For more information on sorting and grouping records in a report, see Lesson 15.)

To add a control that calculates a value for data found in a report grouping, follow these steps:

1. Click the **Sorting and Grouping** button on the Design toolbar. The Sorting and Grouping dialog box opens (see Figure 16.4). Click the first row of the dialog box. Use the drop-down arrow to select the field that you want to use to group the information in the report.

Figure 16.4

The Sorting and Grouping dialog box enables you to add Group Headers and Group Footers to the report.

2. When you select the field, a Group Properties box appears in the bottom of the Sorting and Grouping dialog box. Click the Group Header or Group Footer box. Use the drop-down arrow to select **Yes** to add a Group Header or Group Footer to the report. (To group the data by the field and enter a summary calculation based on the field, choose both.)

3. Close the Sorting and Grouping dialog box. If the field you want to group the data by already appears in the report, drag the field's control to the Group Header.

If the control that you want to group the data by does not appear on the report, create a new control and assign it the correct label. To bind the new control to the correct field, double-click the control. The Text Box Properties dialog box appears.

4. On the **Data** tab of the Text Box Properties dialog box, click the **Control Source** box. Use the drop-down list to select the field that will be bound to the control. Close the Text Box Properties dialog box.

5. To create the summary expression for the group, create another new control in the Group Footer. Type a name in the new control's label. Double-click the control to open its Properties dialog box.

6. On the **Data** tab, click the **Control Source** box, and then click the **Expression Builder** button. Use the Expression Builder to create a formula that sums, averages, or acts on a particular field using one of the other available formulas. (Refer to steps 4–8 in the earlier section, "Adding a Totals Control," if you need help creating the expression.)

 Remember the Equal Sign If you type a function directly into the **Control Source** box (and do not use the Expression Builder to build the formula), make sure you place an equal sign (**=**) before the expression.

7. Figure 16.5 shows a group total formula that calculates the subtotals for the company expenses by department. When you create expressions, make sure to format the results for the correct data type. For example, dollar amounts should be formatted for Currency. Set the format for the control on the **Format** tab of the control's Properties dialog box.

Access offers you almost endless possibilities for calculated controls in your reports. Make sure that you use Print Preview to check the results of your expressions and their position on the report. Keep in mind that even the most brilliantly designed formulas will have little effect on the reader of your report if the report layout is sloppy.

Creating a Chart

A very good way to summarize information in a report is to provide the reader with a pictorial representation of the data—a chart. Charts can provide a way to track information over time or to look at how a certain piece of information relates to the whole. For example, you may want to build a pie chart that shows the percentage of expenses by department and how they relate to the total expenses.

Figure 16.5

You can use calculated controls to provide group totals and other summary calculations for groupings of information in your reports.

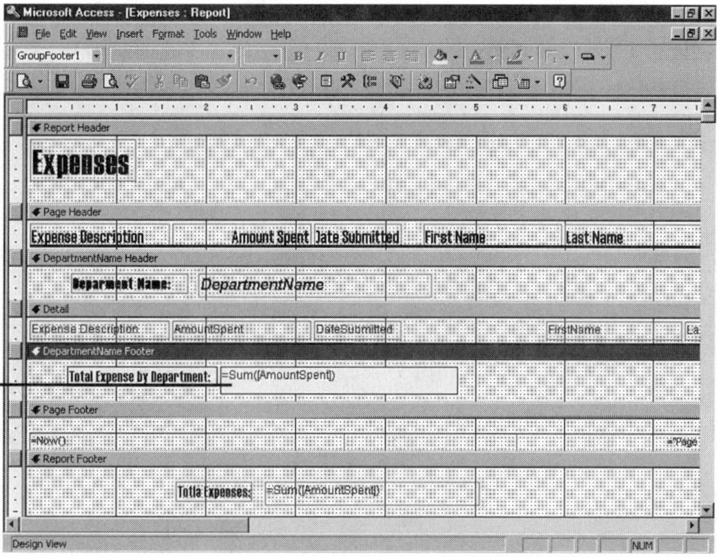

Group Subtotal control ─

[screenshot of Microsoft Access Expenses Report in Design View showing Report Header "Expenses", Page Header with Expense Description, Amount Spent, Date Submitted, First Name, Last Name; DepartmentName Header; Detail section; DepartmentName Footer with "Total Expense by Department: =Sum([AmountSpent])"; Page Footer; Report Footer with "Total Expenses: =Sum([AmountSpent])"]

Charts can be created for use as forms or reports. The Chart Wizard is available in both the New Form and New Report dialog boxes.

To create a new chart, follow these steps:

1. Open the database that contains the table or query on which you want to base the chart.

2. On the **Report** tab, click the **New** button.

3. In the New Report dialog box, select the **Chart Wizard**. From the drop-down list at the bottom of the dialog box, select the table or query on which you want to base the chart. Click **OK** to continue.

4. The first screen of the Chart Wizard asks you to select the field in the table or query that you want to include in the chart. Select fields in the **Available Field** box and add them to the **Field for Chart** box. Click **Next** to continue.

Selecting Fields for the Chart Most charts that you create from your database data will be simple x, y charts—they have two axes. Two axes charts include line graphs, simple bar charts, and pie charts. The information on the x-axis is usually textual—for example, the name of an employee or a kind of newt. The y-axis contains the related numerical information, such as sales in dollars or number of newts counted.

5. The next screen asks you to choose the type of chart that you want to create (see Figure 16.6). The type of chart you select depends on what you are trying to depict with the information. For example, bar charts are best for showing change over time. Pie charts are good for showing how the parts of something relate to the whole. Line charts are good for tracking upward and downward changes over a time period. Click the **chart type** you want to use; then click **Next**.

Figure 16.6

The Chart Wizard asks you to select the type of chart you want to create.

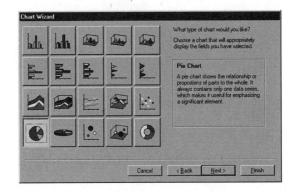

6. The Chart Wizard gives you a chance to manipulate how the information will be shown on the chart. You can drag buttons that represent the various fields in the chart to a specific place. Fields that contain data represent the y-axis of the chart and should appear on the chart itself. Usually, the x-axis field goes outside the chart to serve as the series for the chart. For example, in a pie chart like the one shown in Figure 16.7, the Sum of Expenses field appears on the chart, whereas the informational field (the name of the department button) appears outside the chart.

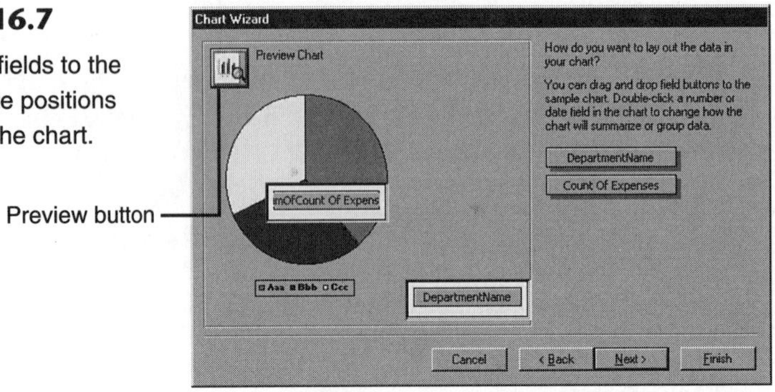

Figure 16.7

Move the fields to the appropriate positions to create the chart.

Preview button

7. Use the **Preview** button to look at the chart before moving to the next step. When the chart looks satisfactory, click the **Next** button.

Do Not Move the Field Markers Unnecessarily The Chart Wizard does a pretty good job placing the fields that will serve as the various axes for your chart. Do not rearrange the fields if the chart appears to be correct.

8. The last Chart Wizard screen asks you to name the chart and decide whether or not you want to include a legend for the chart. Legends provide a way for the viewer of the chart to make sense out of the data. Definitely include a legend for pie charts and bar charts. Click the **Finish** button.

The completed chart appears as a report in the Print Preview window. You can switch to Design view by clicking the **View** button on the toolbar. Editing a chart can be somewhat problematic, and if the chart is unsatisfactory, you may want to build a new chart using the Wizard.

You can edit the chart (somewhat) in Design view. The chart is actually an embedded object (linking and embedding objects are covered in Lesson 17, "Integrating Data from Other Applications") on a blank report.

To edit the chart using Graph 97 (the application that the Wizard used to create the chart), make sure that you are in Design view. Then double-click your chart. When Microsoft Graph 97 appears, the Graph 97 window contains your chart and a datasheet for the chart. The datasheet is the result of the data choices that you made when the Chart Wizard walked you through the chart creation process. However, the datasheet that appears here displays a set of default values for a sample chart rather than the actual data that is represented in your chart.

Microsoft Graph 97 has its own toolbar and menus, giving you access to a wide variety of commands relating to charting your data. You can use Microsoft Graph 97 to change the graph type that you are using, add vertical or horizontal gridlines behind the graph, or change the colors that are used in the graph.

Editing a chart using Graph 97 can be a somewhat frustrating experience. Again, if your chart is lacking, you may want to re-create it using the Chart Wizard.

Adding Custom Pages to Reports

As you already know, reports are great at summarizing the information in your tables and queries. You can take this concept one step further and set up reports that contain two parts—the main report, which may list the data in great detail, and a subreport that summarizes the information given in the main report. You can also use the idea of multiple-part reports to include images and charts on certain pages of the report.

When you expand Report Header and Report Footer areas to include charts, subreports, or linked or embedded objects, you are in effect creating custom pages. Custom pages can help you build a report that not only contains all the data necessary but also provides summary information in the form of subreports or charts. Summary information is especially useful when a reader wants to skip to the bottom line immediately.

Adding Subreports to a Report

The technique used to place a subreport in a main report is very similar to the technique that you used to create a main form containing a subform (see Lesson 13, "Designing Queries," for more information on subforms). An example of when to use a subreport is a report that breaks down the company's expenses by employee. It may also be useful to see the information broken down by department—which would require a second report (if you did not group information by including Group Headers or Group Footers in the report). Attaching the much more specific report on department expenses to the report on expenses for employees (which could be quite a number of pages) enables you to present the data in two very different ways in the same report.

You can place the subreport in any nonrepeating section of the main report, such as the Report Header and Report Footer. If you place the subreport in the Report Header, you can then place a page break in the report so that the subreport and the other Report Header information prints on the first page and the main report prints on subsequent pages. (See the section "Inserting Page Breaks in a Report" for information on placing a page break in the report.)

You may want to create as a subreport the report that you want to place on another report. If the subreport already exists, it's just a matter of placing a new control on the report currently in Design view to build the compound report.

To add the control for a subreport, click the **Subform/Subreport** button on the Toolbox. Drag out a rectangle to accommodate the controls and labels in the subreport. Placing the subreport control in the main report activates the Subreport Wizard (make sure the **Wizard** button on the Toolbox is on).

The Wizard gives you the option of using an existing report or building a new report for the subreport. If you already created a report for this purpose, select it and then click **Finish** to return to Report Design view. Alternatively, to build a new report using the Subreport Wizard, complete the steps in the report building process. The Wizard places your new report in the main report as a new control.

 Drag and Drop to Create Subreport   You can also create a subreport by opening the main report in Design view and dragging another report from the Database window **Report** tab onto the main report. Size the main report Design view window so that you can still see the Database window and then drag the appropriate report (which will serve as the subreport) onto one of the main report areas (such as the Report Header). A new subreport control is created for you. You can also use the drag-and-drop technique to create subforms on main forms.

You can view the subreport by double-clicking its control (click right in the middle). A second window opens, showing you the subreport in Design view. You can modify the design of the subreport at this point. To return to the main report, close the subreport window. Figure 16.8 shows a subreport control in the Report Header of a main report.

Figure 16.8

The subreport appears as a control in the main report.

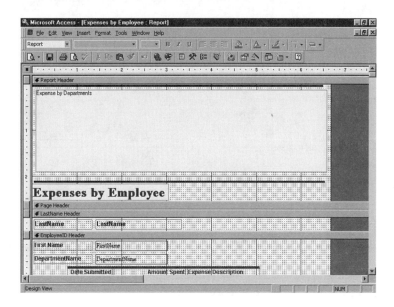

To view the completed compound report, switch to the Print Preview window. Make sure to save the changes that you have made to the report.

Inserting Page Breaks in a Report

When you add a subreport to the beginning of a main report, it pushes the main report down on the first page or may, if the subreport runs several pages, bury the beginning of the main report somewhere within the report's page run. You can use a page break to separate the end of the subreport from the beginning of the main report.

To add a page break to a report, make sure that you are in Design view. Click the **Page Break** tool in the Toolbox. Place the mouse pointer where you want to place the page break and click the left mouse button. A page break symbol appears on the left side of the section, showing you exactly where the page break will fall. For example, the page break in Figure 16.9 falls between a subreport and the main report.

After placing your page break, you can view the report in Print Preview mode to look at the changes. When you complete the design changes to your compound report, make sure to save the changes.

Figure 16.9

Placing a page break between a subreport and the main report.

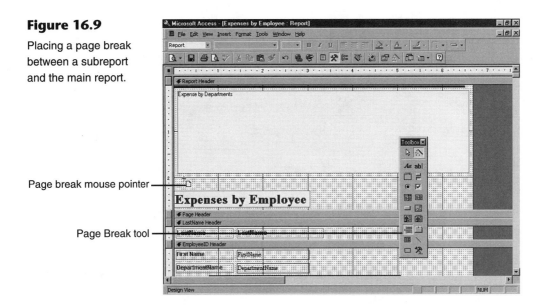

Page break mouse pointer

Page Break tool

Inserting an Image into a Report

You can add graphics to a report. For example, you may want to add your company logo to the top of a report in the Report Header.

The technique for adding an image to a report is the same as adding an image to a form (see Lesson 12 for more information). To add a graphic to a report, follow these steps:

1. In Design view, use the **Image** button on the Toolbox to create a new control for the image.

2. The Insert Picture dialog box appears. Specify the location and the graphic file you want to insert in the report. Click **OK** to continue.

3. The image appears in the report (see Figure 16.10).

4. To size the image to fit your control box, double-click the control; the Image Properties dialog box appears. On the **Format** tab of the Image Properties dialog box, change the Size Mode to **Zoom**.

Placing graphics and other images in your reports adds visual strength to them. In addition to placing pictures and logos in your reports, you can insert charts and other items created in other programs. (See Lesson 17 for more information on linking and embedding objects in Access.)

Figure 16.10

You can place graphics in your report in Design view.

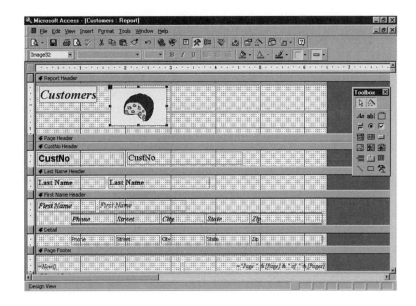

Getting the Most from Your Reports

As you can see from this lesson, reports are extremely important because all your work in Access will be judged by their appearance. Reports are really the only objects in your databases that others ever see. You can maximize their visual impact by using different report templates (click **Format**, **AutoFormat** to choose various looks for your report), adding graphics to your reports, or taking advantage of the various report Wizards in Access (the Wizard's help you design visually appealing reports).

You've already worked with the AutoReport, Chart Wizard, and Report Wizard. Access also provides one other tool to help you create good-looking reports: the Label Wizard. The Label Wizard walks you through the steps of creating mailing labels and enables you select a label type by Avery number. This straightforward Wizard is extremely useful when you have a large number of records in a table (such as a customer or employee table) and want to prepare a mass mailing.

 Creating Mailing Labels To create mailing labels from a table or query, select the Label Wizard in the New Report dialog box and then select the appropriate table or query in the drop-down box. When you click **OK**, the Wizard opens a screen from which you choose the Avery label that you plan to use for the labels. The Wizard's other screens enable you to choose the font type and size and to place the fields from the table or query on a sample label that serves as the template for the labels you will print.

Review Questions

The Certified Microsoft Office User Exams are task oriented. The following types of questions are not representative of the test. These questions are designed to help you understand the required tasks and methods of performing those tasks prior to taking the test.

1. Which Access tool do you use to create calculated controls in reports?

2. If you want to add a label or control that will only appear at the beginning or end of the report, which areas would you place them in?

3. If you want to add a control that will appear at the bottom of every page, which area of the report would you place it in?

4. If you want the information in the Report Header to appear on its own page, what would you do?

5. True or False: Access charts are limited to line graphs.

Review Question Answers

1. The Expression Builder provides all the formulas and expressions you need to build calculated controls in your reports. For more information, see the section "Making Calculations on a Report."

2. Controls and labels that you place in the Report Header or the Report Footer appear only at the top or bottom of the report, respectively. For more information, see the section "Adding a New Label to a Report."

3. Controls that you place in the Page Footer appear at the bottom of each page of the report. For more information, see the section "Inserting Date and Page Number Controls."

4. To create a custom page for the Report Header, place a page break at the bottom of the header information. For more information, see the section "Inserting Page Breaks in a Report."

5. False: Access provides a number of different chart types for you to graphically represent the data in your tables and queries. For more information, see the section "Creating a Chart."

Practice Lab

The Microsoft Access Expert User Exam lists various Required Tasks for the two Skill Areas covered in this lesson. The following practice lab covers many of these tasks.

 Required Tasks   Four Required Tasks for the "Produce Reports" Skill Area are modify a report, label a report, customize headers and footers, make a calculation on a report, and add custom pages. One Required Task for the "View Information" Skill Area is present information in a chart.

Copy the **lesson16.mdb** database from the CD that accompanies this book to a folder on your computer using Windows Explorer. Open the database.

Modify and Label a Report

Open the **Products by Category** report. Add a label to the upper-left side of the Report Header that reads "Products by Category." Make the label Arial, 14 point, bold, italic. Resize the label to accommodate the text. Save the changes you make to the report. View the report in Print Preview mode.

Customize Headers and Footers

Add a control to the Products by Category report that places the current date in the Page Footer area. Place the date control to the left of the Page Footer area and label the control **date**. Add a control to the right side of the Page Footer area that places the page number in the Page Footer. Label the control **Page Number**. Save the changes you make to the report. View the report in Print Preview mode.

Make a Calculation on a Report

Open the **Product Categories** report in Design view. Add a control to the Report Footer that provides a total (sum) for the UnitsInStock control in the report. Place a subtotal for UnitsInStock in the CategoryID Footer. Save the changes you make to the report. View the report in Print Preview mode.

Add Custom Pages

Open the **Employee Expenses** report. In the Report Header, add a label above the subreport control that reads "Expenses by Department". Place a page break below the subreport control to force the Report Header onto its own page. Save the changes to the report. View the report in Print Preview modes.

Present Information in a Chart

Create a pie chart for the Products table that uses the Product Name and UnitsInStock fields. Save the pie chart as **Products in Stock Chart**.

Open the database **lesson16a.mdb** on the CD to see completed versions of the reports you created in this the lab.

Integrating Data from Other Applications

This lesson covers "Integrate Information from Other Applications" skills for the Expert User level.

In this lesson, you learn the following Required Tasks for your exam:

▶ Import data

▶ Link data

▶ Add pictures to records

Understanding Object Linking and Embedding

Access offers several different ways for you to integrate information from other applications into your Access databases. You can import information, link or embed information, and even copy and paste information. Access also provides ways to export information to other applications such as Microsoft Excel and Microsoft Word.

A sharing strategy embraced by most Windows applications is OLE. OLE stands for object linking and embedding, and it is basically two different strategies for taking items created in one application and placing them into another application such as Microsoft Access. The application in which these items or *objects* are created is called the *source* application in the case of linking and the *server* application in the case of embedding. The application into which you place the object (whether linking or embedding) is called the *destination* application—in this case, Microsoft Access.

 The Word *Object* The word *object* is probably one of the most overused terms in the computer lexicon. *Object* can describe certain kinds of programming, database objects, and items linked or embedded into applications. You should always understand the particular context in which the word *object* is being used.

You can place linked or embedded objects in your database objects. For example, you can place an OLE field in a table and store linked or embedded photos of your employees in that particular field. Or you can place an embedded or linked graph in a report to help your clients understand a complex set of statistics.

Linking Objects

When you link an object to your database, you are creating a connection between the source application file and Access. The object does not reside in the Access database file, but is represented there by a linking code. When you need to update the file, you do so in the original source application, and the results of the update appear in the Access database. For example, you can link a Microsoft Excel chart to an Access report. When you double-click the chart in the report, the chart's source application—Microsoft Excel—starts and the linked file opens in it.

Linked objects reside outside the destination file. Therefore, they do not increase the size of the designation file such as an Access database file. The easiest way to link an object to another application item is to use copy and paste. In the following example, an Excel chart is an object linked to a report in an Access database.

To link an Excel chart to an Access report, follow these steps:

1. Open an Access database and open a report in Design view.

2. Open the application from which you want to link the object, in this case Microsoft Excel. Open the file that will serve as the linked object (see Figure 17.1).

Figure 17.1

Open the source application and file that you want to link to the Access database object.

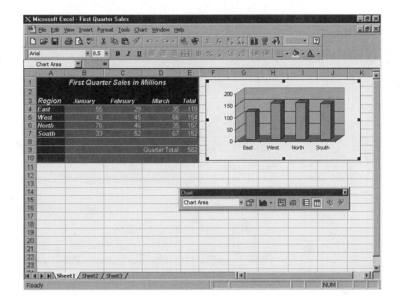

3. Select the worksheet cells or the chart you want to link to the Access object (in this case a report).

4. Click **Edit**, **Copy**.

5. Click the **Access** button on the Windows taskbar to return to Access and the Report Design window.

6. Activate the area of the report that you want to link the object into. For example, to place the linked object in the Report Header, click the Report Header area.

7. Click **Edit**, **Paste Special**. The Paste Special dialog box opens. The object that you copied to the Clipboard appears in the Paste Special As box (see Figure 17.2).

8. Click the **Paste Link** radio button in the Paste Special dialog box; then click **OK**. The chart or other object is now linked to the Access report.

The linked object appears in the report in Design view (see Figure 17.3) and in the Print Preview window when you switch views. You cannot activate the linked object from the Print Preview window, however, just as you cannot edit any of the controls in a report in Print Preview.

Figure 17.2

The Paste Special dialog box gives you the option of linking the copied item to the Access object.

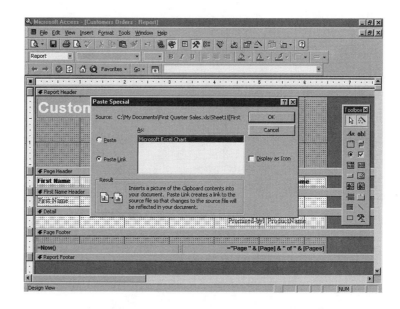

Figure 17.3

The linked object appears in the Access report. Double-click the object to start the source application.

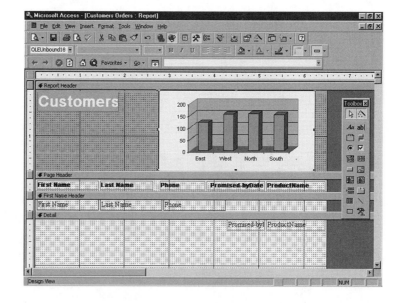

When you double-click the linked chart in the Report Design window, you return to Excel (if Excel is closed, the application opens automatically) and the linked item is loaded into the Excel window. Any changes you make to the object (such as changing the spreadsheet data that the chart is based on and thereby changing the chart itself) in the source application (Excel) appears in the destination application (Access) when you return to the report.

Embedding Objects

Embedded objects work differently than linked objects do. An embedded object becomes part of the destination file and so increases its size. It is basically a transplanted copy of the original file. Because the embedded file resides in the destination file, updating the original file in the original application does not update the embedded copy.

Embedded objects are dynamic, however. When you activate an embedded object, the server application opens in a window inside the destination application. In many cases, the menu system of the server application temporarily replaces that of the destination application. In essence, you are running the server application from inside the destination application.

Adding Pictures to Records

Embedding objects in an Access form or report is similar to linking an object to an Access item. You can also use embedding to add preexisting pictures to the records in your database. These picture files can be in several different formats and can be clip art or scanned images.

 Graphics File Formats Graphics come in various file formats. You can tell the particular format by the file's extension: Windows Bitmap (.BMP), AutoCAD Format 2-D (.DXF), Computer Graphics Metafile (.CGM), CorelDRAW (.CDR), Encapsulated PostScript (.EPS), HP Graphics Language (HPGL) file, Kodak Photo CD (.PCD) file, PC Paintbrush (.PCX) file, and Tagged Image File Format (.TIF) file to name a few.

To embed pictures in your table records, you must first create an OLE field for the embedded objects.

To create an OLE field in a table, follow these steps:

1. In Design view, open the table for which you want to create the OLE field.

2. Create a new field in the field grid, as shown in Figure 17.4. Type a name for the field and then select **OLE Object** as the data type.

3. Save the changes that you've made to the table's structure.

4. Return to Datasheet view.

Now that you have the OLE Object field set up in the table, you can insert OLE objects into the field in the various records. To embed graphics files into the fields, follow these steps:

1. Click the OLE Object field in the record that you want to place the object in. To insert the object, click the **Insert** menu and then click **Object**. The Insert Object dialog box appears as shown in Figure 17.5.

Figure 17.4

You can embed (or link) objects such as picture files in table fields with the OLE Object data type.

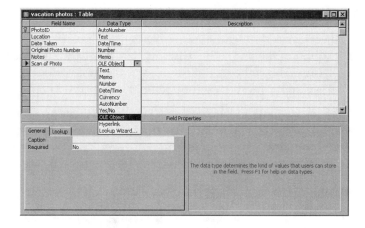

Figure 17.5

The Insert Object dialog box enables you to embed a newly created object or an existing object.

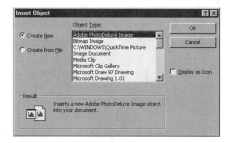

2. The Insert Object dialog box enables you to embed and link objects from a wide range of source applications. There will be an object type for nearly every piece of software you have installed on your computer.

3. To create an item from scratch, select the object type that you want to use and then click **OK**. The application that creates the particular object type opens, enabling you to create the new object.

4. To embed an existing file (such as a scanned photo, a Photo CD image, or other graphics file), click the Create from File radio button. The Insert Object dialog box asks you to supply the filename and location of the file you want to embed in the field.

5. If you know the location and name of the file, type it in the **File** box. Otherwise, click the **Browse** button and use the Browse dialog box to locate the file. When you locate the file, select it and then click **OK**.

6. The filename and location appears in the File box as shown in Figure 17.6.

Figure 17.6

When you embed an
existing object into an
Access table field, you
must specify the name
of the file and its
location.

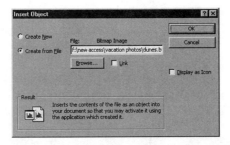

 Link Rather Than Embed   If you would rather link the graphics file to the OLE field
in the table, click the Link check box in the Insert Object dialog box.

Click the **OK** button to embed (or link) the object. You will not see the actual object in the
table field; a file type name appears, designating it. For example, a bitmap image says
Bitmap Image, or an Excel spreadsheet is tagged as Microsoft Excel Worksheet.

 Graphics File Associations May Differ   The value that appears in the table field
that you embed your object in may vary from computer to computer. The value depends on which application is associated with that particular file type on your computer. Bitmap files are associated with Windows Paint by default and use the Bitmap
Image value in the table field. If you have Microsoft Photo Editor installed, the image
value in the table field may read Photo Image (the Photo Editor becomes your *associated* image editor). The value in the field does not affect how the image is embedded
or linked.

To actually view the object, double-click the field to start the source or server application
(depending on which application on your computer is associated with the file type that
you embedded). You can even edit the objects after you enter the application. Any changes
that you make are saved with the embedded or linked object. Figure 17.7 shows two embedded bitmap images in a table. The first embedded object was double-clicked, which
opened the server application (in this case Windows Paint).

In the case of the embedded object, the changes are reflected in the stored object itself,
which now resides in the Access table. When you are working with a linked object, the
changes are stored in the original source file, which can be viewed in the destination application or the original server application.

Figure 17.7

Embedded images in
the OLE Object field
appear as file type text
entries in the table.
Double-click the image
to see the file in the
server application.

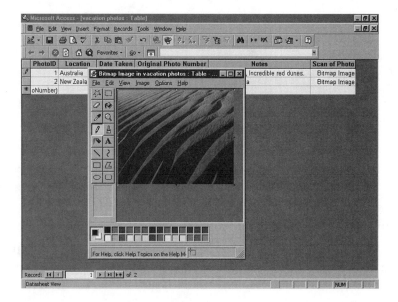

Viewing Images in Forms

A great way to view the objects that you embed or link into a table is to design a form for the table. In Form view, you will be able to actually see the embedded images.

Use AutoForm to create a new form based on the current table. The picture files found in the OLE Object field will be displayed in the form. If the form field does not accommodate the size of the picture file, switch to Form Design view and edit the size of the control for the OLE Object field. Figure 17.8 shows a form based on a table that has an OLE Object field. The actual image embedded in the table field appears in the form.

 Creating Forms with OLE Fields You can create your form by using the Form Wizard, by creating the form from scratch in Design view, or by clicking the **New Object** button on the toolbar and selecting **AutoForm**. If you select the OLE field as one of the fields for the form, the Form Wizard automatically provides the appropriate control. This statement also holds true for AutoForm, which uses all the fields in the table to create the form. If you want to build the control from scratch, you should use the **Object Frame** button in the toolbox.

Importing Data from Other Applications

Access makes it very easy for you to import a number of file types. You can import data from other database software packages such as Microsoft FoxPro, and you can also import spreadsheet files from programs such as Microsoft Excel.

Figure 17.8

Forms provide a way
to view OLE Object
field items without
starting the server
application.

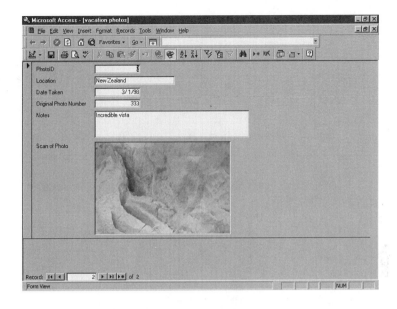

You can import the data into an existing database, or you can create a new database for the
imported information. If you import an Excel worksheet file that has been used to keep
records and contains repeated and redundant data, you can then use the Table Analyzer to
normalize the imported spreadsheet into several related Access tables.

To import an Excel worksheet into Access, follow these steps:

1. Open a new database or open an already existing database. Click the **File** menu,
   point at **Get External Data**, and click **Import**. The Import dialog box opens.

2. Select the file type that you want to import in the Files of Type box. Figure 17.9
   shows an Excel file that has been selected for importing. Notice that the Files of
   Type box has been changed to Microsoft Excel.

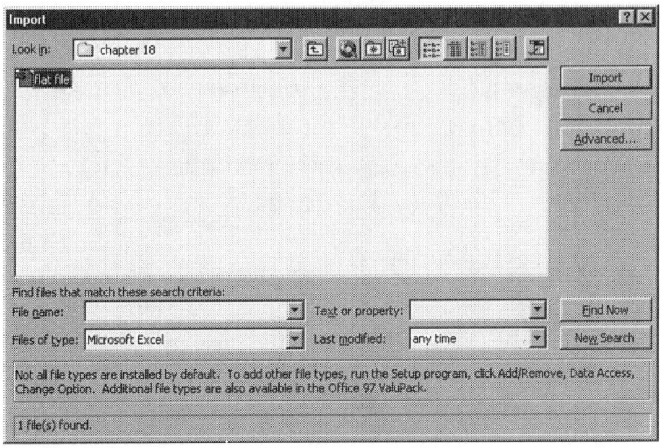

Figure 17.9

The Import dialog box
enables you to select
the file type and the
file you want to import
into Access.

3. Locate and select the file in the Import dialog box and click the **Import** button.

4. The Import Spreadsheet Wizard appears and walks you through the import process. The first step is to tell the Wizard which of the sheets in the Excel workbook that you are importing is the sheet you want to create a new table from. Select the sheet on the Wizard screen and then click the **Next** button.

5. The next Import Spreadsheet Wizard screen asks whether the first row in your spreadsheet contains column headings that can be used for field names when the data is placed in a table (see Figure 17.10). If column headings in the spreadsheet (the first row in the spreadsheet) can serve as the field names for the table fields, click the **First Row Contains Column Headings** check box. Click **Next** to continue.

Figure 17.10

The Import Spreadsheet Wizard can use the column headings in the spreadsheet (the first row of information in the spreadsheet) as the field names for the new table created during the import process.

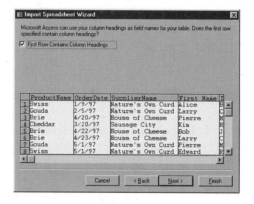

   Before Importing Spreadsheets, Define Column Headings   When you import a spreadsheet into Access, it is worth your while to set up the column headings in the spreadsheet to serve as the field names for the table that the import process will create.

---

6. The next Wizard screen asks whether you want to store the imported data in a new table or in an existing table. You will want to import most spreadsheets into a new table (you can always use an Append query later to move the data into an existing table). Select the **New Table** radio button and click **Next** to continue.

7. The next Wizard screen enables you to edit the field names (using the spreadsheet column heading names as the default) for the new table. You can also choose to index certain fields and not import some fields (see Figure 17.11). Make the appropriate changes and click **Next**.

8. The next Wizard screen asks whether you want the Wizard to create a primary key for the new table or whether you want to choose your own primary key.

If a field in the imported spreadsheet contains unique values for each record, you can designate that field as the primary key; otherwise, you will want Access to create a new primary key field for the table. Make your selection and click **Next**.

Figure 17.11

The Wizard enables you to edit the field names for the new table, index fields if necessary, and prevent some fields from being imported.

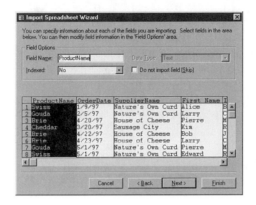

9. The last screen asks you to type a name for the new table. Type the name and click the **Finish** button.

The table appears on the Table tab of the current Database window. You can now edit the table structure, use Delete or Append queries to manipulate the records in the new table, or use the Table Analyzer to split the table into several related tables.

Exporting Data from Access to Other Applications

You can also export data from your Access objects to other applications, such as spreadsheets and word-processing documents. For example, the data you have in a table or in a query might be better off in an Excel spreadsheet so that you can use Excel's statistical features. Or you may want to create a form letter in Microsoft Word and mail it to your clients, using the client information in an Access table.

Access is tightly integrated with the other applications found in Microsoft Office 97. Exporting Access information to these software packages (such as Word or Excel) is extremely straightforward.

Copying and Pasting

You can copy or cut data from Access and paste it into other applications such as Microsoft Excel and Microsoft Word. To copy or cut data from Access, open the database object (most likely a table or query) that holds the information. Select the data that you want to copy or cut.

You can select a record by clicking the record selector, or you can select an entire field column by clicking the field selector. To select the entire table, click the **Select All** button in the upper-left corner. You can start another application via the **Start** button on the taskbar. When the application is running, choose the spreadsheet (in the case of Excel) or document into which you want to paste the information.

In Excel or Word, you can click the **Paste** button on the toolbar, or click the **Edit** menu and then click **Paste**, to place the Access data into a spreadsheet or a document. When you paste the data into Excel spreadsheets, the text formatting that you assigned to the information in Access is carried over into Excel. Access information pasted into Word appears in a table format.

Using OfficeLinks

Although copying and pasting can take care of some of your data transfer needs, Access provides a tool called OfficeLinks for sharing larger amounts of information with other applications.

The Database toolbar includes the OfficeLinks drop-down button; its drop-down list has three choices: Merge It (with Word), Publish It with Microsoft Word, or Analyze It with Microsoft Excel.

Merge It

When you select **Merge It** from the OfficeLinks drop-down list, the currently selected table or query in the Database window supplies the data for a Microsoft mail merge. The Microsoft Mail Merge Wizard helps you link the selected data (in a table or query) to a currently existing form letter or other Word document. You can also choose to create a document from scratch.

Publish It with Microsoft Word

This OfficeLinks choice places the data in the currently selected database object into a new Word document as a text file. For example, you can take report information and place it in Word. Having the data in Word in a text format gives you greater flexibility in presenting information from Access in a written report or other summary document.

Analyze It with Microsoft Excel

When you click **Analyze It with MS Excel**, Excel is opened and the currently selected table or query is placed into a spreadsheet. The spreadsheet that is created by this method has the same name as the table or query in your Access database.

Excel offers an incredible array of mathematical functions and charting possibilities. You can use Excel to analyze mathematical information in your tables and queries.

Access offers great flexibility for both importing and exporting data. The applications in Microsoft Office have been created with data integration in mind.

Review Questions

The Certified Microsoft Office User Exams are task oriented. The following types of questions are not representative of the test. These questions are designed to help you understand the Required Tasks and methods of performing those tasks prior to taking the test.

1. What is the major difference between embedded and linked objects?

2. What must you do to a table's structure if you want to embed pictures in a field?

3. When you import spreadsheet data into Access, what type of object does Access create to hold the information?

Review Question Answers

1. Embedded objects are saved as part of the Access database file. Linked objects reside outside of the database file in the link's source file. For more information, see the section "Understanding Object Linking and Embedding."

2. To embed pictures in an Access table field, you must create an OLE Object field. For more information, see the section "Adding Pictures to Records."

3. When you import spreadsheet data into Access, it must be placed in a table. You can use an existing table, or you can have Access create a new table to hold the imported information. For more information, see the section "Importing Data from Other Applications."

Practice Lab

The Microsoft Access Expert User Exam lists lists three Required Tasks for the "Integrate Information from Other Applications" Skill Area. The following practice lab covers these tasks.

 Required Tasks The three Required Tasks for the "Integrate Information from Other Applications" Skill Area are import data, link data, and add pictures to records.

Copy the **lesson17.mdb** database from the CD that accompanies this book to a folder on your computer using Windows Explorer. Also copy the two graphics files, **dunes.bmp** and **glacier.bmp,** and the **flat file.xls** and **first quarter sales.xls** worksheets to the folder.

Import Data

Open the **lesson17.mdb** database. Import the **flat file.xls** file into Access as a new table called **Customers**. Use the column headings in the spreadsheet as the field names for the new table. Also allow Access to create a primary key for the table.

Linking Data

Open the **Sales Report** in the **lesson17.mdb** database in Report Design view. Start Excel and open the first **quarter sales.xls** workbook. Link the chart in the workbook into the Report Header of the Access Sales Report (adjust the size of the Report Header if necessary). Return to Excel and edit the monthly totals for the West Region as follows: January: 63, February: 55, March: 76. Return to Access and view the updated chart. View the report in the Print Preview window.

Add Pictures to Records

Open the **Vacation Photos** table in the **lesson17.mdb** database. Add an OLE Control field to the table. Embed **dunes.bmp** and **glacier.bmp** into the first two records of the table in the OLE Control field.

Open the database **lesson17a.mdb** on the CD to see completed versions of the tables and reports you created in this the lab.

LESSON 18

Access and the Internet

This lesson covers two Utilize Web Capability skills for the Expert User level.

In this lesson, you learn the following Required Tasks for your exam:

- ▶ Create hyperlinks
- ▶ Build order forms for Internet use

Using Access Internet Integration Tools

Access 97 provides a number of tools to integrate your database and its objects with the Internet. You can add hyperlinks to your database objects that enable users to quickly open a particular Web page on the World Wide Web.

You can also create forms that receive data input from individuals accessing your World Wide Web site. You can even publish Access reports to the Web, making it easy for you to summarize data in the database and make it available on your Web page.

Creating Hyperlinks in Database Objects

Hyperlinks provide an easy way to jump to another document, image, or other linked file. Hyperlinks basically tie together two items: the item containing the link and the item that is reached via the link.

In the case of World Wide Web (WWW) hyperlinks, you are tying a field in a database table (or a control in a form) to a Web address on the World Wide Web. Clicking the hyperlink field opens the appropriate application (in the case of the Web, Microsoft Internet Explorer) and takes you to the location referenced in the hyperlink.

Creating a Hyperlink in a Table Field

You can create hyperlinks in a field in a datasheet or in a label, text box, combo box, command button, or image control on a form. To create a Web hyperlink in a table, follow these steps:

1. Open the database you want to work with. In Design view open the table for which you want to create the hyperlink field.

2. In the Field Grid box, enter a new field name for the field in the Field Name column.

3. Click the drop-down arrow in the Data Type column and select **Hyperlink,** as shown in Figure 18.1.

4. Save the changes that you've made to the table structure and switch to the table's Datasheet view.

In Datasheet view you specify the information that enables you to jump to the hyperlinked item when you click the hyperlink in the field. Hyperlinked items can reside on your local drive, network, or on the World Wide Web. Suppose that you have a table of curriculum suppliers and that you have placed a Hyperlink field in the table's structure that will enable you to jump to the supplier's Web pages. The actual address of a particular supplier's Web page is the value that you place in the Hyperlink field in the table.

Figure 18.1

To create a hyperlink in a table field, you must set the Data Type for the field to Hyperlink.

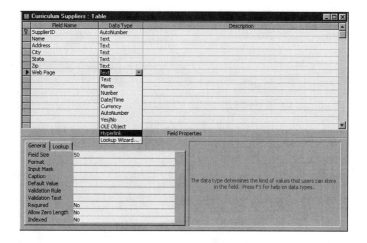

Placing a Hyperlink in a Table Field

Web sites are located by their URLs. *URL* stands for Uniform Resource Locator, and URLs serve as the addresses for all the sites residing on the Web. For example, the URL for Microsoft's Web site is `http://www.microsoft.com/`. The URL for Macmillan Publishing is `http://www.mcp.com`.

The Access Web toolbar contains a number of special Web-related tools, including tools to help you work with hyperlinks. Right-click any of the current toolbars to select **Web** from the shortcut menu.

To place a Web address in the Hyperlink field, follow these steps:

1. Click the Hyperlink field in Datasheet view. Click the **Insert Hyperlink** button on the Table toolbar to open the Insert Hyperlink dialog box.

2. Type the location of the hyperlink file in the Link to File or URL text box. For a Web page, type **http://** and then the address of the Web page (see Figure 18.2). Complete your entry and click **OK**.

 Type the URL Directly in the Field   You can also place URLs and other Hyperlink field destinations directly in the field itself. Click the Hyperlink field and type the appropriate Web address or other file location.

Figure 18.2

Designate the Web
address or the location
of the file that you
want to place in the
Hyperlink field.

Web toolbar

Insert Hyperlink button

Web Toolbar button

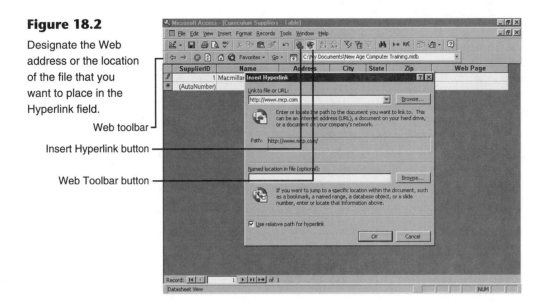

The hyperlink appears in the field in blue and is underlined (see Figure 18.3).

Figure 18.3

After closing the Insert
Hyperlink dialog box,
the hyperlink appears
in the field.

Hyperlink

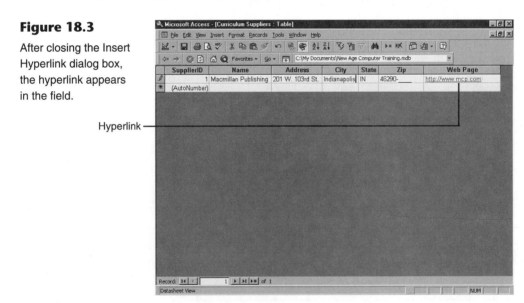

Copy URLs from the Web Toolbar   You can use the Access Web toolbar to copy URLs to the fields or controls in your Access databases. Click the **Web Toolbar** button on the Standard toolbar for the currently open object type (such as a table). Open a particular Web site, using the drop-down list on the Web toolbar in Microsoft Access. You can pull the site from your Favorites list. Internet Explorer opens and displays the Web page. Select the URL that appears in Explorer's Address box. Then press **Ctrl+C** to copy the address to the Windows Clipboard, return to the hyperlink field in your database table, and paste the URL into the field using the **Edit**, **Paste** commands.

A small hand appears when you place the mouse pointer on the Hyperlink field that contains the Web address. Click the hyperlink to jump to the designated location. In the case of Web hyperlinks, Microsoft Internet Explorer opens (or your current default browser if Internet Explorer is not your default browser); the Web page designated in the hyperlink address also opens (see Figure 18.4).

 If you are not on a network that maintains a constant connection to the Internet, make sure that you connect to your Internet service provider using your modem and dial-up connection before you attempt to jump to the Web page designated in the Hyperlink field.

After you use the hyperlink, its color changes to purple, letting you know that you have previously jumped to the address found in the field. After viewing the Web page using Internet Explorer, close the Internet Explorer window and return to Access.

Figure 18.4

Click the hyperlink to jump to the location designated in the field.

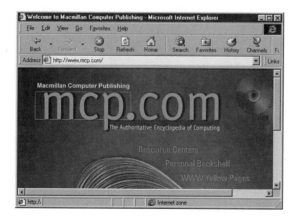

Wrong Colors? The color of the new hyperlink and the color of the used hyperlink depend on how Access is configured. To configure the color of items in Access, click **Tools**, **Options**, and the Options dialog box opens. The default color for hyperlinks is blue when unused and purple after you've used them to jump to the particular link.

Placing a Hyperlink in a Form or Report

You can also tie hyperlinks to the labels and images that you place on your forms and reports. When you create a form or report based on a table that includes hyperlinks, the hyperlinks automatically appear in the Hyperlink field control on the form or report as any other data would. For example, you may want to put your company's logo in the Form Header of a form and tie a hyperlink to it for your company's Web page. Then to access the particular Web page, all you have to do is click the company logo on the form.

To place a hyperlink in a form or report, follow these steps:

1. Open the form or report in Design view and create a new label or image to serve as the control to which you will attach the Hyperlink. (See Lessons 14, "Working with Advanced Queries," and 16, "Modifying Report Design," for more information on inserting labels and images in forms and reports.)

2. Insert the new label or image, and double-click the label or image box. The item's Properties box appears.

3. Click the **Format** tab on the image's or label's Properties box. In the Hyperlink Address box, type the URL for the Web site (see Figure 18.5). Close the Properties box and make sure you save the changes to the form or report.

Figure 18.5

Designate the URL address for the hyperlink in the Hyperlink Address box on the Format tab.

When you click the picture or label in Form or Report view, the hyperlink will activate and take you to the designated Web location.

Saving Access Objects in HTML Formats

Although it demands some understanding of Web publishing, Access enables you to create an Access object, such as a form, and save it in a format that allows you to receive data input (into your database) from a Web page on the World Wide Web.

For example, your company may have a Web page in which an Access form enables customers to order products that your company sells. The customers input their orders on the page, and the data is placed in the appropriate table in your Access database.

The programming language used to build the content that you find on Web pages is called Hypertext Markup Language (HTML). Each item on a Web page is tagged with a specific tag created using the HTML language. The purpose of HTML tags is to format information for viewing with a Web browser (such as Microsoft Internet Explorer). Using HTML to design a Web page is very similar to using a word processing package such as Microsoft Word to design a flyer or brochure. Items in a brochure, for instance, are tagged to be bold or to use a certain font size or to appear in a certain color. A brochure may also include linked graphics that are tagged to show their directory location on your computer.

You can create two different types of content for the World Wide Web from your Access database objects:

- ▶ Static HTML
- ▶ Dynamic HTML

Static HTML enables you to export an object in Access, such as a report, into the HTML format (saving Access objects as Static HTML is discussed later in this lesson). The report is then in a format that can be published to the Web. The report is an unchangeable, static object on the Web page, however, and provides no interaction (such as data input or data updates) for viewers.

Dynamic HTML provides the potential for sending updated database information to a Web page or receiving data input into your database from an object on a Web page, such as a form. Two Dynamic HTML file formats are available:

- ▶ HTML extension file (HTX)
- ▶ ActiveX Server Page (ASP)

HTX is a type of file that contains all the Web formatting information that an HTML file does, but does not contain the static data found in an HTML file. Rather, the HTX file works with an Internet Database Connector (IDC) file that helps display the information found in a table or query to a Web page.

Access can also save your database objects as ASP files. This file format takes advantage of *ActiveX controls*, which are very much like OLE objects in that they can be used to receive information from an application outside of Access. (See Lesson 17, "Integrating Data from Other Applications," for a discussion of OLE.) ActiveX controls were primarily created to enhance the connectivity of applications such as Access with the World Wide Web. An ActiveX object (such as an Access form) in a Web page can collect data via the Web and then deposit it in the appropriate Access file.

To build Dynamic HTML links to your databases using HTX and ASP files, you must have access to an Internet server that is using Microsoft Internet Information Server software. Internet Information Server is considered a key component of Microsoft BackOffice and is used on networks that are using Microsoft NT Server as the network operating system.

Microsoft Office 97 comes with a wizard—the Web Publishing Wizard—that enables you to easily create a new Web page that incorporates the HTX and ASP objects you build in Access so that they can placed in a designated folder on the Microsoft Internet Information Server.

Building Internet Order Forms

Building an Internet order form using an existing form in an Access database requires you to complete two fairly complex tasks. First you must create an Open Database Connectivity (ODBC) data source involving the database that will receive the data input on your World Wide Web form. Second, you must save a preexisting form in the database as an ASP object, and it will serve as the order form on a World Wide Web page.

Creating the ODBC Data Source

The ODBC data source supplies the Web form that you create with a link to the database that accepts the data input into the form. For example, if you build a Web order form for your bicycle supply business, the Web order form needs a way to link itself to the tables in your database that accept data for customer information, product information, and order information. The ODBC data source provides this link.

To create an ODBC data source for your database, follow these steps:

1. Click the **Start** button on the Windows taskbar. Point at **Settings** and then click **Control Panel**. The Control Panel dialog box opens.

2. Double-click the **32bit ODBC** icon in the Control Panel. The ODBC Data Source Administrator opens (see Figure 18.6).

3. Click the **Add** button. The Create New Data Source dialog box opens. When you are asked to select the driver for your new data source to use, select the **Microsoft Access Driver** from the list. Click **Finish**. The ODBC Microsoft Access 97 Setup dialog box opens.

Figure 18.6

The ODBC Data
Source Administrator
enables you to add a
new ODBC data
source for your
database.

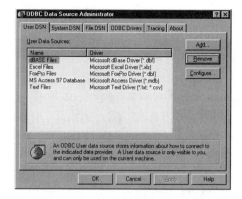

4. Type a name for the data source in the Data Source Name box and specify the
    database file that serves as the source (see Figure 18.7).

5. Click the **Select** button to select a database to serve as the source. The Select
    Database dialog box opens. This dialog box functions the same as any Open
    dialog box you have used to open a database using Access. Move to the appropri-
    ate folder on your computer and select a database file.

6. Click **OK** to return to the ODBC Microsoft Access 97 Setup dialog box.

Figure 18.7

The ODBC Microsoft
Access 97 Setup
dialog box is where
you name your data
source and specify the
Access database that
will serve as the
source.

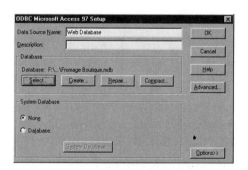

7. Click **OK** to return to the ODBC Data Source Administrator. Your new data
    source appears on the list. Click **OK** to close the Administrator.

After you create the new ODBC data source, you are ready to convert your Access form to
an ASP file that accepts data input from a Web page and places the data in your ODBC
Data Source database.

Saving an Access Form as an ASP File

To create the Web form, start Access and open the database that you designated as the ODBC data source. Click the **Form** tab in the Database window. Now you're ready to create the Web form.

Follow these steps to save the selected form in the ASP format:

1. Click the **File** menu and then click **Save As/Export**. The Save As dialog box opens. Select the **To an External File or Database** radio button and then click **OK**. The Save Form As dialog box opens.

2. Click the drop-down arrow in the Save as Type box at the bottom of the dialog box and select **Microsoft Active Server Pages**. In the Save In box, designate the folder that you place your Web documents (the folder may be on the Internet Information Server). Figure 18.8 shows an Access form being saved to a Web directory as an ASP file. Click **Export**. The Microsoft Active Server Output Options dialog box opens.

Figure 18.8

Save the form as an ASP file to the folder on your Internet Information Server.

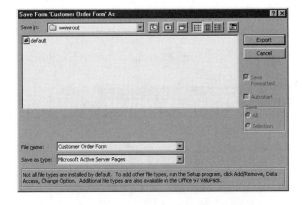

3. In the Microsoft Active Server Pages Output Options dialog box, you must specify the data source that the new Web form is linked to. In the Data Source Name box, type in the name of the data source that you created in the "Creating the ODBC Data Source" section. Type the URL for your Internet Information Server in the Server URL box (see Figure 18.9). Click **OK**.

After you save the form as an ASP file, you can attach it to your Web page (using HTML tags) or access the file directly using a Web browser such as Microsoft Internet Explorer.

To inspect the form, open Internet Explorer and type the location of the ASP file in the Address box, as shown in Figure 18.10. Press the **Enter** key, and the form loads into the Internet Explorer window. Click any field in the form, and you will find that it accepts data entry. This data is entered into the appropriate tables in the database.

Figure 18.9

The Microsoft Active
Server Pages Output
Options dialog box is
where you specify the
data source for the
form and the URL of
your Web page.

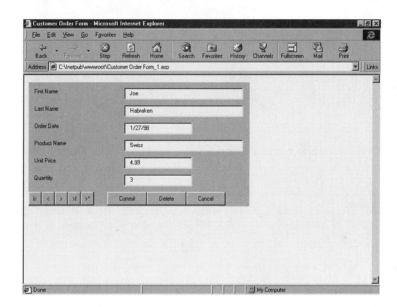

Figure 18.10

You can use Microsoft
Internet Explorer to
view and test the Web
order form.

As you can see, after you create the appropriate data source, creating the Web form is just a matter of exporting a currently existing form in the Data Source database. Web forms are an excellent way to add potential clients to a client list or to take orders directly from customers using your World Wide Web page.

Exporting Reports as Static HTML

You can also export reports, tables, and queries as Static HTML files. This approach basically takes a snapshot of the current data in the report or table and places it in a format that can be used for Web pages.

Click **File**, **Save as HTML**. The Publish to the Web Wizard opens. The first screen explains that the Wizard helps you create Web publications from Access objects. Click **Next**.

The next screen provides a tabbed dialog box that looks like the Database window. Select the object tab (such as Reports), and all the objects of that particular type in the database will be listed. Select the check box for an object that you want to save in the HTML format (see Figure 18.11).

Figure 18.11

You can use the Publish to the Web Wizard to save reports, tables, or queries as Static HTML files.

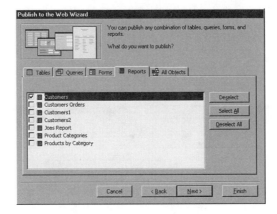

When you click **Next,** the Wizard gives you the option of choosing an HTML template as a format for the new HTML file and provides several format choices. Select a format and click **Next**.

The next Wizard screen is where you select the file type for the new HTML object. The default choice for file type is Static HTML, so you can proceed to the next screen by clicking **Next**.

The final screen asks you to select a folder in which to save the HTML file. You can select any folder on your computer or send the HTML file directly to the folder that contains your Web page documents. Designate a folder and click **Finish**.

The new HTML file resides in the folder that you selected. You can use Internet Explorer to open the file. Start Internet Explorer and type the file location and name in the **Location** box. Press the **Enter** key, and the file appears in the Internet Explorer window. Static HTML files provide no data entry or editing capabilities. These files are very much like a graphic placed on a Web page and differ greatly from the Dynamic Web form that you created using the ASP file.

Although creating Dynamic and Static HTML files from Access objects may seem fairly straightforward, you still need to understand some of the basics of Web page design and the Hypertext Markup Language to do anything constructive with these new object types. You may want to become familiar with one of the Web page creation tools, such as Microsoft FrontPage, which will help you integrate the Web-ready files that you create in Microsoft Access into your corporate or personal Web pages.

Review Questions

The Certified Microsoft Office User Exams are task oriented. The following types of questions are not representative of the test. These questions are designed to help you understand the Required Tasks and methods of performing those tasks prior to taking the test.

1. What is the purpose of hyperlinks in an Access database table?

2. What is the major difference between Static HTML files and Dynamic HTML files created in Access?

3. What part does an ODBC data source play in creating a order form for a Web page?

Review Question Answers

1. Hyperlinks enable you to jump to another file or a location on the World Wide Web. Hyperlinks can be placed in Hyperlink fields in Access tables or can be linked to controls in forms or reports. For more information, see the section "Creating Hyperlinks in Database Objects."

2. Static HTML enables you to take a snapshot of an Access object, such as a table or report, and publish it to your Web site as a static item. Dynamic HTML enables you to save forms in the ASP or HTX format, which creates Web objects that provide interaction between your database and output to or input from your Web page. For more information, see the section "Saving Access Objects in HTML Formats."

3. The ODBC data source links the Web order form to the database that receives the data input from the form. For more information, see the section "Creating the ODBC Data Source."

Practice Lab

The Microsoft Access Expert User Exam lists create hyperlinks and build order forms for Internet use as Required Tasks for the "Utilize Web Capability" Skill Area. The following practice lab covers these tasks.

 Required Tasks The two Required Tasks for the "Utilize Web Capability" Skill Area are to create hyperlinks and build order forms for Internet use.

Copy the **lesson18.mdb** database from the CD that accompanies this book to a folder on your computer using Windows Explorer. Open the database.

Create Hyperlinks

1. Open the Resources table. Create a Hyperlink field for the table. Create hyperlinks for the first two records in the table (Macmillan Publishing and Microsoft Corporation) using these Web addresses: `http://www.microsoft.com/` for Microsoft and `http://www.mcp.com` for Macmillan Publishing.

Build Order Forms for Internet Use

2. Create a new ODBC data source for the **lesson18.mdb** database. Create a form for the Orders query (use all the fields in the query). Save the new form as **Orders**. Use the **Save as HTML** command on the Access **File** menu to start the Publish to the Web Wizard. Save the Orders form in the ASP file format. If you have access to a corporate Internet Information Server, ask your administrator for permission to save the Web form to the Internet server. This step enables you to use a Web browser such as Internet Explorer to view the form. If you do not have access to an Internet server, create the ODBC source and ASP file so that you understand the steps required to create a new Dynamic Web object.

3. Use the Publish to the Web Wizard to save the Orders form in Static HTML format. Use a Web browser to view the HTML object.

Fine-Tuning Your Databases

This lesson does not cover any of the Required Tasks for the Access Certification test. It does provide, however, information that will help you improve, document, and maintain the databases you create using the Required Tasks discussed in this book.

Using the Performance Analyzer

You've already learned that a database is made up of a number of Access objects:

- ▶ Tables hold the data.

- ▶ Forms enable you to view and enter data.

- ▶ Queries enable you to sort and select records based on criteria.

- ▶ Reports enable you to get the database information into a format that is suitable for printing.

Your database is truly only as good as the objects that it contains.

One way to fine-tune the objects in your database is to use the Database Performance Analyzer. You can use this Access tool to optimize the performance of any database object in a particular database: tables, forms, queries, and reports. (You can also use the Performance Analyzer to fine-tune Access macros and modules.) In addition, you can use the Table Analyzer to analyze tables in more detail; the Table Analyzer is discussed in the section "Using the Table Analyzer" later in this lesson.

The main benefit of the Performance Analyzer is increased speed. After you optimize a query or a report, it will do its job faster. The Analyzer also points out potential relationships between tables that you have not taken advantage of for your queries, forms, and reports.

To use the Performance Analyzer to analyze an object, follow these steps:

1. Open the database that you want to optimize.

2. Click the **Tools** menu, point to **Analyze**, and then click **Performance**. The Performance Analyzer window opens (see Figure 19.1).

3. The Performance Analyzer window has a tab for each object type (much like the Database window in which you open your objects). Select a tab and then click the check box next to a particular object to analyze it. You can select several or all the objects on a tab; to select all the objects, click the **Select All** button.

Figure 19.1

The Performance Analyzer can help you fine-tune the objects in your database.

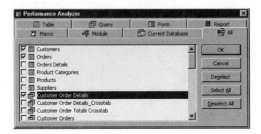

View All the Objects in the Database   You can view all of the objects in the database in one list by selecting the **All** tab in the Performance Analyzer window.

4. After you choose the objects you want to optimize, click the **OK** button to continue.

The Performance Analyzer scrutinizes the selected object or objects, and if you watch the screen closely, you can see that it inspects the objects associated with the one it is currently analyzing. For example, when you analyze a report, the Analyzer also looks at the source of the data for the report (the tables and/or queries).

When the analysis is complete, the Performance Analyzer dialog box displays the Analyzer's recommendations (see Figure 19.2). It gives you a list of possible fixes for improving the performance of the particular database object.

The optimization tips come in three categories: Recommendations, Suggestions, and Ideas. Each type of tip is represented by an icon: Recommendations by an exclamation point, Suggestions by a question mark, and Ideas by a light bulb.

To view the details on a particular optimization, click it. The information appears in the Analysis Notes box of the Performance Analyzer dialog box.

Figure 19.2

The Performance Analyzer makes recommendations that will help you optimize an object or objects listed.

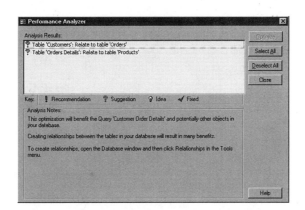

 Check Mark Means the Object Has Been Optimized   A fourth icon appears in the Key of the Optimization dialog box. A check mark represents an analysis result that has been fixed. For more information, see the section "Optimizing the Object" later in this lesson.

Understanding the Optimization Tip Types

Each type of optimization tip has its own idiosyncrasies as to how much direct assistance it provides. Recommendations are the easiest to implement and usually result in a performance gain if you implement them on the object. Suggestions are usually associated with some kind of potential trade-off, and you should look closely at the Analysis Notes before implementing them.

Suppose you are trying to optimize a particular report. A typical Recommendation or Suggestion provided by the Analyzer may suggest changing the way that the data is compiled for the report. Usually, you would require the report to pull data from several related tables. A Recommendation or Suggestion to optimize the report could be to construct a query that pulls the data together in one place. Then when you build the report from the query, the report runs optimally.

Compared to Recommendations or Suggestions, Ideas are more general. For example, the Analyzer may provide an Idea that says you should relate an analyzed table to other tables in the database. That is, you should identify the potential relationships that can exist between the current table and the other tables in the database. In contrast, a Suggestion for another table that has been analyzed might actually name a table in the database that should be related to the analyzed one.

Optimizing the Object

After you view the details of each optimization possibility, you will want to use some and reject others. The Performance Analyzer can perform the Recommendations and Suggestions. Select the Recommendation or Suggestion, and then click the **Optimize** button in the Performance Analyzer dialog box.

The Analyzer creates the recommended or suggested object or carries out any other steps that were detailed in the Recommendation or Suggestion. After carrying out a Recommendation or Suggestion, the Analyzer places a check mark next to the tip, letting you know that the optimization has been carried out.

You must implement Ideas yourself. Click a particular Idea to read the suggestions it offers in the Analysis Notes box. When you have finished reading the Idea and are ready carry out its suggestions, close the Performance Analyzer dialog box by clicking the **Close** button.

Optimizations performed by the Analyzer may not make an obvious performance change, but they do help speed certain operations and are more apparent in very large databases.

Using the Table Analyzer

Creating tables that do not contain redundant data (except when planned redundancy is used to relate two tables) is one of the keys to creating a relational database in Access. The concept of table normalization is discussed in Lesson 9, "Building a Relational Database." Access actually provides a tool that can help you normalize a database table or imported spreadsheet file—the Table Analyzer. Using the Table Analyzer is quite straightforward because a wizard controls the process.

 Spreadsheet Normalization The Table Analyzer is an excellent tool for normalizing imported spreadsheets from programs such as Microsoft Excel. See Lesson 17, "Integrating Data from Other Applications," for more information on importing data into Access.

To use the Table Analyzer Wizard, follow these steps:

1. Click the **Tools** menu, point to **Analyze**, and then click **Table**.

2. This first screen of the Table Analyzer Wizard explains why duplicate information in tables can cause problems. Examples are available (click the appropriate button) that discuss how duplicate information wastes table space and can lead to data entry mistakes. After viewing the examples on this screen, click **Next** to continue.

3. The next Wizard screen explains what the normalization process is and how it will potentially solve the problems in your table. Again, examples are offered to help you understand the process. When you are satisfied that your table needs to be normalized, click the **Next** button.

4. On the next screen, the Wizard asks you to select a table (the table you want to analyze) that contains fields where values have been repeated. Click the appropriate table in the Tables box. Click the **Next** button to continue.

 New Tables Created During Analysis New tables are created during the normalization process, but the original table still exists after you analyze it. You can delete the original table if you no longer need it after normalization.

5. The next screen asks whether you want the Wizard to determine which fields in the selected table should be placed in new tables, or whether you want to place the fields yourself. Even if you select the radio button for the Wizard, you will be able to adjust the new field locations (see Figure 19.3). Select the Wizard radio button and click **Next**.

Figure 19.3

The Table Analyzer Wizard gives you the option of selecting fields for placement in new tables or allowing the Wizard to normalize the table.

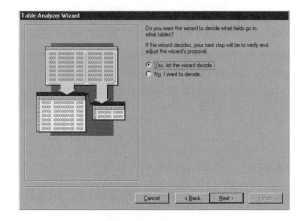

Placing the Fields in New Tables

The Table Analyzer Wizard creates new tables and attempts to place the appropriate fields in these new tables as shown in Figure 19.3. The Wizard also creates special Lookup fields in the original table so that the new tables will have a relationship with it.

In many cases, the Table Analyzer Wizard does not create the number of new tables warranted by the fields in the original table. For example, if you are normalizing a spreadsheet that contains customer orders where customer, product, and supplier information is documented, you may want to create a table during the normalization process for the Supplier table as well. In Figure 19.4, the Table Analyzer Wizard has created only one new table from a table like the one described in the example.

The Table Analyzer Wizard enables you to rename any of the tables created. Select a table and click the **Rename** button. Type a new name for the table in the Table Analyzer Name box and then click **OK**.

You can also rearrange the grouping of the fields in the new tables and create additional tables. Drag a new field into the group box to create a new table. The Wizard creates a relationship between the table you create and the table from which you dragged the field. The Name dialog box opens for the original table. Rename the table if you want and then click **OK**. After you move a field or create a new table, the **Undo** button is available; you can use it to Undo your most recent action.

Figure 19.4

The Table Analyzer Wizard moves fields where values were repeated from the original table into a new related table.

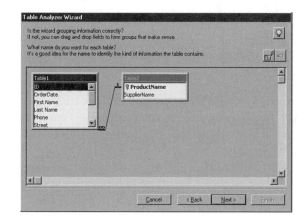

When you create new tables by dragging a field into the group box, a primary key field is created for the new table. A later screen in the Table Analyzer Wizard enables you to adjust the fields that are currently assigned as the primary key for the tables.

Figure 19.5 shows a group of new tables created from a table (imported from an Excel spreadsheet) that originally grouped fields for customer data, product data, order data, and supplier data in one table.

Figure 19.5

Tables created by normalization of an imported spreadsheet.

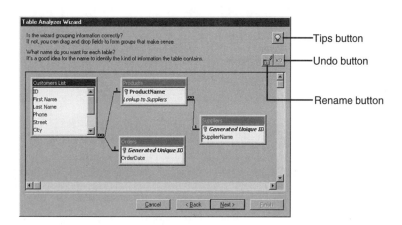

Tips button
Undo button
Rename button

You can also drag the relationship Lookups (the fields marked Lookup, which join tables) that the Wizard has created to new locations so that the new tables have the appropriate kinds of relationships with the other tables.

After you create the tables that you need and arrange the fields the way you want them, click the **Next** button.

Completing the Process

The next screen in the table analysis process enables you to check the primary keys that have been specified for the tables created during the normalization process. You are asked whether the bold fields currently found in the tables are satisfactory as primary keys for the tables.

You can leave the currently bolded field as the primary key for a table, or you can specify a new field in a table as the primary key by selecting it and then clicking on the **Set Unique Key** button. If a table does not contain a field that would be appropriate for the primary key, you can create a new field in the table by clicking the **Add Generated Unique Key** button. This Table Analyzer Wizard screen also equips you with an Undo button and a Tips button (see Figure 19.6).

In the example, the Customer List table has an ID field, but it has not been designated the key field. To make it the key, click the field and then click **Set Unique Key**. When you are sure that each table has a primary key, click the **Next** button.

Figure 19.6

Tables created by normalization of an imported spreadsheet.

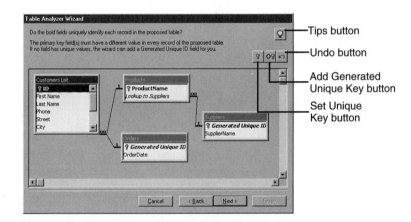

Tips button

Undo button

Add Generated Unique Key button

Set Unique Key button

The next screen or screens ask you to correct any typographical errors in the tables. For example, you may have field data that has been repeated, such as a supplier's name, but the name of the supplier has not been entered consistently (it is misspelled or not entered exactly as it has been in other cases). You will be asked to correct the value so that it matches the way in which the particular information was entered in other records. After providing the appropriate values for the inconsistent entries, click the **Next** button.

The final Table Analyzer screen asks whether you want to create a query that will return a result that duplicates the field groupings found in the original table you normalized using the Table Analyzer. It is a good idea to create the query. You can always delete it from the Query tab later if you find no particular use for it. Click the **Finish** button to end the normalization process. If you chose to create the query, Access builds and displays it onscreen.

The new query takes the name of your original table, and the original table's name changes to include _old_ to identify it. You can now delete the original table. The new tables created from the normalization process can now be filled with appropriate fields and data and then used to create forms, queries, or reports.

Documenting Database Objects

Access provides another tool that doesn't particularly enhance or improve your database objects, but does provide a detailed report regarding an object. You can use the Object Documenter to print a report that provides information on an object such as the date it was created, the date it was last modified, details on its makeup (the fields in the table or the controls in a form or a report), and even information on who has permission to delete, read, or change the object.

To start the Object Documenter, click the **Tools** menu, point to **Analyze**, and then click **Documenter**. The Object Documenter is very much like the Performance Analyzer in that the opening dialog box enables you to specify the object type and the particular object you want to document. Click the appropriate tab to select the object category. Then click the check box for the specific object or objects that you want to document.

After you make your selections, click the **OK** button. The Object Documenter examines the object (or objects) and builds a report detailing its attributes.

The documentation report appears in the Print Preview window so that you can look at it and decide whether you want to print it. When you are ready to print the report, click the **Print** button.

Figure 19.7

A documentation report for a table gives you information ranging from the attributes of each field in the table to the relationships that the table has with other tables in the database.

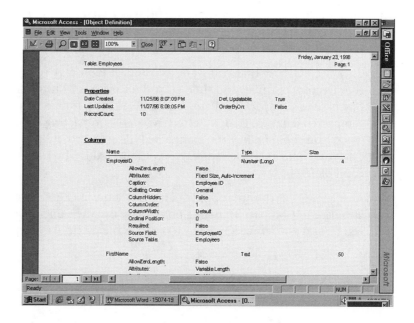

Object documentation reports provide the anatomy of your database. You may even be able to glean ideas for improving a particular object from the report or to use the information to create objects in other databases that serve a similar purpose. Be advised, however, that documenting an entire database generates a large number of hard copy documents. You may want to refrain from printing all the Object Documenter reports.

Compressing a Database

As you work with your database and delete records and tables over time, the database becomes fragmented and no longer uses your disk space efficiently. This situation can cause your database to run more slowly.

Compacting a database makes a copy of the database and rearranges how the database file is stored on your hard drive or disk. This process defragments the database file and frees up disk space.

To compact a database, complete the following steps:

1. Close the current Database window. Your menu selections dwindle to **File**, **Tools**, and **Help**.

 Make Sure the Database Is Not in Use If you work in a multiuser environment (a network in which a number of people can use the database file) make sure that no one is currently using the database you want to compact.

2. Click the **Tools** menu, point to **Database Utilities**, and then click **Compact Database**. Specify the database file that you want to compact in the Database to Compact From dialog box.

3. Click the database that you want to compact (you may have to switch to a different directory or drive) and then click the **Compact** button. Access opens the Database to Compact To dialog box and asks you for a database name to save the compacted database under. Because you are compacting the database to save disk space, you should allow the compacted file to overwrite the fragmented file. Click the same database name that you selected in the Database to Compact From dialog box.

4. After you select the appropriate database name, click the **Save** button in the Database to Compact To dialog box. If you use the same database filename, you will be asked whether you want to replace the original file; click **Yes**.

Access compacts the database and saves it under the current name. Compared to the original fragmented database, the compacted version takes up less disk space and potentially runs faster.

Repairing a Database

Database files can become damaged for many reasons—for example, a problem related to a particular storage device, such as your hard drive, or some sort of network problem when you access the database via the network. Even a sudden loss of power, which prevents you from exiting Access appropriately, can damage a database file. Fortunately, in most cases Access can detect whether a database is damaged when you try to open it or try to compact it. And at that time, Access will ask whether you want to try to repair the problem.

Before you try to repair a database, you should make a backup copy of it. The repair process can fail, making the database unusable.

You can use Windows Explorer to copy the database file: Close the database file and then start Windows Explorer. Select the database file in the Windows Explorer window and then click **Edit**, **Copy**. Use Paste to place the file in the folder from which you want to open the copy.

To begin the repair process, complete the following steps:

1. Make sure the database is closed. Again your menu choices become limited as they did when you compacted the database.

2. Click the **Tools** menu, point to **Database Utilities**, and then click **Repair Database**. The Repair Database dialog box opens.

3. Select the database that you want to repair and then click the **Repair** button. Access attempts to repair the database.

Upon completion, Access displays a report on the status of the repair. Most repairs are successful.

Review Questions

The Certified Microsoft Office User Exams are task oriented. The following types of questions are not representative of the test. These questions are designed to help you understand the Required Tasks and methods of performing those tasks prior to taking the test.

1. Does Access give you a way to improve the performance of your database objects?

2. Which Access feature can help you normalize a database table?

3. What should you do to your database file before you try to repair it?

Review Question Answers

1. Yes, you can use the Performance Analyzer to fine-tune any database object you create. For more information, see the section "Using the Performance Analyzer."

2. You can use the Table Analyzer to normalize a database table. For more information, see the section "Using the Table Analyzer."

3. You should create a backup copy of the database before you attempt to repair it. For more information, see the section "Repairing a Database."

Practice Lab

The following practice lab relates to skills not included in the Microsoft Access certification exam. This lab does, however, give you practice with the skills covered in this lesson.

1. Use the Performance Analyzer to analyze objects in a database that you have created or any of the databases included on the companion CD-ROM. Fine-tune the objects that you analyze, using the information provided by the Performance Analyzer.

2. Copy the **lesson19.mdb** from the CD-ROM to a folder on your computer. Open the database. Use the Table Analyzer to normalize the Customers table in this database.

3. Compact either a database that you have created or any other database that you have copied from the CD-ROM.

Access Security

This lesson does not cover any Required Tasks for the Access Certification test. It does provide, however, information that will help you deal with security issues related to your Access databases.

Securing Your Databases

Access provides two different approaches for protecting the information in your databases. The most straightforward method is to password-protect the database. When you open a password-protected database, you are prompted to provide the password.

Another approach that can be very useful if you share the database on a network with other users is to define different user levels. This technique gives other users of the database different levels of access to the database's objects and is similar to the methods that are used to grant the various permissions on a computer network.

Assigning a Password to a Database

To add a password to a database, the database must be closed (if you are on a network, all other users must close the database as well). You actually begin the process of adding a password to a database by claiming exclusive rights to the database in the Open dialog box.

 Be Careful with Passwords Passwords are meant to be kept secret. When you choose a password, do not choose a word that is easy to guess, such as your first name. Also, you must remember your password; writing down passwords can, again, only lead to others learning your password.

To password-protect the database, follow these steps:

1. Click the **File** menu and then click **Open** (or use the **Open** button on the Database toolbar). When the Open dialog box appears, select the database file you want to add the password to.

2. In the Open dialog box, click the **Exclusive** check box as shown in Figure 20.1. This option means that you want exclusive rights to the database file.

3. Now that you've opened the database using the exclusive rights parameter, you can set up the password for the file. Click the **Tools** menu, point at **Security**, and then click **Set Database Password**. The Set Database Password dialog box opens. Its purpose is to allow you to type in a password and then verify it by typing it in a second time.

4. Type your password in the Password box. The password appears as a series of asterisks, as shown in Figure 20.2.

5. Press the **Tab** key and retype the password to verify it.

Figure 20.1

In the Open dialog box, click the Exclusive check box to assign exclusive rights to the database.

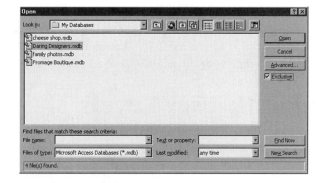

Figure 20.2

The Set Database Password dialog box is where you choose and verify a password for your database.

 Case-Sensitive Passwords Passwords are case sensitive; using all lowercase characters can help you remember the password.

6. Click **OK** to close the Set Database Password dialog box.

The password will not be required again until you open the database. When you open a password-protected database, the Password Required dialog box appears. Type in your password and then click **OK** to open the database file.

If you type an incorrect password or if someone tries to get into the database without knowing the correct password, Access states the obvious—Not a valid password.

Your only recourse is to click **OK** and try the password again. You must type it in correctly (it's case sensitive, remember) to open the database.

 Removing the Password You can *unset* or remove a password for a database file. First, you must open the database and deselect the **Exclusive** check box in the Open dialog box. Then click the **Tools** menu, point to **Security**, and click **Unset Database Password**. Enter the correct password in the next dialog box and then click **OK**. The database no longer requires a password when you open it.

When you password-protect a database, you own the exclusive rights to it. The only way another user can open the database is for you to give him or her the password. Then you no longer have exclusive rights to the database. Access also offers a security strategy that enables you to set security levels for those who have access to the database.

Working with User Levels

If the exclusivity of password protecting a database will not work in your database environment, you can set different levels of security for each user of the database. Setting security levels, however, is really necessary only if you are sharing a database with others on a network.

In many multiuser environments, the network administrator grants network security rights as well as database level rights. However, in some circumstances, you may have to serve as the administrator for a particular database, so you should know how to assign the various security levels.

Assigning Users to Security Groups

Groups will define security levels for your database; each group can have a different level of access to the objects in the database. The default groups already defined in Access are User and Admins. To begin the process of securing a database, the users have to be assigned to a group. The Admins group has *complete* access to the database. The User group has *limited* access to the database.

For example, you may assign only yourself and one other person to the Admins group, which has full access to the database and its objects—an administrator's level of use. People assigned to the User group have limited access to the database and its objects (viewing, printing, and so on).

To assign users to a group, follow these steps:

1. Open the database for which you want to set the security levels.

2. Click the **Tools** menu, point to **Security**, and then click **User and Group Accounts.** The User and Group Accounts dialog box opens (see Figure 20.3).

The User and Group Accounts dialog box has three tabs: Users, Groups, and Change Logon Password.

Figure 20.3

The User and Group Accounts dialog box is where you assign users to groups, assign passwords to users, and create new security groups.

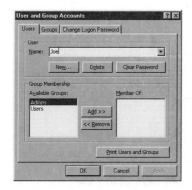

Users

The Users tab is where you assign new users to the groups. For example, suppose you want to include a particular user in the Admins group. In the **Users** tab of the User and Group Accounts dialog box, type the user's name in the **Name** box and then click the **New** button.

The New User/Group box opens with the user's name in it. Press the **Tab** key and type a Personal ID in the **Personal ID** box. The Personal ID or PID identifies a user in the user list. The PID must have at least 4 characters (the maximum is 20) and it is case sensitive. After you establish the PIDs for your various users, you can then assign the users to any of the groups that appear on the Users tab (refer to Figure 20.3).

Groups

The Groups tab is where you create new groups. For example, you may want to create a group that has access to most of the objects in the database (such as a Human Resources department) but not complete rights to all objects, as the Admins group does. Click the **New** button and then assign the group a name and a PID as you did for a new user. When you return to the Users tab, the new group appears in the Available Groups box (refer to Figure 20.3).

Change Logon Password

You can use the Change Logon Password tab to create a new password or to change an old password for a particular user. When new users are initially assigned to the various groups, the Logon Password is blank, so a password will have to be assigned.

After you establish the group accounts and place various users in them, you are ready to establish the security levels for the objects in the database. The easiest way to do so is to use the Access Security Wizard.

Using the Security Wizard

The Security Wizard actually creates a secured copy of your original database and uses the objects in the copy when it assigns the various security parameters to the database.

To use the Security Wizard, follow these steps:

1. Click the **Tools** menu, point to **Security**, and then click **User-Level Security Wizard**. Figure 20.4 shows the first screen of this Wizard.

2. The Wizard screen lists the different object types in a database (tables, queries, forms, and so on). Each object type has a check box that is currently selected. To exclude an object type from the security set up, deselect the check box with a click.

Figure 20.4

The User-Level Security Wizard enables you to decide which objects in the database will be secured.

3. Click **OK** after you tell the Wizard which object types to secure.

The User-Level Security Wizard creates a new database and exports copies of all the objects from the original database into the new database. The objects in the new database are secured according to the object types you selected earlier.

All permissions to these objects are revoked, and users in your User group (or other groups you created using the tools discussed in the section "Assigning Users to Security Groups") will not be able to access any of the secure objects. (Consequently, you must change the rights available to the User group, using the techniques discussed next.) Table relationships and any linked tables are also re-created in the new database, and the new database is encrypted. (The unchanged original database remains as a backup if you decide that your security setup is unneeded or unwanted.)

Encrypted databases are coded so that utility programs or word processors cannot decipher them. When you encrypt a database, only the owner (Admins in the cases discussed in this lesson) can open the database and assign the various security levels to other users.

Because only members of the Admins group have access to the secured objects in the database, you need to grant permissions to the User group so that users can work with certain objects.

To grant permissions to groups and users, follow these steps:

1. On the **Tools** menu, point to **Security** and then click **User and Group Permissions**.

2. On the **Permissions** tab, click **Users** or **Groups** and then click the user or group whose permissions you want to assign in the **User/Group Name** box (see Figure 20.5).

3. Click the type of object in the **Object Type** box and then click the name of the object to assign permissions for in the **Object Name** box.

4. Under **Permissions**, either select the permissions you want to assign or clear the permissions you want to remove for the group or user; then click **Apply**. To assign permissions for additional objects for the current user or group, repeat these steps.

Figure 20.5

The User and Group Permissions dialog box is where you assign rights to the objects in the secure database.

To assign additional users or groups rights to the objects in the database, repeat the steps above as necessary. When you have completed assigning the various permissions, click **OK** to close the User and Group Permissions dialog box.

Data Protection on Forms

The security techniques discussed so far in this lesson require you to work with passwords, user groups, and permission levels. A very simple way to protect data in your database without dealing with all the potential headaches involving security issues is to protect certain fields on the forms that you create. This method enables other users to view the information in your database via a form, but does not permit them to change the values in certain fields on the form.

To protect a field or fields on a form, follow these steps:

1. Open the form in Form Design view.

2. Right-click any field and select **Properties**.

3. Select the **Data** tab and click the **Locked** property box.

4. Click the drop-down arrow and select **Yes** to lock the field, as shown in Figure 20.6. Close the Properties dialog box for the field.

Figure 20.6

You can lock fields on your forms so that other users can view the data, but cannot change it.

You can lock as many fields as you want on the form. However, if you decide to lock most of the fields on the form, you might want to make the entire form read-only instead. Then other users can view the form, but not make any changes to the data.

To make a form read-only, follow these steps:

1. Open the form in Design view. The gray box at the intersection of the two rulers in Design view (the upper-left corner of the form) is the Form Selector button. Click the **Form Selector** button to select the entire form (a black square appears in the Form Selector button).

2. Click **View**, **Properties**. The form's Properties box opens.

3. Select the **Data** tab and click the **Allow Editing** box.

4. Click the drop-down arrow in the **Allow Editing** box and select **No** as shown in Figure 20.7.

5. You may also want to set **Allow Additions** and **Allow Deletions** to **No** to also prevent these actions.

6. Complete the changes to the form's properties and close the Properties dialog box.

Figure 20.7

You can make an entire form read-only in the form's Properties dialog box.

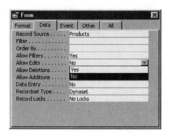

When you view the form in Form view, you cannot make any changes to the form. The form will not accept any input from the keyboard in any of its fields.

A final comment should be made concerning databases and security in general. The need for passwords and user levels really should be dictated by the value of the data in your database. If you are working with extremely sensitive, highly proprietary data, it may make sense to use a database password, or assign user levels in a multiuser environment.

On the other hand, if your only real problem is that other users of your database are inadvertently changing data, you may just need to lock certain fields in the forms or make the form read-only. The decision to make a database secure requires you as the administrator of the database to control who has rights to the database and what levels of access those rights contain.

Review Questions

The Certified Microsoft Office User Exams are task oriented. The following types of questions are not representative of the test.

1. What is the first step you must take before you can password-protect a database?

2. What is the easiest way to select the objects that will be secured in a secure database and to create an encrypted version of a current database?

3. Which view do you use to lock fields in a form or to make the form read-only?

Review Question Answers

1. When you open the database that you want to password-protect, you must select the **Exclusive** check box in the Open dialog box. For more information, see the section "Assigning a Password to a Database."

2. The Security Wizard provides the easiest route for selecting the objects that you want to assign permission to in a secure database. The Wizard also automatically creates an encrypted version of the database. For more information, see the section "Using the Security Wizard."

3. You must be in Form Design view to lock fields in a form or to make the entire form read-only. For more information, see the section "Data Protection on Forms."

Practice Lab

The following practice lab relates to skills not included in the Microsoft Access certification exam. This lab does, however, give you practice with the skills covered in this lesson.

1. Copy the **lesson20.mdb** from the CD-ROM that accompanies this book to a folder on your computer. Password protect the database.

2. Remove the password protection on **lesson20.mdb**.

3. Open the **Product** form in the **lesson20.mdb** and lock the UnitsInStock field and the UnitPrice field.

4. Open the **Customer** form in the **lesson20.mdb** and make the form read-only.

LESSON 21

Getting Help

This lesson does not cover any of the Required Tasks for the Access Certification test. It does provide, however, information on how to use the Access Help system, which will assist you in learning the required skills for the Microsoft Access Certification exam.

Using the Office Assistant

Access offers you a number of ways to get help as you create and work with your Access objects. You can ask the Office Assistant for help, get help on a particular part of the screen with the What's This tool, and choose topics from the Help system. You can even get additional help via Microsoft's Access Web page.

The Office Assistant provides a very flexible way to get help as you work in Access. By default, the Office Assistant is turned on and sits in a little box on top of your work area, as shown in Figure 21.1. You can turn the Office Assistant off by clicking the **Close** (**x**) button in its top-right corner.

Figure 21.1

The Office Assistant offers a flexible way to get help in Access.

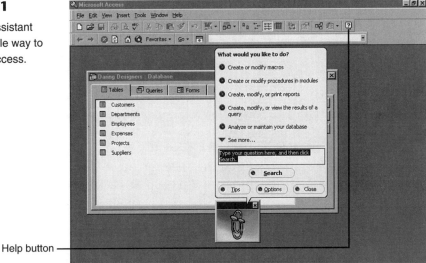

Help button ——

To turn the Office Assistant on again, click the **Help** button in the Standard toolbar or select **Help, Microsoft Access Help**.

 Other Assistants   If you installed Microsoft Office with a Custom installation and you chose to install the additional assistants, you can choose a character other than the paper clip. Just right-click the **Office Assistant** and select **Assistant** from the short-cut menu. Then click the **Back** and **Next** buttons to find an assistant that you prefer; click **Apply** to change the character.

Working with the Office Assistant

When you turn on the Office Assistant, a bubble appears next to (or above) its box asking you what kind of help you want. You can do any of the following:

▶ Type a question in the text box to tell the Office Assistant what kind of help you need.

▶ Select one of the Office Assistant's guesses about what you need help with.

▶ Click the **Tips** button to get any tips that the Office Assistant can provide for the task you're performing.

▶ Click the **Options** button to customize the way the Office Assistant works.

▶ Click **Close** to close the bubble (but leave the Office Assistant onscreen).

If you close the Help bubble, you can reopen it at any time by clicking the **Help** button on the Standard toolbar, pressing **F1**, selecting **Help, Microsoft Access Help**, or clicking the Office Assistant window.

Asking the Office Assistant a Question

If you need help on a particular topic, simply type a question into the Office Assistant text box and follow these steps:

1. If the Office Assistant's Help bubble doesn't appear, click the **Help** button on the Standard toolbar.

2. Type a question into the text box. For example, you might type **How do I print?** to get help printing your work.

3. Click the **Search** button or press the **Enter** key. The Office Assistant provides some topics that might match what you're looking for.

4. Click the option that best describes what you're trying to do. A Help window appears with instructions for the specified task. If none of the options describe what you want, click the **See More** arrow to view more options or type a different question in the text box.

The Help window that contains the task instructions is part of the same Help system that you can access with the **Help, Contents and Index** command. See "Managing Help Topics You've Located" later in this lesson for information about navigating this window.

Using the Access Help Topics

A more conventional way to get help is through the **Contents and Index** command on the **Help** menu. When you open the Access Help system, move through the topics listed to find the topic you're interested in.

The Help system has three tabs (**Contents**, **Index**, and **Find**), so you can get help in various ways. To access the Help system:

1. Select **Help, Contents and Index**.

2. Click on the tab for the type of help you want.

3. Click the topic you're interested in (if there's a list) or type in your topic and press the **Enter** key.

The following sections contain specific information about each tab.

Using the Contents Tab

The **Contents** tab of the Help system is a series of books you can open. Each book contains one or more Help topics, and some books contain chapters. Chapters break down a broader topic into more specific areas of information. Figure 21.2 shows a Contents screen.

Figure 21.2

The Contents tab provides another way to get help in Access.

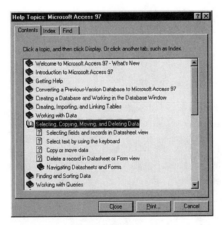

To select a Help topic from the **Contents** tab, follow these steps:

1. Select **Help**, **Contents and Index** to open the Help window.

2. Click the **Contents** tab if necessary.

3. Double-click the book that describes, in broad terms, what you want help with. A list of Help topics appears below the book.

4. Double-click a Help topic to display it.

5. When you finish reading a topic, click **Help Topics** to go back to the main Help screen; or click the window's **Close** button (**x**) to exit from Help.

If you want to refer to the Help topic again and do not want to close the Help window, click its **Minimize** button.

Using the Index

The Index is an alphabetical listing of indexed terms associated with every available Help topic. By typing in an index term or part of an index term, you can get a list of topics that match the particular index entry.

To select a Help topic from the **Index** tab:

1. Type the first few letters of the topic you're looking for. The index list jumps quickly to that spot.

2. Double-click the topic you want to see.

Finding Help topics by keywords is one more way to get help in Access (see Figure 21.3).

Figure 21.3

You can use the Index tab to move quickly to a particular Help topic.

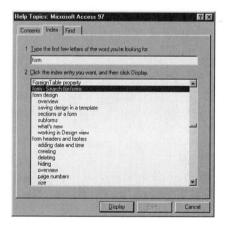

Using Find

The Index is great if you know the name of the Help topic you're looking for, but what if you're not sure? That's where Find comes in handy. Find searches both the titles and the contents of Help topics and retrieves all the topics in which the word(s) you typed appear.

 Build the Find Index   The first time you use Find, you'll be asked to build the Find index. Click **Next**, **Finish** to create the list.

To select a Help topic from the **Find** tab:

1. Type the topic you're looking for in the top box.

2. If more than one line appears in the middle box, click the line that most closely matches your interest.

3. Browse the topics that appear at the bottom and click the one that matches the help you need (see Figure 21.4).

Figure 21.4

Find enables you to quickly narrow your search of Help topics.

4. Click the **Display** button or press the **Enter** key.

The Find tab really offers the most extensive search of the Help system for a keyword or phrase. Use the Find tab when you can't seem to find the information that you need on the Contents tab or can't seem to come up with the right index term for the topic on the Index tab.

Managing Help Topics You've Located

No matter which of the four avenues you choose for finding a Help topic (the Office Assistant, Contents, Index, or Find), you eventually end up at a Help screen like the one shown in Figure 21.5. From there, you can read the information onscreen or do any of the following:

1. Click an underlined word (a glossary term) to see a definition of it.

2. Click a button to jump to another Help screen.

3. Print a hard copy of the information by clicking the **Options** button and then selecting **Print Topic**.

4. Copy the text to the Clipboard (for pasting into a program such as Microsoft Word or Windows Notepad) by clicking the **Options** button and then selecting **Copy**.

5. Return to the main Help topic that brought you to this subtopic by clicking the **Back** button.

Figure 21.5

The Office Assistant Help screen offers several subtopics.

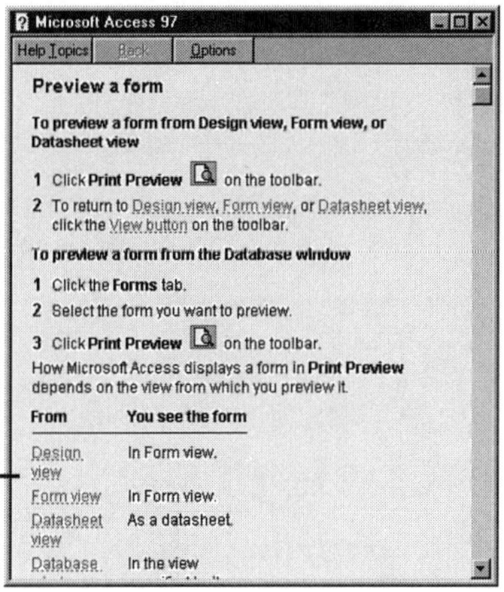

Glossary terms ——

Return to the main Help Topics screen by clicking the **Help Topics** button. If you are finished with the Help system, close the Help window by clicking the **Close** (x) button.

Access on the Web   The **Help** menu also provides another help avenue—access to Microsoft's Web site, where you can find additional Help information. Establish your Internet connection, select **Help**, **Microsoft on the Web**, and choose from the Web pages listed on the submenu to jump directly to one of them.

Getting Help with Screen Elements

If you need help with the function of a particular button or tool on the screen, you can get specific help. Just follow these steps:

1. Click the **Help** button in the toolbar.

2. Click the screen element for which you want help. A box appears explaining the element.

Review Questions

The Certified Microsoft Office User Exams are task oriented. The following types of questions are not representative of the test. These questions are designed to help you understand the required tasks and methods of performing those tasks prior to taking the test. Knowledge of the Access Help system is not a required Skill Area, but an understanding of the Help system will aid you in becoming an expert Access user.

1. To search for help using a term that is not part of a Help topic's title, which Help dialog box tab would you use?

2. To ask a question of the Access Help system, which Help tool would you use?

3. When the various Help topic books are displayed on the Help dialog box Contents tab, what must you do to see the various subtopics?

Review Question Answers

1. The Find tab provides the tools to search the titles and contents of the various Help topics using keywords. For more information see the section "Using Find."

2. The Office Assistant helps you find various Help topics by answering the questions that you pose in the Assistant's Search box. For more information, see the section "Using the Office Assistant."

3. Double-click any of the Help topic books to see a list of subtopics (chapters) associated with the main topic. For more information, see the section "Using the Contents Tab."

Practice Lab

The following practice lab relates to skills not included in the Microsoft Access certification exam. This lab does, however, increase your familiarity with the skills covered in this lesson:

1. Use the Office Assistant to find help on creating Access Switchboards.

2. Using the information provided by the Assistant, create a Switchboard for one of the databases that you copied from the companion CD.

3. Use the Index tab of the Help dialog box to find help on subforms.

APPENDIX A

Student Preparation Guide

The purpose of this appendix is to provide information about the certification tests—how to register, what the tests cover, how the tests work, and so on.

Studying for the Tests

You aren't required to take a training course to pass the Certified Microsoft Office User exams, but you certainly need to be sure you can successfully complete the tasks that the exams cover. Although a training class provides guidance, support, and practice, it may not be convenient or necessary for you.

This book provides the tutorial, review questions, and practice to help you complete your exams successfully. You can use the book in a classroom situation, or you can work through the lessons on your own. You don't have to work through the book from front to back, as each lesson stands on its own. Therefore, if you're familiar with an area, you can skip that lesson and go on to another. The Practice Labs at the end of each lesson give you a chance to get familiar with the tasks, and the CD-ROM that's included with the book has samples of the completed exercises.

Levels of Certification

The Certified Microsoft Office User exam for Microsoft Access 97 has one level of certification: **Certified Microsoft Expert User**. You should be able to handle a wide range of everyday tasks without difficulty. In addition, you should be able to handle complex assignments involving advanced formatting and functionality.

Microsoft also has a special Office 97 certification, the Certified Microsoft Office Expert. To attain this level, you must be an Expert User in each Microsoft Office application (Access, Excel, Word, PowerPoint, and Outlook) and have taken the Office Integration Exam to prove you can integrate these applications.

The specific topics covered at each level are listed in the "Required Tasks" section of this appendix. In this book, these tasks are broken down into lessons. A list at the beginning of each lesson specifies the tasks that lesson covers and the subject area they fall under in the tests.

Required Tasks

Each exam involves a list of required tasks that you may be asked to perform. The list of possible tasks is categorized by Skill Area. The tear-out card provided with this book lists the Microsoft Access Skill Areas and tasks covered by the Access Expert User exam and gives you a roadmap of where those topics are covered in the book.

A Microsoft Access Expert User should be able to do the following:

▶ Create relational databases for individual or small workgroup use

▶ Create and edit tables

▶ Create and edit forms

▶ Create and edit queries

▶ Create and edit reports

▶ Import information from other programs into Access

▶ Integrate Access with the Internet using hyperlinks and World Wide Web forms

The skill areas covered in the exam and the required tasks for those Skill Areas are listed in Table A.1.

Table A.1 Expert user skills.

Skill Area	Required Tasks
Create a Database	Plan a database
	Create a table
	Enter data into a table
	Modify data in a table
	Enter data into a form
	Navigate through a table
	Delete data from a table
Use Forms	Create a simple form
	Modify a form
	Create controls on a form
	Modify controls
	Add a record using a form
	Show related records on a form
Modify a Database	Open a database
	Modify field properties
	Modify field layout
	Modify the presentation of a database

continues

Table A.1   Continued

Skill Area	Required Tasks
View Information	Present information in a chart
	View information in a form
	View multiple records
	Switch between views
Organize Information	Sort data on single fields
	Sort data on multiple fields
Locate Information	Find a specific record
	Create a simple query
	Create a query with multiple criteria
	Add filters (selection and form)
	Remove filters
Refine Results	Add fields to a query
of a Query	Remove fields from a query
	Sort a query
	Join tables in a query
	Remove joins in a query
	Save a query
Analyze Data	Build summary queries
	Calculate fields
	Set Crosstab queries
Create Subforms	Identify appropriate use for subforms
	Add a record with a main form
	Add records with subforms
	Merge two tables into a form
Build a Relational	Identify relationships

Skill Area	Required Tasks
Database	Relate tables
Integrate Information	Import data
from Other Applications	Link data
	Add pictures to records
Utilize Web Capability	Create hyperlinks
	Build order forms for Internet use
Maintain Data Integrity	Identify criteria for data integrity
	Validate text
	Set required properties
	Set validation rules
	Set lookup fields
	Use expressions in calculated controls
Build a Form	Title a form
for Other Users	Modify form design
	Improve accuracy in forms
	Enhance design of a form
Produce Reports	Create a report
	Modify a report
	Label a report
	Customize headers and footers
	Make a calculation on a report
	Group data in a report
	Sort data in a report
	Add custom pages
Print	Print a report
	Print a form
	Print the results of a query

Registering for the Exams

Certified Microsoft Office User exams are administered by Approved Certification Testing (ACT) centers. To find the nearest ACT center, call 800-933-4493. You'll have to call the ACT center to find out about its test policies and schedules, whether it accepts walk-ins or requires advanced registration, how the exams are conducted, and the charge for the tests. The typical retail price of each exam is $50.00 in the United States, but that price can vary from center to center. You must pay for the tests in advance. There is no refund for missed exam appointments or failed tests.

Exams are currently available only in English, although Microsoft plans to offer the Office 97 exams in Japanese. The exams will be offered in other languages as soon as the courseware in those languages becomes available.

Taking the Tests

Certified Microsoft Office User exams are not multiple-choice or true-false tests. Instead, they are based on the types of tasks you may encounter in the everyday world. When you take the test, you sit at a computer that uses Windows 95 or Windows NT Workstation, work with Microsoft Access 97, and use the features of Access to perform the tasks outlined for you.

You can't use notes, manuals, laptops, tape recorders, or other aids during the tests. Access Help is available, but using it may cut down on the time you have available to complete the exam tasks.

Exams are 1 hour or less (some as short as 30 minutes). Your score is based on the number of tasks you successfully perform in the allotted time. This assessment measures your productivity and efficiency, as well as your skill and knowledge.

Each test has a minimum score. If your score meets or exceeds that minimum, you pass the test. If not, you may take the test as many times as you need until you pass. However, you won't get a refund if you don't pass the test.

You see your test results as soon as your test is completed. Successful candidates receive a certificate a week or two after the testing. Test scores are confidential; only you and Microsoft see them.

To keep up to date on the Certified Microsoft Office User exams, check Microsoft's Web site at `http://www.microsoft.com/office/train_cert/`.

Glossary

alphanumeric characters   The letters of the alphabet and other nonnumeric symbols.

autoForm   A form that uses all the fields in the table as it displays the data one record at a time. Click the New Object button on the toolbar to create an AutoForm.

best fit   Double-clicking a column divider in a datasheet widens the column to the left of the mouse pointer to accommodate the longest entry that has been entered in it.

bitmap image   A particular file format for graphics. Bitmap files such as .bmp, .pcx, and .jpg are rasterized (made up of many dots); in contrast, formats such as encapsulated PostScript are vector based.

bound control   A control in a form or report tied to a particular field in the associated table or query. The opposite of the bound control is the unbound control, which can contain expressions that calculate values.

chart   A graphical representation of numerical data in a table, query, form, or report. Charts for Access objects can be created using the Graph 97 program that ships with Access and the other members of Microsoft Office software package.

combo box   A box that provides a drop-down list of choices in a table, form, or report, and gives you the option of typing in an entry not found on the list.

command button   A button that can be placed on a form to invoke certain commands such as printing. Command buttons can also be tied to macros.

compact   The act of defragmenting a database file to increase its performance. Compacting a database file also frees up disk space on your hard drive.

control   Objects on a form or report that display data, perform actions, or decorate the form or report. Bound and unbound controls provide dynamic boxes in a form or report that call data from a specific field in a table or use a formula designed in the Expression Builder to calculate an answer.

control format   You can format controls so that they display their contents with a certain number of decimal places or as currency. Control formats are set in the control's Properties box.

criteria   Conditional statements that you devise for queries.

crosstab query   This query displays its results in a spreadsheet-like format that enables you to cross-tabulate the information in the report. For example, row headings could be customer names, and the column headings could be product names. The intersection of each row and column provides a crosstab summary of each customer's purchases of each product.

custom pages   Adding page breaks to Access reports enables you to create custom pages in the Report Header and Footer Areas. These custom pages can serve as the title page for the report or as a summary page.

data   The discrete pieces of information that you place in your database tables.

data integrity   The validity of the data entered into an Access table. Access provides several strategies for ensuring data integrity, such as default values, Lookup fields, and referential integrity.

database object   An item that can be part of a database. Objects can consist of data manipulation and viewing containers such as tables, forms, and reports, or objects can be software miniprograms that you create using macros and the Visual Basic application language that comes with Microsoft Access.

Detail Area   The main area of the Design window for forms and reports. The Detail Area is where the controls representing fields or calculations are placed when a form or report is being designed.

dialog box   Software packages use these boxes to gather information from you, the user.

dynamic HTML   Access objects (tables and forms) exported as .htx or .asp files can be used to receive new data via the Web. Data input received through these objects updates the associated table in your Access database (see HTML).

export   The act of moving data out of Access and into other applications. You can cut and paste information from Access directly into other applications. You can also export Access tables into Excel where they are treated as worksheets.

Expression Builder   A tool for building mathematical formulas and other expressions that can be placed in controls in forms and reports. The Expression Builder can also be used to build expressions in the Query Design window.

external data   Information that resides outside Access in another format. Access can import data from Excel and Lotus spreadsheets.

field   A particular piece of information, such as a name or address, found in a record. Fields appear as columns in the Datasheet view of a table. In Table Design view, the fields in the table are the rows in the field grid box.

field properties   Control parameters that dictate how information in a field will be stored, handled, or displayed.

filtering records   A method of viewing certain records in a datasheet. To filter by selection, select an example of a field parameter you want to view by. To filter by form, type a filter parameter into a specific field.

footer   The area at the bottom of a printed page. It is also the bottom area in Form Design view and Report Design view. Items placed in the Page Footer area repeat on every page of the form or report. Items placed in the Form Footer or Report Footer appear at the end of the report.

foreign key   A primary key field is placed redundantly in a second table to provide a relationship between the two tables. The secondary occurrence of the key field is called the foreign key.

form   This object supplies a record-by-record view of database records. Forms are excellent vehicles for data input and editing.

freezing fields   When you freeze a particular field in a datasheet, the field remains in view when you scroll to the extreme edges of the data area.

groups   Areas of a report in which certain information is grouped together, such as a subtotal for a set of selected fields. In a report, you can also group information, such as all the records by a particular field.

header The area at the top of a printed page. In Form Design view and Report Design view, the header area is at the top of the design area. Items placed in the Page Header area repeat on every page of the form or report. You can also have section headers and group headers in reports that place information at the top of a summary group or report section.

HTML Hypertext Markup Language is the set of tagging codes used to publish documents on the World Wide Web. HTML tells a Web browser such as Internet Explorer how to display the text and graphics that are contained in the Web document or home page.

hyperlink In Access a field type that enables you to jump to another document or item. Placing a URL in a hyperlink field enables you to connect to Web sites by clicking the field.

import The act of taking data that resides outside Access and placing it in a new or existing Access table.

input mask A defined pattern for all the data that is entered in a particular field. Input masks are assigned to fields during table design.

join The act of creating relationships between tables based on a field that is common to both tables. The field itself does not require the same name in both tables, but it must contain the same type of data. Joins can be created between tables in the Relationships window or in the Query Design window.

label The tag for a bound or unbound control in a form or a report. The label usually contains the name of the field that the control is associated with.

landscape The page is oriented with the width greater than the length—for example, 11" by 8.5" for a typical piece of paper.

list box A box that provides a drop-down list of choices in a table, form, or report.

many-to-many relationship A relationship between tables in which each record in the first table has many possible matches in the second table and the records in the second table have many potential matches in the first table. Access cannot create direct many-to-many relationships. Tables with a many-to-many relationship are "bridged" by an intermediary join table that has a one-to-many relationship with each table involved in the many-to-many relationship.

normalization The act of breaking a table that has fields in which data is repeated into smaller related tables. Access has automated the normalization process via the Table Analyzer.

object linking and embedding (OLE) The process of placing information that originates in one application into another application. Linking ties outside information to an object such as a table, but the linked file resides outside the database table. Embedded information, such as a graph or a graphic, becomes part of the database file that it is placed in, increasing the size of the database file. Linked and embedded objects retain all the properties that they had (such as formatting capabilities) in their native application.

objects   (1) Items that originate in source or server applications and are linked or embedded into a destination application. Objects can consist of a spreadsheet, graph, or graphic image—just about anything that can be created in an application. (2) Objects also refer to database items such as tables, forms, and reports.

OfficeLinks   A set of commands that make it easy for you to export data from Access to other Microsoft products. You can use OfficeLinks to export tables to Excel or create a mail merge using Access data in a Microsoft Word form letter.

OLE field   A special field that is placed in an Access table; the field uses linked or embedded objects as its source. For example, an OLE field in a table can hold embedded photos.

one-to-many relationship   A relationship between tables in which a record in the first table can be matched to more than one record in the second table.

one-to-one relationship   A relationship between tables in which each record in the first table can be matched to only one record in the second table.

optimization   The Performance Analyzer can be used to optimize any of your database objects; it provides Recommendations, Suggestions, and Ideas for improving object performance.

primary key   A field that uniquely identifies each record in a table. The table is indexed automatically by the primary key field.

properties   All the objects in an Access database and the database file itself have properties that refer to the formatting and other attributes related to the particular object or file. For example, the properties of a control dictate the source of the control, such as a particular field. The properties of an object such as a form include information on the table that the form was based on.

query   A way to ask a table or tables certain questions. A Select query lists the records that satisfy a certain question or parameter. An Action query actually does something to a table such as deleting records that satisfy a certain request. Queries can also return totals or the answers to other mathematical expressions.

record   A collection of data pertaining to a particular person, place, or thing. Appears as a row in a datasheet.

relational database   A database that groups information in discrete tables. Relationships exist between the tables in this type of database. An example is a small business database in which the customer information, product information, supplier information, and employee information reside in different tables but can be tied together by queries, forms, and reports.

repair   Database files can become corrupted or damaged. Use the Repair command to try to fix any damage that a file may have suffered. Because this process does entail some risk to your data, make sure to create a copy or backup the database file before beginning the process.

report   This object pulls together data from a table or a number of tables and presents the information in a readable, well-designed format.

sections   Additional areas that you can add to a report. For example, you can add a group section that provides a subtotal for certain information or provides some other type of summary information.

sorting   The capability to reorder table records numerically or alphanumerically in either ascending or descending order. The physical order of the information in the records remains the same; however, the data is displayed based on the sort parameters.

subform   A form that you can place in a control on an already existing form. This feature enables you to see data from two different tables as you work with the form.

subreport   A previously created report that can be placed in a control on a second report. Subreports are excellent vehicles for placing a short summary report on a longer, more detailed main report.

table   An object consisting of data in rows and columns. It is used for data input and editing in your database.

template   A blueprint or foundation for a database that can include ready-made tables, forms, reports, and other database objects.

toolbox   A group of design tools used to create forms and reports in their respective Design views.

URL   Short for Uniform Resource Locator, the URL provides the address that you use to locate a particular Web site on the World Wide Web.

user levels   Different degrees of access to a database's objects. User levels are assigned to user groups. The group that you belong to dictates your level of access to the objects.

validate   To ensure data integrity, data validation can be based on a default value, a list of values, or on data in another table using table relationships that invoke referential integrity.

Wizard   An interactive feature that walks you through a particular process such as creating a form. Wizards use a series of dialog boxes to get answers to specific questions and then create a particular object or complete a particular task based on those answers.

World Wide Web (WWW)   An electronic patchwork of interconnected HTML documents on computers all over the world. The Web is navigated via a Web browser that enables you to view the various pages.

zoom   The ability to increase or decrease the degree of detail you can see on an object that is displayed in the Print Preview window. You can zoom out to see the design of the entire page or zoom in to view specific data. You can also use Zoom in the Query Design, Form Design, and Report Design windows to zoom out on the field or control information that you are working with.

INDEX

A

Access dialog box,
18-20, 25
ACT centers (Approved
Certified Testing), 312
action queries, 178
Append, 207-209
Delete, 209-210
adding
criteria to queries,
181-182
*clearing the Design
grid, 183*
multiple criteria, 183
operators, 182
custom pages to
reports, 241
fields
creating forms, 145
database tables, 76
to queries, 180
graphics to controls,
170-171
images to records (embed-
ding objects), 253-255
new records (compound
forms), 167
subreports to
reports, 242
Advanced Find dialog
box, 27
advanced sorts (records),
84-86
saving as queries, 86
Analyze It, OfficeLinks
(exporting data), 260
Append queries, 207-209

applications
copying and pasting data,
259-260
database integration, 250,
253
*embedding objects,
254-256*
*linking objects,
250-251*
destination (OLE), 250
exporting data to, 259
importing data from,
257-258
OfficeLinks, 260
source (OLE), 250
ASP (Active Server Pages)
dynamic HTML objects,
270
saving forms as, 272-273
assigning
passwords (database
security), 290-292
users (to security groups),
292-293
AutoForm
creating forms, 136
viewing images (embed-
ding and linking
objects), 256
AutoFormat command
(Format menu), 245
AutoForms (table data
entry), 51-52
closing AutoForms, 52
updating tables, 53
Autonumber fields
(Datasheet data entry), 48
AutoReport (creating
reports), 216-217

B

blank databases,
    creating, 18
        Access dialog box, 18-20
        starting MS Access, 18
borders, formatting (custom
    forms), 143
bound controls
    (forms), 154
building
    crosstab queries (in
        Design view), 207
    Internet order forms, 270
        ODBC data sources,
            270-271
        saving as ASP files,
            272-273
    relational databases,
        104-109
        deleting table relation-
            ships, 111
        editing table
            relationships, 111
        many-to-many table
            relationships, 110
        one-to-many table
            relationships, 110
Byte field size, 122

C

calculated controls, 235
    creating, 233
        Expression Builder,
            156-157
        dates and page
            numbers, 233-234
    forms, 154
    group subtotals, 237-238
    Totals controls, 235-236
        math functions, 236
calculations
    fields
        expressions, 200-202
        summary queries,
            196-198
    form, 158
        Expression Builder,
            158-159
        formatting
            controls, 159
case-sensitivity (passwords),
    291

certification
    levels, 308
    required skills, 308-311
Chart Wizard, 239
charts, report, creating,
    238-241
Clear Grid command
    (Edit menu), 183
clearing Design grid (adding
    criteria to queries), 183
Close the Replace dialog box,
    96
closing
    AutoForms (table data
        entry), 52
    tables, 54
colors
    control, formatting, 169
    object hyperlinks, 268
Column command (Insert
    menu), 76
Column Sizing tool (chang-
    ing field widths), 73
Column Width dialog
    box, 73
columnar layout (creating
    forms), 138
columns, *see* fields
Combo Box control, 163
Combo Box Wizard, 160
combo boxes (forms), 163
    creating, 160-162
commands
    Edit menu
        Clear Grid, 183
        Copy, 62, 251
        Cut, 62
        Delete Column,
            65, 181
        Delete Record, 64
        Paste, 62
        Paste Special, 251
        Replace, 95
        Select Record, 64
    File menu
        Open, 290
        Print, 172
    Find
        finding records, 92
        Replace feature,
            95-96
        setting parameters,
            92-93
        wildcards, 94-95

Format menu
    AutoFormat, 245
    Font, 74
    Hide Columns, 75
    Unhide Columns, 75
Help menu, Contents and
    Index, 302
Insert menu,
    Column, 76
Records menu
    Data Entry, 63
    Remove Filter/Sort, 63
View menu
    Form Header/Footer,
        139
    Table Names, 189
compressing databases, 286
content (database table
    fields)
    changing, 60
    editing, 61
    replacing, 60
Contents and Index com-
    mand (Help menu), 302
Contents tab (Help system),
    302
Control Panel dialog
    box, 270
Control Properties dialog
    box, 155
controls
    calculated, creating with
        Expression Builder,
        156-157
    Combo Box, 163
    field, resizing, 147
    form
        bound, 154
        calculated, 154
        entering in Form
            Footer, 155
        Expression Builder,
            156-157
        unbound, 154
    formatting (form calcula-
        tions), 159
    modifying, 168
        formatting text and
            colors, 169
        graphics, adding,
            170-171
        tab order,
            changing, 168
    moving (report design),
        226-227

report
   modifying, 225
   calculated, 233-238
Copy command (Edit menu), 62, 251
copying
   data
      database tables 62
      to other applications, 259-260
   URLs (from the Web Toolbar), 267
Create New Data Source dialog box, 270
criteria
   operators, 182
   query, adding, 181-183
crosstab queries, 178, 203
   building in Design view, 207
   Crosstab Query Wizard, 205
CustomerID numbers (combo boxes), 162
Customize dialog box, 18
customizing
   forms, 141
      creating titles, 141
      formatting text and borders, 143
      Forms Toolbox, 141-143
   report pages, 241
      adding subreports, 242
      enhancing visually, 245
      inserting images, 244
      inserting page breaks, 243
Cut command (Edit menu), 62

D

data
   database table, moving and copying, 62
   entering into forms, 147
   integrity (tables), 116
      default values, 116-117
      formats, 123
      input masks, 123-126
      lookup fields, 128-130

   referential integrity, 126-128
   required fields, 121
   sizing fields, 122-123
   validation rules, 118-121
   table entry
      in Datasheet view, 48-50
      with AutoForms, 51-52
Data Entry command (Records menu), 63
Data Integrity message box, 121
Database to Compact From dialog box, 286
Database to Compact To dialog box, 286
Database toolbar icons, 24-25
Database Wizard, 18
databases, 6
   compressing, 286
   creating, 17
      blank, 18-20
      Database Wizard, 20-24
   integrating application information, 250
      Analyze It, 260
      copying and pasting data, 259-260
      embedding objects, 253-256
      exporting data, 259
      importing data, 257-258
      linking objects, 250-251
      OfficeLinks, 260
      Publish It, 260
   integration application information (embedding objects), 255
   objects
      documenting, 285-286
      Performance Analyzer, 278-280
      viewing, 24-25
   opening, 25
      files, finding, 27-28
      Open dialog box, 26

   relational, 6
      building, 104-111
      normalizing, 11-12
      objects, 7-10
      planning, 10-11
   repairing, 287
   security, 290
      forms, 296-297
      passwords, 290-292
      Security Wizard, 294-295
      user groups, 292-293
      user levels, 292
   tables, 64
      adding fields, 76
      AutoForm data entry, 51-52
      closing, 54
      Datasheet view data entry, 48-50
      deleting records, 64
      editing field content, 61
      field content, changing, 60
      field properties, changing 76-77
      field widths, changing, 72-73
      fields, deleting, 65
      fonts, changing, 74
      hiding fields, 75-76
      inserting new records, 63
      moving and copying data, 62
      moving fields, 70-71
      navigating, 50-51
      printing, 53
      record heights, changing, 74
      replacing field content, 60
      Table Analyzer, 281-284
Datasheet view
   creating tables, 39
   inserting table records, 63
   table data entry, 48-50
      AutoNumber fields, 48
datasheets
   layout (creating forms), 138
   summary queries, 199
   table views, 32

date calculated controls, **233-234**
default values
  Datasheet data entry, 50
  field data integrity, 116-117
Delete Column command (Edit menu), 65, 181
Delete queries, 209-210
Delete Record command (Edit menu), 64
deleting
  database table
    fields, 65
    records, 64
  table relationships, 111
Design grid
  clearing (adding criteria to queries), 183
  dragging fields into, 180
Design view
  crosstab queries, building, 207
  database table fields, moving, 71
  forms, creating, 136, 144-145
    adding fields, 145
    adjusting field labels and controls, 147
    moving fields, 146
    saving the form, 147
  modifying reports, 232
    adding new labels, 232
    creating calculated controls, 233-238
  reports, creating, 225
    moving labels and controls, 226-227
    selecting fields for groups and sorting, 225
  tables, creating, 32
    field properties, 36-37
    field setup, 33
    primary keys, 37
    saving structure, 38
  reports, modifying, 216
destination applications (OLE), 250
Detail queries, 187
dialog boxes
  Access, 18-20, 25
  Advanced Find, 27

  Close the Replace, 96
  Column Width, 73
  Control Panel, 270
  Control Properties, 155
  Create New Data Source, 270
  Customize, 18
  Database to Compact From, 286
  Database to Compact To, 286
  Expression Builder, 156-158
  File New Database, 19-21
  Find, 93
  Find in Field, 92
  Font, 74
  Grouping Intervals, 220
  Import, 257
  Insert Hyperlink, 265
  Insert Object, 253
  Insert Picture, 170, 244
  Join Properties, 108
  Join Type, 108
  New, 21
  New Database, 20-21
  New Form, 136, 144, 149
    creating charts, 239
  New Query, 179, 186, 189, 205
  New Report, 216-218
  New Table, 33, 39-40
  ODBC Microsoft Access 97 Setup, 270
  Open, 25-27, 290
  Password Required, 291
  Paste Special, 252
  Performance Analyzer, 279
  Print, 53, 172, 207
  Properties, 148, 158, 171
  Relationships, 107, 111
  Replace in Field, 96
  Row Height, 74
  Save As, 38, 147, 185
  Set Database Password, 290
  Show Table, 105, 127, 179, 189, 196
  Sorting and Grouping, 225, 237
  Summary Options, 187
  Tab Order, 168
  Text Box Properties, 234-235, 238

  User and Group Accounts, 292
    Change Logon Password tab, 293
    Groups tab, 293
    Users tab, 293
documenting database objects, 285-286
Double field size, 122
drag and drop (moving fields), 71
dragging fields (into the Design grid), 180
dynamic HTML (object formats), 269
  ASP (ActiveX Server Pages), 270
  HTX, 269
dynasets (queries), 178

E

Edit menu commands
  Clear Grid, 183
  Copy, 62, 251
  Cut, 62
  Delete Column, 65, 181
  Delete Record, 64
  Paste, 62
  Paste Special, 251
  Replace, 95
  Select Record, 64
editing
  field content (database tables), 61
  table relationships, 111
embedding objects, 253
  adding images to records, 253-255
  viewing images in forms, 256
exams
  levels of certification, 308
  registering for, 312
  required skills, 308-311
  study tips, 308
  taking, 312
Expert User certification (required skills), 308-311
exporting
  data (to other applications), 259
  reports (as static HTML), 273-274

Expression Builder,
201-202
creating calculated
controls, 156-157,
233-235
*date and page number,
233-234*
*group subtotals,
237-238*
*Totals controls,
235-236*
form calculations, 158
operators, 159
validation rules, 121
Expression Builder dialog
box, 156-158
expressions (query fields),
200
Expression Builder,
201-202

F

fields, 48
adding (creating forms),
145
Autonumber, 48
calculating
expressions, 200-202
*summary queries,
196-198*
columns, freezing, 86
data integrity, 116
*default values,
116-117*
formats, 123
input masks, 123-126
*lookup fields,
128-130*
referential, 126-128
required fields, 121
sizing, 122-123
*validation rules,
118-121*
database table, 7, 72
adding, 76
changing, content, 60
deleting, 65
editing content, 61
hiding, 75-76
moving, 70-71
*properties, changing,
76-77*

replacing content, 60
*widths, changing,
72-73*
default values (Datasheet
data entry), 50
indexes, 210-211
moving (creating forms),
146
multiple (sorting records
by), 83-84
nonprimary key (table
relationships), 104
OLE (creating forms), 257
properties (Design view),
36-37
query
adding, 180
*hiding or
showing, 181*
removing, 181
resizing labels and
controls (creating
forms), 147
setting up
(Design view), 33
single (sorting records by),
82
table
*objects hyperlinks,
264-267*
*placing with Table
Analyzer, 282-283*
table layout
(field selector), 32
File New Database dialog
box, 19-21
files
database, finding, 27-28
formats (graphics), 253
filters
record, 84, 96
by form, 98
by selection, 97
saving as queries, 178
Find command
(records), 92
Help topics, 303-304
Replace feature, 95-96
setting parameters,
92-93
wildcards, 94-95
Find dialog box, 93
Find in Field dialog box, 92
Find Unmatched
queries, 210

finding
database files, 27-28
records (Find
command), 92-96
Font command (Format
menu), 74
Font dialog box, 74
fonts, database table,
changing, 74
Form Design view, 159
combo boxes, creating,
160-163
controls, creating
*bound/unbound
controls, 154*
*entering in Form
Footer, 155*
*Expression Builder,
156-157*
Form Design window, 140
Form Footer (entering new
controls), 155
Form Header/Footer com-
mand (View menu), 139
Form Wizard
creating forms, 136-139
columnar layout, 138
datasheet layout, 138
subforms
*adding new
records, 167*
creating, 164-166
tabular format, 164
*viewing related records,
167*
Format menu commands
AutoFormat, 245
Font, 74
Hide Columns, 75
Unhide Columns, 75
formatting
control text and
color, 169
fields (data integrity), 123
text and borders (custom-
izing forms), 143
forms
calculations, 158
*Expression Builder,
158-159*
*formatting controls,
159*
combo boxes, 163
creating, 160-162

controls
  *entering in Form
    Footer, 155*
  *Expression Builder,
    156-157*
creating, 136, 144-145
  adding fields, 145
  *adjusting field labels
    and controls, 147*
  AutoForm, 136
  Design view, 136
  *Form Wizard,
    136-139*
  moving fields, 146
  OLE fields, 257
  queries, 137
  saving the form, 147
customizing, 141
  creating titles, 141
  *formatting text and
    borders, 143*
  *Forms Toolbox,
    141-143*
database, 7
entering data, 147
filtering records, 98
multiple records, viewing,
  148
order (Internet
  integration), 270-272
printing, 172
saving as ASP files,
  272-273
securing data, 296-297
subforms
  *adding new
    records, 167*
  creating, 164-166
  tabular format, 164
  *viewing related records,
    167*
table (object hyperlinks),
  268
viewing images in
  (embedding objects),
  256
views, switching between,
  139-140
**Forms Toolbox (custom
  forms), 141-143**
formulas
  expressions (Expression
    Builder), 201-202
  summary query grid, 197

**fragmented databases,
  compressing, 286**
freezing field columns, 86

G

graphics
  adding to records (embed-
    ding objects), 253-255
  control, adding, 170-171
  file formats, 253
  inserting into reports, 244
  viewing in forms (embed-
    ding objects), 256
**grouping data (Report
  Wizard), 219-220**
**Grouping Intervals dialog
  box, 220**
groups
  security (assigning users),
    292-293
  subtotals (calculated
    controls), 237-238

H

**Height-Sizing tool (changing
  record heights), 74**
Help system
  Office Assistant, 300-301
    asking questions, 301
    What's This tool, 300
  screen elements, 305
  topics, 302-305
    Contents tab, 302
    *Find command,
      303-304*
    Index tab, 303
**Hide Columns command
  (Format menu), 75**
hiding fields
  database tables, 75-76
  to queries, 181
**HTML (HyperText Markup
  Language)**
  object formats (Internet
    integration), 269
  static (exporting reports
    as), 273-274
**HTX dynamic HTML objects,
  269**
**hyperlinks, object (Internet
  integration), 264-268**
**HyperText Markup
  Language, *see* HTML**

I

icons (Database toolbar), 24
images
  adding to records (embed-
    ding objects), 253-255
  file formats, 253
  inserting into
    reports, 244
  viewing in (embedding
    objects), 256
Import dialog box, 257
**Import Spreadsheet Wizard,
  258**
**importing data (from other
  applications), 257-258**
Index tab (Help system), 303
indexes (field), 210-211
**input masks, fields (data
  integrity), 123-126**
**Insert Hyperlink dialog box,
  265**
**Insert Object dialog
  box, 253**
**Insert Picture dialog box,
  170, 244**
inserting
  database table
    records, 63
  images into reports, 244
  page breaks in
    reports, 243
Integer field size, 122
integration, 250
  copying and pasting data,
    259-260
  exporting data, 259
  importing data, 257-258
  Internet tools, 264
    *building order forms,
      270-272*
    *exporting reports,
      273-274*
    *HTML object
      formats, 269*
    *object hyperlinks,
      264-268*
  objects
    embedding, 253-256
    linking, 250-251
  OfficeLinks, 260
integrity (data tables), 116
  default values, 116-117
  formats, 123

input masks, 123-126
lookup fields, 128-130
referential integrity,
126-128
required fields, 121
sizing fields, 122-123
validation rules, 118-121
**Internet (integration tools),
264**
building order forms,
270-272
exporting reports,
273-274
HTML object formats, 269
object hyperlinks,
264-268

J-L

**Join Properties dialog
box, 108**
**Join Type button (Relation-
ships dialog box), 108**
Join Type dialog box, 108
**joining query tables,
190-191**
removing join lines, 191

keyboard shortcuts
copying and moving table
data, 62
editing field content, 61
navigating tables, 50
**keys (checking with Table
Analyzer), 284**

labels
adding to reports, 232
field, resizing, 147
moving (report design),
226-227
layout (creating tables), 32
datasheets, 32
fields, 32
records, 32
linking objects, 250-251
viewing images in
forms, 256
Long Integer field size, 122
**lookup fields (data
integrity), 128-130**
columns, 129

M

macros (database), 10
**mailing labels (creating from
tables or queries), 245**
**Main Switchboard window
(Database Wizard), 23**
maintenance
Make Table queries, 210
repairing databases, 287
**many-to-many table rela-
tionships, 110**
**math functions (Totals
controls), 236**
**menus (changing field
widths), 73**
**Merge It, OfficeLinks
(exporting data), 260**
**Microsoft Access,
starting, 18**
**Microsoft Office Clip Art,
170**
modifying
controls, 168
*formatting text and
colors, 169*
*graphics, adding,
170-171*
*tab order, changing,
168*
database tables
*field widths,
changing, 72-73*
moving fields, 70-71
*record heights,
changing, 74*
reports, 232
adding new labels, 232
*creating calculated
controls, 233-238*
modules, database, 10
moving
database table data, 62
fields
creating forms, 146
database tables, 70
in Design view, 71
labels and controls (report
design),
226-227
**multiple criteria (adding to
queries), 183**
**multiple fields (sorting
records), 83-84**

**multiple records (viewing in
forms), 148**
multiple tables
creating queries, 189
Query Wizard, 187
**multiple-table reports
(Report Wizard), 221-222**

N

navigating tables, 50-51
keyboard shortcuts, 50
**New Database dialog box,
20-21**
New dialog box, 21
**New Form dialog box, 136,
144, 149**
creating charts, 239
**New Query dialog box, 179,
186, 189, 205**
**New Report dialog box,
216-218**
**New Table dialog box, 33,
39-40**
**nonprimary key fields (table
relationships), 104**
**normalization, spreadsheet
(Table Analyzer), 281**
**normalizing databases,
11-12**
**NorthWind database rela-
tionships, 110**

O

**Object Linking and Embed-
ding,** *see* **OLE**
objects, 250
database, 7
*documenting,
285-286*
forms, 7
macros, 10
modules, 10
*Performance
Analyzer, 278-280*
queries, 8
reports, 8
tables, 7
viewing, 24-25
database templates, 21
embedding, 253
*adding images to
records, 253-255*
*viewing images in
forms, 256*

HTML formats (Internet integration), 269
hyperlinks (Internet integration), 264-268
linking, 250-251
viewing images in forms, 256
ODBC (Open Database Connectivity) (building order forms), 270
data sources, 270-271
ODBC Microsoft Access 97 Setup dialog box, 270
Office Assistant (Help), 300-301
asking questions, 301
What's This tool, 300
OfficeLinks (exporting data to applications), 260
OLE (Object Linking and Embedding), 250
fields (creating forms), 257
objects
embedding, 253-255
linking, 250-251
one-to-many table relationships, 110
one-to-one table relationships, 110
Open command (File menu), 290
Open Database Connectivity, *see* ODBC
Open dialog box, 25-27, 290
opening databases, 25
file, finding, 27-28
Open dialog box, 26
operators
criteria, 182
Expression Builder, 159
validation rule, 120
optimizing
objects (Performance Analyzer), 280
tables (Table Analyzer), 281-284
order forms, building (Internet integration), 270-272

P

page breaks (inserting into reports), 243

page number calculated controls, 233-234
parameters, Find command, setting, 92-93
Password Required dialog box, 291
passwords (security), 290-292
case-sensitivity, 291
removing, 291
Paste command (Edit menu), 62
Paste Special command (Edit menu), 251
Paste Special dialog box, 252
pasting data, 259-260
Performance Analyzer
database objects, 278-279
optimizing objects, 280
dialog boxes, 279
pictures, *see* images; graphics
planning databases, 10-11
primary keys
checking with Table Analyzer, 284
Design view, 37
Print command (File menu), 172
Print dialog box, 53, 172, 207
Print Preview (printing and viewing reports), 223
printing
forms, 172
query results, 207
reports (Print Preview), 223
tables, 53
properties
database fields (Design view), 36-37
fields, changing, 76-77
Properties dialog box, 148, 158, 171
Publish It (OfficeLinks), exporting data, 260

Q

queries, 178
action, 178
Append, 207-209
creating with Simple Query Wizard, 208

creating, 178
multiple tables, 189
query by example, 180
Query Design view, 178
Query Wizard, 185-188
creating forms, 137
criteria, adding, 181-183
crosstab, 178, 203
building in Design view, 207
Crosstab Query Wizard, 205
database, 8
Query Design window, 9
Delete, 209-210
Detail, 187
dynasets, 178
expressions, 200
Expression Builder, 201-202
fields
adding, 180
hiding or showing, 181
indexes, 210-211
removing, 181
Find Unmatched, 210
mailing labels, creating from, 245
Make Table, 210
printing results, 207
records, sorting, 184
running, 185
saving, 185
filters as, 178
sorts as (records), 86
Select, 178
Summary, 187, 196
datasheets, 199
Query Grid Totals section, 196-197
Totals row, 198
tables
joining, 190-191
removing join lines, 191
Update, 210
Query Design view, 178
creating queries, 178
query by example, 180
joining tables, 190-191
multiple tables, 189
removing table join lines, 191

Query Design window, 9, 209
Query Wizard, 178, 185-188
  multiple tables, 189
  selecting multiple tables, 187

R

ready-made table relationships, 106
records, 48
  adding
    to compound forms, 167
    images (embedding objects), 253-255
  database table
    changing heights, 74
    deleting, 64
    inserting, 63
  filtering, 96
    by form, 98
    by selection, 97
  finding (Find command), 92-96
  forms, viewing multiple, 148
  freezing columns, 86
  query, sorting, 184
  related subform, viewing, 167
  sorting, 82
    advanced sorts, 84-86
    by multiple fields, 83-84
    by single fields, 82
  table layout, 32
Records menu commands
  Data Entry, 63
  Remove Filter/Sort, 63
referential integrity
  data fields, 126-128
  joining query tables, 191
  table relationships, 107
registering for exams, 312
related records, subforms, viewing, 167
relational databases, 6
  building, 108
    deleting table relationships, 111

    differentiating relationship types, 109
    editing table relationships, 111
    many-to-many table relationships, 110
    one-to-many table relationships, 110
    table relationships, 104-108
  normalizing, 11-12
  objects, 7
    forms, 7
    macros, 10
    modules, 10
    queries, 8
    reports, 8
    tables, 7
  planning, 10-11
relationships (table), 104, 108
  creating, 105-107
  deleting, 111
  differentiating types, 109
  editing, 111
  Join Type option, 108
  many-to-many, 110
  one-to-many, 110
  one-to-one, 110
  referential integrity, 107
  types, 107
Relationships dialog box, 107, 111
Relationships window, 106
Remove Filter/Sort command (Record menu), 63
removing
  fields to queries, 181
  join lines (query tables), 191
  passwords (database security), 291
repairing databases, 287
Replace command (Edit menu), 95
Replace feature (Find command), 95-96
Replace in Field dialog box, 96
Replication ID field size, 123
Report Design view (modifying reports), 224

Report Header (adding new labels), 232
Report Wizard (creating reports), 218-219, 222
  grouping data, 219-220
  multiple-table, 221-222
  sorting data, 220
reports
  adding custom pages, 241
    images, inserting, 244
    page breaks, inserting, 243
    subreports, 242
  charts, 238-241
  creating, 216
    AutoReport, 216-217
    Design view, 225-227
    mailing labels, 245
    Report Wizard, 218-222
  database, 8
  enhancing visually, 245
  exporting as static HTML, 273-274
  modifying, 224, 232
    adding new labels, 232
    controls, 225
    creating calculated controls, 233-238
    Design view, 216
  printing and viewing (Print Preview), 223
  table (object hyperlinks), 268
required fields (data integrity), 121
requirements (certification), 308-311
resizing, field labels and controls (creating forms), 147
Row Height dialog box, 74
rows, *see* records
running queries, 185

S

Save As dialog box, 38, 147, 185
saving
  filters as queries, 178
  forms as ASP files, 272-273

newly created
   forms, 147
   queries, 185
   table structure
     (Design view), 38
**screen elements (Help
  system), 305**
security (databases), 290
   form protection,
     296-297
   passwords, 290-292
   Security Wizard,
     294-295
   user groups, 292-293
   user levels, 292
Select queries, 178
**Select Record command
  (Edit menu), 64**
**selecting fields, grouping
  and sorting (report design),
  225**
**Set Database Password dialog
  box, 290**
**setup, database fields (Design
  view), 33**
**Show Table dialog box, 105,
  127, 179, 189, 196**
**showing fields to queries,
  181**
**Simple Query Wizard
  (creating Append Wizard),
  208**
Single field size, 122
**single fields (sorting
  records), 82**
**sizing fields (data integrity),
  122-123**
sorting
   data (Report Wizard), 220
   query records, 184
   table records, 82
     advanced sorts, 84-86
     *by multiple fields,
      83-84*
     by single fields, 82
     freezing columns, 86
**Sorting and Grouping dialog
  box, 225, 237**
**source applications (OLE),
  250**
spreadsheet table views, *see*
  datasheets
**spreadsheets, normalization
  (Table Analyzer), 281**

static HTML
   exporting reports as,
     273-274
   object formats, 269
study tips (tests), 308
Subform Wizard, 166
**Subform/Subreport Wizard,
  165**
subforms
   adding new records, 167
   creating, 164-166
     tabular format, 164
   viewing related
     records, 167
**subreports, adding to
  reports, 242**
**Summary Options dialog
  box, 187**
summary queries
   calculating fields, 196
     datasheets, 199
     *Query Grid Totals
      section, 196-197*
     Totals row, 198
   crosstab queries, 203
     *building in Design
      view, 207*
     *Crosstab Query
      Wizard, 205*
Summary query, 187
**SupplierID numbers (combo
  boxes), 162**
**switchboards (Database
  Wizard), 23**
**switching between forms,
  139-140**

T

**tab order, changing (modify-
  ing controls), 168**
Tab Order dialog box, 168
**Table Analyzer (database
  tables), 281**
   checking primary
     keys, 284
   field placement, 282-283
   spreadsheet
     normalization, 281
**Table Names command
  (View menu), 189**
**Table Wizard (creating
  tables), 40-43**

tables
  creating
    Datasheet view, 39
    *Design view, 32-33,
     36-38*
    layout, 32
    Table Analyzer, 281
    Table Wizard, 40-43
  data integrity, 116
    *default values,
     116-117*
    formats, 123
    input masks, 123-126
    *lookup fields,
     128-130*
    *referential integrity,
     126-128*
    required fields, 121
    sizing fields, 122-123
    *validation rules,
     118-121*
  database, 7, 64
    adding fields, 76
    *AutoForm data entry,
     51-52*
    closing, 54
    *Datasheet view data
     entry, 48-50*
    deleting fields, 65
    deleting records, 64
    *field content,
     changing, 60*
    *field content,
     editing, 61*
    *field properties,
     changing, 76-77*
    *field width, changing,
     72-73*
    fields, 7
    fonts, changing, 74
    hiding fields, 75-76
    *inserting new
     records, 63*
    *moving and copying
     data, 62*
    moving fields, 70-71
    navigating, 50-51
    printing, 53
    *record heights,
     changing 74*
    records, 7
    *replacing field content,
     60*
    *Table Analyzer,
     281-284*

fields
indexes, *210-211*
objects hyperlinks,
264-267
*placing with Table
Analyzer, 282-283*
filtering records, 96
by form, 98
by selection, 97
finding records (Find
command), 92-96
forms (objects
hyperlinks), 268
mailing labels, creating
from, 245
multiple
creating queries, 189
Query Wizard, 187
query
joining, 190-191
*removing join lines,
191*
relational databases, 6
relationships, 104, 108
creating, 105-107
deleting, 111
*differentiating types,
109*
editing, 111
Join Type option, 108
many-to-many, 110
one-to-many, 110
one-to-one, 110
*referential integrity,
107*
types, 107
reports (objects hyper-
links), 268
sorting records, 82
advanced sorts, 84-86
*by multiple fields,
83-84*
by single fields, 82
freezing columns, 86
**tabular format (subforms),
164**
templates (database), 21
tests
levels of certification, 308
registering for, 312
required skills, 308-311
study tips, 308
taking, 312

text
control, formatting, 169
formatting (custom
forms), 143
**Text Box Properties dialog
box, 234-235, 238**
titles, form, creating, 141
toolbars
Database (icons), 24-25
Web Toolbar (copying
URLs from), 267
topics (Help system), 302-305
Contents tab, 302
Find command, 303-304
Index tab, 303
**Totals calculated controls,
235-236**
math functions, 236
**Totals row (calculating
fields), 198**
**Totals section (summary
query grid), 196-197**
formulas, 197
**troubleshooting databases
(repairing), 287**

U

**unbound controls (forms),
154**
**Unhide Columns commands
(Format menu), 75**
**unsetting passwords (secu-
rity), 291**
Update queries, 210
**updating tables (AutoForms),
53**
**URLs (Universal Resource
Locators)**
copying from Web
Toolbar, 267
entering into fields, 265
**User and Group Accounts
dialog box, 292-293**
users (security levels), 292
assigning to groups,
292-293

V

**validation rules (field data
integrity), 118-119**
entering, 118

Expression Builder, 121
operators, 120
View menu commands
Form Header/Footer, 139
Table Names, 189
viewing
database objects, 24-25
*Database toolbar icons,
24-25*
images in forms (embed-
ding objects), 256
related subform
records, 167
reports (Print Preview),
223
views
Datasheet
*creating database
tables, 39*
*table data entry,
48-50*
Design
*building crosstab
queries, 207*
*database tables,
creating, 32-33,
36-38*
*forms, creating, 136,
144-147*
modifying reports, 232
moving table fields, 71
*reports, creating,
225-227*
form, switching between,
139-140
Form Design, 159
*combo boxes, creating,
160-162*
*controls, creating,
155-157*
Query Design, 178
*creating queries,
178-180*
*joining tables,
190-191*
multiple tables, 189
*removing tables join
lines, 191*
Report Design (modifying
reports), 224-225
spreadsheet table, *see*
datasheets

W

Web Toolbar (copying URLs from), 267
What's This tool (Office Assistant), 300
widths, field, changing, 72-73
wildcards (Find command), 94-95
windows
    Query Design, 9
    Relationships, 106
wizards
    Database, 20-24
        switchboards, 23
        templates, 21
    Table (creating database tables), 40-43
WWW (World Wide Web)
    HTML object formats, 269
    object hyperlinks, 264-268
        forms and reports, 268
        table fields, 264-267

Hardware & Software Requirements

486 DX speed processor or higher, 12MB RAM, VGA video adapter, CD-ROM drive, Microsoft Windows 95, Microsoft Access 97

Licensing Agreement

By opening this package, you are agreeing to be bound by the following:

This software product is copyrighted and all rights are reserved by the individual software developer and/or publisher. You are bound by the individual licensing agreements associated with the software contained on the disk. THIS SOFTWARE IS PROVIDED FREE OF CHARGE, AS IS, AND WITHOUT WARRANTY OF ANY KIND, EITHER EXPRESSED OR IMPLIED, INCLUDING BUT NOT LIMITED TO THE IMPLIED WARRANTIES OF MERCHANTABILITY AND FITNESS FOR A PARTICULAR PURPOSE. Neither the book publisher nor its dealers and distributors assumes any liability for any alleged or actual damages arising from the use of this software. (Some states do not allow exclusion of implied warranties, so the exclusion may not apply to you.)